GRAND COMPLICATIONS®

VOL. VIII

WATCHES INTERNATIONAL®

THE ORIGINAL ANNUAL OF THE WORLD'S WATCH COMPLICATIONS AND MANUFACTURERS®

tourbillon international®

GRAND COMPLICATIONS®

THE ORIGINAL ANNUAL OF THE WORLD'S WATCH COMPLICATIONS AND MANUFACTURERS®

SPECIAL ALARM EDITION

First published in the United States in 2012 by

TOURBILLON INTERNATIONAL
A MODERN LUXURY MEDIA COMPANY

11 West 25th Street, 8th Floor
New York, NY 10010
Tel: +1 (212) 627-7732 Fax +1 (312) 274-8418
www.modernluxury.com/watches

Caroline Childers
PUBLISHER

Michel Jeannot
EDITOR IN CHIEF

Lew Dickey
CHIEF EXECUTIVE OFFICER

Michael Dickey
PRESIDENT

John Dickey
EXECUTIVE VICE PRESIDENT AND CO-CHIEF OPERATING OFFICER

Jon Pinch
EXECUTIVE VICE PRESIDENT AND CO-CHIEF OPERATING OFFICER

JP Hannan
CHIEF FINANCIAL OFFICER

Richard Denning
GENERAL COUNSEL

In association with RIZZOLI INTERNATIONAL PUBLICATIONS, INC.

300 Park Avenue South, New York, NY 10010

ISBN: 978-0-8478-3751-9

PRINTED IN ITALY

COVER: LANGE 1 TOURBILLON PERPETUAL CALENDAR (A. LANGE & SÖHNE)

PIAGET EMPERADOR
COUSSIN
Piaget Manufacture movement 855P
Mechanical self-winding perpetual calendar
Dual time, day/night indicator
White gold, sapphire case-back
PIAGET
www.piaget.com

HUBLOT
THE ART OF FUSIO
MASTERPIECE
KEY OF TIME
Masterpiece Key of Time.
Vertical tourbillon positioned at 6 o'clock.
5-day power reserve indicator. Speed of time
indicator, from 4x slower to 4x quicker,
giving the wearer the ability to manage their
own time. Manufactured entirely by Hublot.
50-piece limited edition.

TIME
4X FASTER
4X SLOWER
HUBLOT
GENEVE
POWER RESERVE
SWISS MADE
HUBLOT
BOUTIQUES
NEW YORK • BEVERLY HILLS • BAL HARBOUR
BOCA RATON • LAS VEGAS • PALM BEACH • ST THOMAS
Tel. 1 800 536 0636

Letter from the President

It's Your Time

In today's world of rapid technological advances, one could argue that no one needs a watch. So why do high-end timepieces continue to be in such demand among purveyors of luxury? We're not experts on the why, but we are when it comes to what is in demand.

We are equally as excited to introduce the latest volume of *Grand Complications* as we are to announce our first foray into China this year with *Watches International Chinese Edition Volume I.* Around the world, there is no greater symbol of luxury than a finely crafted timepiece. As our audience knows, this publication represents the most elite collection of complicated mechanical timepieces. Mechanical movements and the various complications they offer have been exploding in popularity over the last decade. Our fascination with mechanical prowess and perfection is a motivation in its own right, distinct from mundane concerns such as punctuality.

Along with this printed piece, we also provide this content digitally and most importantly, in app format on the iPad. With over 40,000 Tourbillon International apps downloaded in this digital age, we understand the importance of allowing our audience to view this content anywhere, anytime.

The master craftsmanship of these pieces ensures that they will go from being treasured collector's items to even more treasured family heirlooms, quietly—or, in the case of watches that include striking functions, audibly—keeping time for the next generation. We hope you enjoy this edition, and look forward to bringing you this authoritative book that helps navigate these works of art.

Michael Dickey

PIAGET EMPERADOR
Piaget Manufacture movement 600P
Mechanical hand-wound tourbillon
World's thinnest shaped tourbillon
3.5mm thickness
White gold, sapphire case-back
Boutique exclusivity
PIAGET
www.piaget.com

cellini

New York City is not for the faint of heart. The streets teem with the most successful people in the world, and the city is notoriously tough on those who don't measure up. This is the environment in which Cellini Jewelers has thrived for more than 30 years, exceeding expectations in the world's most demanding city with an unsurpassed selection of rare timepieces and sublime jewelry, all presented by a gracious staff of experts dedicated to consummate service.

AHEAD OF HIS TIME

Leon Adams, Cellini's founder and president, has always been passionate about *haute horlogerie*. It led him to open his first boutique inside the Hotel Waldorf-Astoria in 1977, and a second on Madison Avenue a decade later.

Cellini opened at the dawn of the current horological renaissance, a time when fine mechanical watches were scarce commodities. By offering an extensive array of hard-to-find timepieces, Cellini struck a chord with collectors, who visited the stores to see watches they could not find anywhere else in the United States.

Through the years, Cellini's reputation grew along with its collection, which was the first in the U.S. to include brands like Audemars Piguet, A. Lange & Söhne, Roger Dubuis and Maîtres du Temps. Today, Cellini covers the spectrum of *haute horlogerie* as an authorized dealer for more than two dozen of the world's best known and most exotic watchmakers. Its phenomenal range appeals to all types of enthusiasts, from budding aficionados in search of their first fine timepiece, to savvy collectors who prize Cellini's unrivaled selection of rare watches.

DB28

This titanium version of De Bethune's DB28 is part of Cellini Jeweler's unsurpassed selection of mechanical timepieces from the world's best known and most exotic watchmakers.

EXPLORING OPULENCE

For those who treasure the natural beauty of jewelry, both of Cellini's boutiques reflect a deep appreciation for all things precious. Freestanding glass cabinets gleam with imaginatively designed, impeccably crafted jewelry creations organized by gemstone.

Diamonds of all colors populate one area, while another is reserved for the vibrant fire reflecting from their white counterparts. Nearby, a rich assortment of gems and pearls—assembled through the years from sources around the world—are used to make glamorous showpieces that feature everything from Burmese rubies and Kashmir sapphires to South Sea pearls and alexandrite, the exceedingly rare Russian gem whose color changes in natural light.

For exceptional glamour, nothing outshines a bespoke setting. Cellini's team of gemologists, designers and craftsmen combine their expertise and artistry to transform these precious gems into jewelry tailored exclusively to your personal style, whether you are looking for a unique engagement ring or a one-of-a-kind necklace.

ABALONE SHELL BRACELET

One-of-a-kind with diamonds, sapphires, tourmalines and tsavorites in 18-karat gold.

SKELETON DOUBLE FLYING TOURBILLON
(Roger Dubuis)

KING POWER AYRTON SENNA
(Hublot)

TWENTY-8-EIGHT REGULATOR A.S.W HORIZONS
(DeWitt)

CALIBRE DE CARTIER MULTIPLE TIME ZONE
(Cartier)

BRANDS CARRIED

A. Lange & Söhne	Jaeger-LeCoultre
Audemars Piguet	Jean Dunand
Bell & Ross	Ludovic Ballouard
Cartier	Maîtres du Temps
Chopard	Panerai
De Bethune	Parmigiani
DeWitt	Piaget
Franck Muller	Richard Mille
Girard-Perregaux	Roger Dubuis
Guy Ellia	Ulysse Nardin
H. Moser & Cie.	Vacheron Constantin
Hublot	Zenith
IWC	

EXCEEDING EXPECTATIONS

But the merchandise is far from the only reason the most discerning connoisseurs opt for Cellini. A knowledgeable staff at both locations provides impeccable service before, during and after a purchase.

Cellini's horological specialists live and breathe watches, and draw upon this wealth of knowledge to help each watch lover find the perfect fit. For those enchanted instead by shimmering works of art, Cellini's jewelry experts put a world of exquisite beauty at your fingertips. The experience they provide puts the emphasis on the client's needs.

Sophisticated horology, irresistible jewels, inviting venues and a dedicated staff—it's no wonder that after nearly three and a half decades Cellini continues to be one of the most respected and successful boutiques of its kind. In this wildly competitive city, where storefronts, skylines and styles change as often as the weather, Cellini's longevity is a testament to the power of an irreplaceable experience.

DIAMOND & SAPPHIRE EARRINGS
Breathtaking heart-shaped diamond earrings edged with sapphires.

CELLINI JEWELERS

Hotel Waldorf-Astoria • 301 Park Avenue at 50th Street • New York, NY 10022 - Tel 212 751 9824

509 Madison Avenue at 53rd Street • New York, NY 10022 - Tel 212 888 0505

800-CELLINI • www.CelliniJewelers.com

RÉTROGRADE MYSTÉRIEUSE
2 5 10
CHANEL
J12
www.chanel.com

Letter from the Publisher

The Fruit of Patience

The cult of speed, combined with profusion and performance, has got the modern world firmly in its grip. Could we relearn how to free ourselves from the frenzied pace of life and break free from the tyranny of time, without fear of losing it? This would mean resisting the temptation of seeking at all costs to hasten the end of a given period of time, and instead accepting the passive or even contemplative state that the waiting process imposes upon us. This path would doubtless bring its own rewards.

Are not the world's finest—and often most complex—creations often the fruit of a lengthy process? From the conception of a child to the wonderful scenery surrounding us, or the monumental pyramids built in Ancient Egypt, the genesis of these works, whether fashioned by the human hand or by nature, whether the fruit of arduous labor or of serene expectation, can last months, years or centuries.

The same goes for the clothes and accessories we wear. The most accomplished creations call for lengthy and meticulous work, the watch being the most remarkable example. From horological complications (minute repeaters, tourbillons, chronographs, calendars or moonphase modules, to mention but a few), to decorations such as enameling, gemsetting or engraving, the making of a single timepiece may take weeks or months of intense work, patience and concentration for the master watchmakers and master artisans. They unstintingly pool their skills in a shared quest for perfection, resulting in exceptional timepieces endowed with mechanisms whose technical sophistication is equaled only by their refined aesthetic appeal.

Let us also pay due respect to the Swiss watchmakers who formerly opted for the traditional "établissage" system which involved producing a watch in stages, in small units, using highly qualified workers and in limited series. Their enlightened choice provided scope for the twin activities of the farmer-watchmakers of these Swiss valleys, as well as for the development of a watch industry based on excellence.

Time, as ever. That which it took to elaborate these unique creations and which also guarantees their longevity. That which embodies the centuries-long existence of many watch manufacturers, testifying to expertise passed on from generation to generation and on which these Houses have built their reputation. And finally, the time which the chronograph is by nature intended to measure and indicate.

High-end watches are clearly imbued with the omnipresence of time. Nonetheless—and therein lies the paradox—it is increasingly becoming a space in which to express poetry and fantasy, making it a timeless, seductive invitation to forget the passing of time.

Caroline Childers

HALLMARK OF GENEVA

The "Hallmark of Geneva" gets a makeover to reinforce its certification!

The Hallmark of Geneva, emblem of Genevan watchmaking, ranks as one of the most distinguished marks of product quality, offering its acquirer, has been established in 1886 and celebrated its 125th anniversary on November 2011.

It represents the guarantee of origin, the craftsmanship, durability and expertise.

The criteria governing the quality requirements for the "Hallmark of Geneva" have been considerably expanded. From now on, the watch in its entirety is to be certified.

This major evolution reinforces the value of the Hallmark of Geneva for customers, in a field where quality of manufacture in accordance with the Genevan horological tradition constitutes an essential and sought-after asset.

Patrimony Traditionnelle 14-day Tourbillon
Ref.: 89000/000R-9655

GENEVE

www.vacheron-constantin.com

VACHERON CONSTANTIN
Manufacture Horlogère, Genève, depuis 1755.

CALIBER RM 051 PHOENIX-MICHELLE YEOH
Manual winding tourbillon movement

Power reserve: circa 48 hours
Black Onyx baseplate
Bridges made of titanium
Variable inertia, free sprung balance
Torque limiting crown
Barrel pawl with progressive recoil
Number of jewels: 21
Balance: Glucydur, 2 arms, 4 setting screws,
inertia moment 10 mg·cm^2, angle of lift 53°
Frequency: 21,600 vph (3 Hz)
Anglage and polishing by hand (excluding Onyx baseplate
and PVD treated parts)
Locking sections hand polished
Sapphire blasted milled sections
Burnished pivots

RICHARD MILLE

CALIBER RM 020
TOURBILLON POCKET WATCH

worn by Baptiste Giabiconi

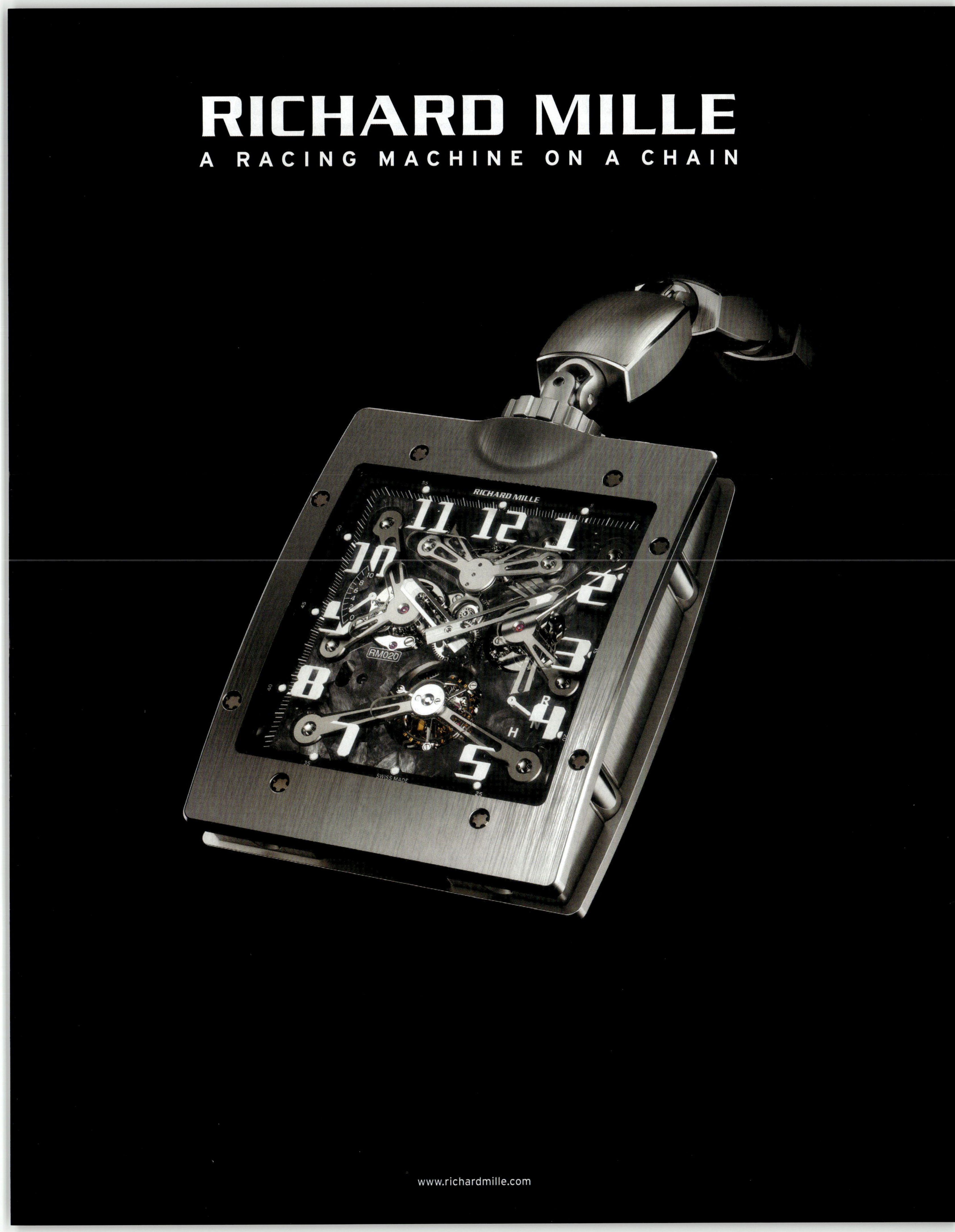

RICHARD MILLE
A RACING MACHINE ON A CHAIN
RICHARD MILLE
RM020
www.richardmille.com

Letter from the Editor in Chief

Innovation is the very essence of horology

With the return of vintage watches and the many anniversaries being celebrated by brands, nothing looks more like a year 2012 model than a model from the 1940s, '50s or '60s! Does this often-played tune actually reflect reality? In aesthetic terms, possibly so. However, on a mechanical level, today's movements bear little resemblance to those of yesteryear.

In its presentation several months ago of the Oscillomax, the all-silicon regulating organ, Patek Philippe picked up an interesting point. "Is the technology on which these developments is based of a sustainable nature, and is it compatible with watchmaking traditions?" asked the brand, before adding, "In response to this legitimate question, let's not forget that, since the first wooden clocks, watchmaking has been constantly evolving. Indeed, innovation is the very essence of its existence."

In addition to Patek Philippe's Silinvar, professionals have also had a chance in recent months to discover the SPRON®610 by Seiko—an alloy that makes an advantageous substitute for Elinvar in the production of balance springs—as well as Bioflex from the Générale Ressorts company—an environmentally friendly alloy for barrel springs. Various research centers in Switzerland and abroad have made horology one of their priorities.

Paradoxically, all these breakthroughs enjoy little visibility among the general public. This isn't because connoisseurs are not interested, but rather because this type of issue tends to remain confined within the watchmaking profession. Nonetheless, the authentic innovations, the kind that further the progress of the watchmaking art, do not lie in a convex watch crystal or a surface treatment coloring.

So why are watchmakers so discreet about their findings? Probably due to the fact that, like Patek Philippe, they are not sure how such progress will be received by an often conservative clientele. Brands' communication strategy tends to rely on the quaint cliché of a watchmaker seated at his wooden workbench—a somewhat dated image celebrating tradition and craftsmanship, and which appeals to a wide audience.

The future will nonetheless bring a number of substantial challenges: we already know that adding an electronic function—such as remote unlocking of a car—to a mechanical watch has not been appreciated by purists. But what about the chemical elements—varnishes, coatings and cementing glues—that are increasingly present in timepieces? Or magnetism, on which Breguet and TAG Heuer are working? Does the use of magnets in a watch movement, involving electron displacement, still have anything to do with mechanical horology?

The question remains open, since there are currently no acknowledged boundaries. However, one thing is for sure: the evolution of watchmaking is currently more than ever based on top-level R&D!

Michel Jeannot

IWC.
Engineered for men.

IWC
SCHAFFHAUSEN
SINCE 1868

The future's safe.

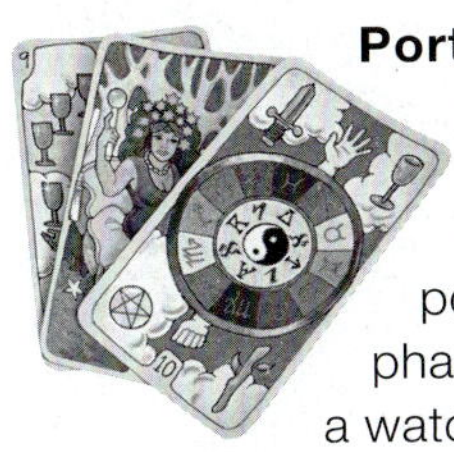

Portuguese Perpetual Calendar. Ref. 5032: One thing at IWC always remains the same: the desire to get even better. Here is one of the finest examples, with the largest automatic movement manufactured by IWC, Pellaton winding and a seven-day power reserve. The perpetual calendar shows the date and moon phase and is mechanically programmed until the year 2499. In short: a watch that has already written the future. **IWC. Engineered for men.**

Mechanical IWC-manufactured movement | Pellaton automatic winding system | 7-day power reserve with display | Perpetual calendar (figure) | Perpetual moon phase display | Antireflective sapphire glass | Sapphire-glass back cover | Water-resistant 3 bar | 18 ct red gold

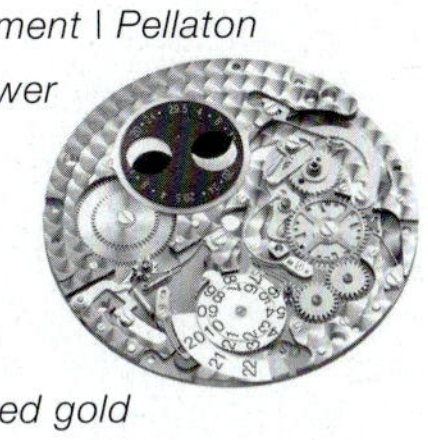

IWC SCHAFFHAUSEN BOUTIQUES

535 MADISON AVENUE NEW YORK, NY 10022 OPENING SOON	THE PALAZZO HOTEL CASINO LEVEL, LAS VEGAS TEL. 702-650-0817	9490C BRIGHTON WAY BEVERLY HILLS, CA 90210 TEL. 310-734-0520

FOR ADDITIONAL INFORMATION OR TO REQUEST A CATALOG, PLEASE CALL 1-800-432-9330, EMAIL CONCIERGE.USA@IWC.COM OR VISIT OUR WEBSITE, WWW.IWC.COM

arije

PARIS • LONDON • CANNES

Arije, in Paris, is more than a boutique, more than just a showcase, and more than one of the most welcoming smiles of Parisian horology: It is a secret. It is a private mystery that is shared amongst friends. Arije is also an address that we would love to keep to ourselves, but that we can't resist sharing with others.

It is a gentle environment, in a unique space that knows how to make time stand still, precisely because it speaks of the language of time, and of the objects that convey it.

Arije, in all honesty, is frankly *somewhere else*, despite the doors that open onto the "golden triangle" of the Avenue George-V. Arije is also present on the famous "Croisette" in Cannes, in the Grand Hôtel du Cap-Ferrat, and in the heart of London's Sloane Street. These noble and exclusive sites for exceptional timepieces offer horological and jewelry enthusiasts a chance to admire approximately 40 eminently prestigious brands.

If there is a secret within the secret, it is the constant focus on respecting other people's sensibilities, regardless of cultural codes and standards: here, almost every language is spoken, and in all cases the language of the heart. This is the hallmark of Arije.

One might say that Arije has the most niche international clientele of watches and jewelry. It is hard to judge, discretion being the watchword in this field, but it is undoubtedly one of the most select that Paris (or anywhere else for that matter) has to offer.

JUMBO CHRONO LIMITED EDITION
(Guy Ellia)

MILLENARY 4101
(Audemars Piguet)

Arije is a byword among devotees of fine objects, who know how to trust the eye and the choices of a house that demonstrates great maturity and a wealth of expertise in its vision of brands, of watches, and of those who create them.

This pervasively elegant and refined atmosphere provides a perfect setting to write, to tell and to experience for a special moment in time, a beautiful story surrounding a particular watch or a jewelry creation.

This is such a rare occurrence within the world of international luxury that has become so systematic and full of stereotypes that one is left to wonder if people don't simply find their way back to Carla Chalouhi's boutique as much for these shared values as for its rare pieces, limited editions or exclusive offerings...

Of course, Arije would not be Arije without the spirit and efforts of its CEO, Carla Chalouhi. The daughter of Arije's founder and herself a cosmopolitan businesswoman with her finger on the pulse of the watch industry, Carla is at the heart of it all; she is the woman behind the watches.

CRAZY FLOWER
(Breguet)

ZEITWERK LUMINOUS
(A. Lange & Söhne)

PATRIMONY TRADITIONNELLE WORLD TIME
(Vacheron Constantin)

PORTUGUESE GRAND COMPLICATION
(IWC)

ROTONDE DE CARTIER ASTROREGULATEUR
(Cartier)

BRANDS CARRIED

A. Lange & Söhne**
Audemars Piguet***
Baume & Mercier**
Bell & Ross*
Blancpain*
Breguet*
Cartier***
Chanel*
Chaumet*
Chopard*
Dior*
Ebel*
Franck Muller*
Girard-Perregaux***

Glashütte Original*
Guy Ellia***
Harry Winston**
Hautlence*
Hublot*
IWC***
Jaeger-LeCoultre*
Jaquet Droz*
Montblanc*
Omega*
Panerai*
Parmigiani***
Piaget**
Pierre Kunz*

Roger Dubuis***
Rolex*
TAG Heuer*
Tudor*
Ulysse Nardin**
Vacheron Constantin*
Van Cleef & Arpels**
Zenith**

* Paris
* London
* Cannes

OYSTER PERPETUAL YACHT MASTER II
(Rolex)

ARIJE

PARIS
50 rue Pierre Charron - Tel +33 (0) 1 47 20 72 40
30 avenue George V - Tel +33 (0) 1 49 52 98 88

LONDON
165 Sloane Street - Tel +44 (0) 20 7752 0246

CANNES
50 boulevard de la Croisette - Tel +33 (0) 4 93 68 47 73

SAINT-JEAN-CAP-FERRAT
Grand-Hôtel du Cap-Ferrat • 71 boulevard du Général de Gaulle - Tel +33 (0) 4 93 76 50 24

www.arije.com
contact: shop@arije.com

MASTER GRANDE TRADITION TOURBILLON À QUANTIÈME PERPÉTUEL
Jaeger-LeCoultre Calibre 987

GRAND COMPLICATIONS®

THE ORIGINAL ANNUAL OF THE WORLD'S WATCH COMPLICATIONS AND MANUFACTURERS®

TOURBILLON INTERNATIONAL
A MODERN LUXURY MEDIA COMPANY
ADMINISTRATION, ADVERTISING SALES, EDITORIAL, BOOK SALES

11 West 25th Street, 8th Floor • New York, NY 10010
Tel: +1 (212) 627-7732 Fax: +1 (312) 274-8418

TO BREAK THE RULES, YOU MUST FIRST MASTER THEM.
THE VALLÉE DE JOUX, THE JURA. FOR MILLENIA, A HARSH, UNYIELDING ENVIRONMENT – A PLACE OF RAW NATURE AND UNFORGIVING CLIMATE. FIRST SETTLED IN THE SIXTH CENTURY BY MONKS WHO SAW IN THIS AUSTERE EXISTENCE A SERENITY AND SPIRITUALITY; MORE RECENTLY, SINCE 1875, THE HOME OF AUDEMARS PIGUET, IN THE VILLAGE OF LE BRASSUS.
THE EARLY WATCHMAKERS OF LE BRASSUS WORKED THE IMPOVERISHED LAND IN SUMMER – AT ONE WITH NATURE AND COMPELLED BY ITS ELEMENTAL POWER. THROUGH WINTER THEY WORKED AT THEIR BENCH, BY THE EVEN, NORTHERN LIGHT, STRIVING TO MASTER, THROUGH THE COMPLEX MECHANICS OF THE WATCHMAKER'S CRAFT, THE ETERNAL MOVEMENT OF THE COSMOS. TODAY WE ARE PROUD TO FOLLOW THIS TRADITION, EXPRESSING THE DYNAMIC COMPLEXITY OF THE UNIVERSE THROUGH THE ART OF FINE WATCHMAKING.
CALIBRE 2120/2808.
PERPETUAL CALENDAR WITH EQUATION OF TIME, SUNRISE AND SUNSET TIME
THE AUDEMARS PIGUET FOUNDATION PROUDLY SUPPORTS GLOBAL FOREST CONSERVATION.
AUDEMARS PIGUET
Le Brassus

GREG SIMONIAN
Westime President

Westime

Los Angeles
Beverly Hills
La Jolla

For the best selection of prestigious watches in Southern California, collectors from around the world head to Westime. Its three boutiques—in West Los Angeles, Beverly Hills and La Jolla—present more than 50 of the most sought-after watch brands in surroundings that reflect California's famous laid-back elegance.

Since its opening 25 years ago, Westime Los Angeles's spacious showroom at the Westside Pavilion has proudly displayed a wide selection of fine timepieces for serious collectors and casual shoppers alike. With the help of experienced staff members who speak more than 12 different languages combined, this is the place where any shopper can discover up-and-coming Swiss watch brands, find watches that complement the hottest fashion trends, or inspect one-of-a-kind grand complication timepieces in the privacy of a VIP viewing room.

Westime Beverly Hills is a multi-story jewel box of a boutique on one of the world's most celebrated shopping streets: Rodeo Drive. Here customers will discover limited edition watches that won't be seen in any other watch store. It's not unusual to meet a master watchmaker from Switzerland in the boutique, who makes his own regular pilgrimage to Westime to greet important clients. Throughout the year, the boutique stages watch auction previews for serious connoisseurs, as well as light-hearted parties that introduce the world of watches to new shoppers in a fun way.

ROYAL OAK OFFSHORE CHRONOGRAPH CARBON
(Audemars Piguet)

Late last year, Westime La Jolla debuted in one of California's most exclusive seaside destinations. The new boutique, located north of San Diego, symbolizes Westime's commitment to introducing the new masters of haute horlogerie to a discriminating clientele. Young, independent watch brands, including Richard Mille, Urwerk, Greubel Forsey, Ikepod and De Bethune, are available in the region for the first time at Westime La Jolla. And of course, the best traditional watch brands—from Zenith to Ulysse Nardin—are thoughtfully represented in the newest Westime location.

Westime's expansion continues this year. In 2012, Westime's flagship Los Angeles store will relocate to a 6,500-square-foot building on Sunset Boulevard, in West Hollywood. The two-level open space will not only showcase an extensive selection of watches, but also an ever-changing line-up of exquisitely crafted accessories, artwork, objects and amenities. Curated by Westime Founder John Simonian and President Greg Simonian, the collections, design, services and décor will transform the new flagship from a place to shop, into a destination where one appreciates the finest things in life at his or her own pace.

Even as it grows, Westime remains a family-owned and -operated business that succeeds by nurturing personal relationships with watchmakers, customers and charitable organizations in its communities.

WESTIME

LOS ANGELES
10800 West Pico Blvd., #197 • Los Angeles, CA 90064 - Tel 310 470 1388 • Fax 310 475 0628

BEVERLY HILLS
254 North Rodeo Drive • Beverly Hills, CA 90210 - Tel 310 271 0000 • Fax 310 271 3091

LA JOLLA
1227 Prospect Street • La Jolla, CA 92037 - Tel 858 459 2222

www.westime.com

OCTA UTC
(F. P. Journe)

KING POWER BLACK MAGIC
(Hublot)

LM1
(MB&F)

RM 004
SPLIT SECONDS CHRONOGRAPH
(Richard Mille)

BRANDS CARRIED

Alpina	Hamilton
Audemars Piguet	Harry Winston
Baume & Mercier	Hublot
Bell & Ross	Ikepod
Blancpain	Jacob & Co
Breitling	Longines
BRM	Ludovic Ballouard
Buben & Zörweg	MB&F
Bulgari	Milus
Chopard	Nixon
Concord	Omega
De Bethune	Pierre Kunz
DeWitt	Richard Mille
Dior	RogueDZN
Dottling	Roland Iten
Ebel	Romain Jerome
FP Journe	Shamballa
Franck Muller	TAG Heuer
Frédérique Constant	Tiffany & Co.
Girard-Perregaux	Tissot
Giuliano Mazzuoli	Ulysse Nardin
Glashütte Original	URWERK
Graham-London	Vertu
Greubel Forsey	Zenith
H. Moser	

Summary

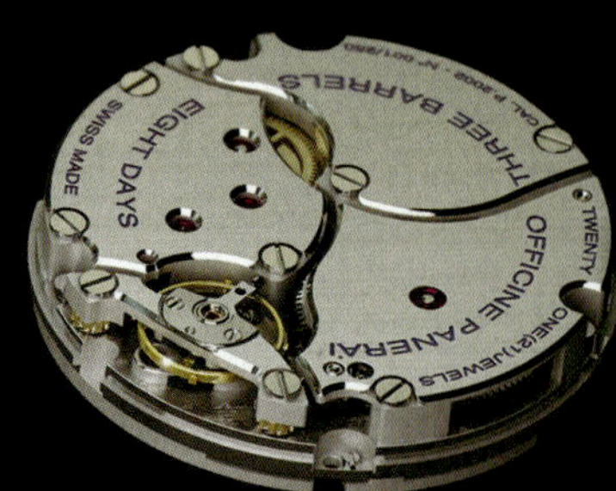

FRANCK MULLER
GENEVE
TWENTY NINE (29) JEWELS
FOUR BARRELS

Web Site Directory

A. LANGE & SÖHNE	www.alange-soehne.com
AUDEMARS PIGUET	www.audemarspiguet.com
BELL & ROSS	www.bellross.com
BLANCPAIN	www.blancpain.com
BREGUET	www.breguet.com
BVLGARI	www.bulgari.com
CHANEL	www.chanel.com
CHRISTOPHE CLARET	www.claret.ch
DE GRISOGONO	www.degrisogono.com
DEWITT	www.dewitt.ch
DIOR HORLOGERIE	www.diorhorlogerie.com
FRANCK MULLER	www.franckmullerusa.com
FRÉDÉRIQUE CONSTANT SA	www.frederique-constant.com
GLASHÜTTE ORIGINAL	www.glashuette-original.com
GRAHAM-LONDON	www.graham-london.com
GUY ELLIA	www.guyellia.com
HUBLOT	www.hublot.com
IWC	www.iwc.com
JACOB & CO.	www.jacobandco.com
JAEGER-LECOULTRE	www.jaeger-lecoultre.com
LONGINES	www.longines.com
PANERAI	www.panerai.com
PATEK PHILIPPE	www.patek.com
PIAGET	www.piaget.com
REBELLION TIMEPIECES	www.rebellion-timepieces.com
RICHARD MILLE	www.richardmille.com
ROGER DUBUIS	www.rogerdubuis.com
STÜHRLING ORIGINAL	www.stuhrling.com
URWERK	www.urwerk.com
VACHERON CONSTANTIN	www.vacheron-constantin.com
ZENITH	www.zenith-watches.com

RELATED SITES

BASELWORLD	www.baselworld.com
SIHH	www.sihh.ch

AUCTION HOUSES

CHRISTIE'S	www.christies.com
SOTHEBY'S	www.sothebys.com

BVLGARI
BVLGARI
Gerald Genta
OCTO BI-RETRO STEEL CERAMIC
ELECTED WATCH OF THE YEAR 2010 BY A SWISS PROFESSIONAL JURY
ATLANTA • BAL HARBOUR • BEVERLY HILLS • BOCA RATON • CHEVY CHASE
CHICAGO • DALLAS • HONOLULU • HOUSTON • LAS VEGAS • NEW YORK
SAN FRANCISCO • SCOTTSDALE • SHORT HILLS • SOUTH COAST PLAZA • BULGARI.COM
M
MONTRE
DE L'ANNEE
2010

BR

Index

PANERAI.COM
LUMINOR
PANERAI
GMT
8 DAYS
REG.
T.M.
TRADITION AND INNOVATION.
LUMINOR 1950 CHRONO MONOPULSANTE 8 DAYS GMT TITANIO - 44MM
PANERAI
LABORATORIO DI IDEE.
Available exclusively at Panerai boutiques and select authorized watch specialists.
BAL HARBOUR SHOPS • BEVERLY HILLS • BOCA RATON • NEW YORK • PALM BEACH

de GRISOGONO
GENEVE
meccanico dG
LIMITED EDITION OF 10 PIECES
Grand Prix d'Horlogerie de Genève
Public Prize • 2009
THE FIRST MECHANICAL WATCH IN THE WORLD WITH A DUAL ANALOGUE AND DIGITAL DISPLAY
MECCANICO dG IN TITANIUM WITH BLACK PVD COATING, HANDWINDING MECHANICAL MOVMENT
WITH DUAL TIME AND MECHANICAL DIGITAL SECOND TIME ZONE
www.degrisogono.com

MECCANICO dG
A TECHNICAL MASTERPIECE

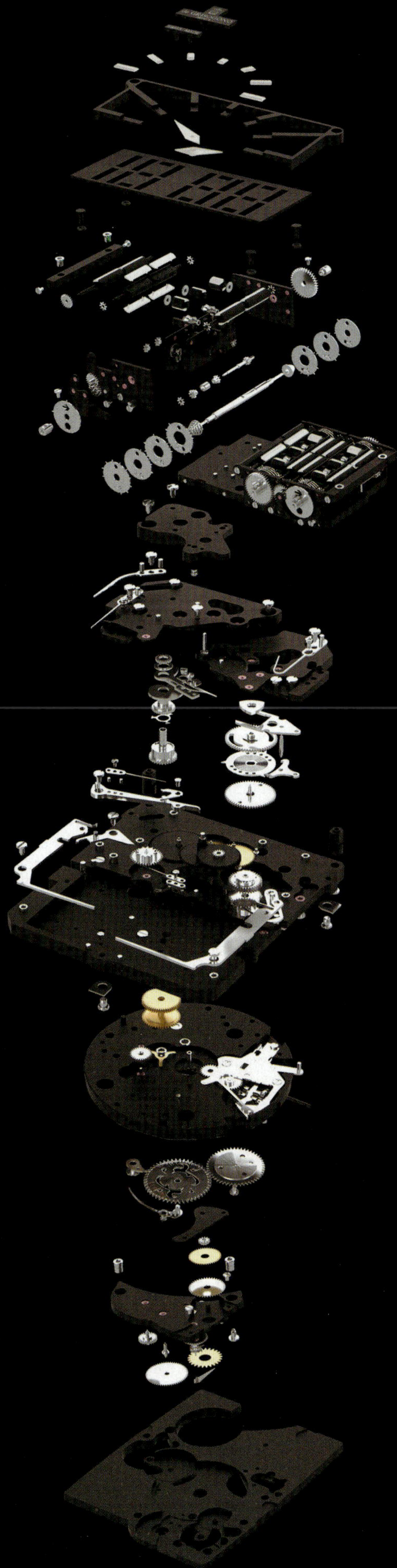

With its double analogue and mechanical digital display, this watch from de Grisogono asserts itself as one of the most exceptional contemporary haute horlogerie models. Its highly sophisticated movement called for years of development, but this marvel of precision is not reserved exclusively for connoisseurs of horological techniques. The accurate and constantly repeated choreography performed by its gear trains, cams and microsegments generates extraordinary emotion and fascinating poetry that can be sensed by everyone. This majestic performance is set off to its best advantage within a case featuring imposing yet elegant lines.

The heart of the watch beats to the tune of **a hand-wound mechanism composed of 651 parts**, all hand-assembled by the company's most skilled and experienced watchmakers. The analogue display of the hours and minutes is located in the upper part of the dial, while the lower area features a mechanical digital display indicating a second time zone. The latter reveals tens of hours, single hours, tens of minutes and single minutes thanks to the action of mobile microsegments driven by a set of **23 cams** combined with gears plus a triggering/synchronisation device. The vertical segments are 4.55 mm high and the horizontal ones have a display length of 1.80 mm. Each segment has four faces: two visible faces opposite each other with coloured inserts and two invisible faces, also opposite. One or more segments rotate 90° to turn one time indication into the next. The jump is instantaneous; while anywhere from 1 to 12 segments move, depending on the time being displayed.

Each year, the digital function is activated 518,400 times and sets 285 million parts into motion.

This exceptional movement lends its full value to this timepiece that is inventing a new watchmaking language. Limited edition of 10 pieces.

Index

JACOB & Co.
EPIC II
JACOB&CO
jacobandco.com
212.719.5887
48 East 57th Street
New York, NY

Index

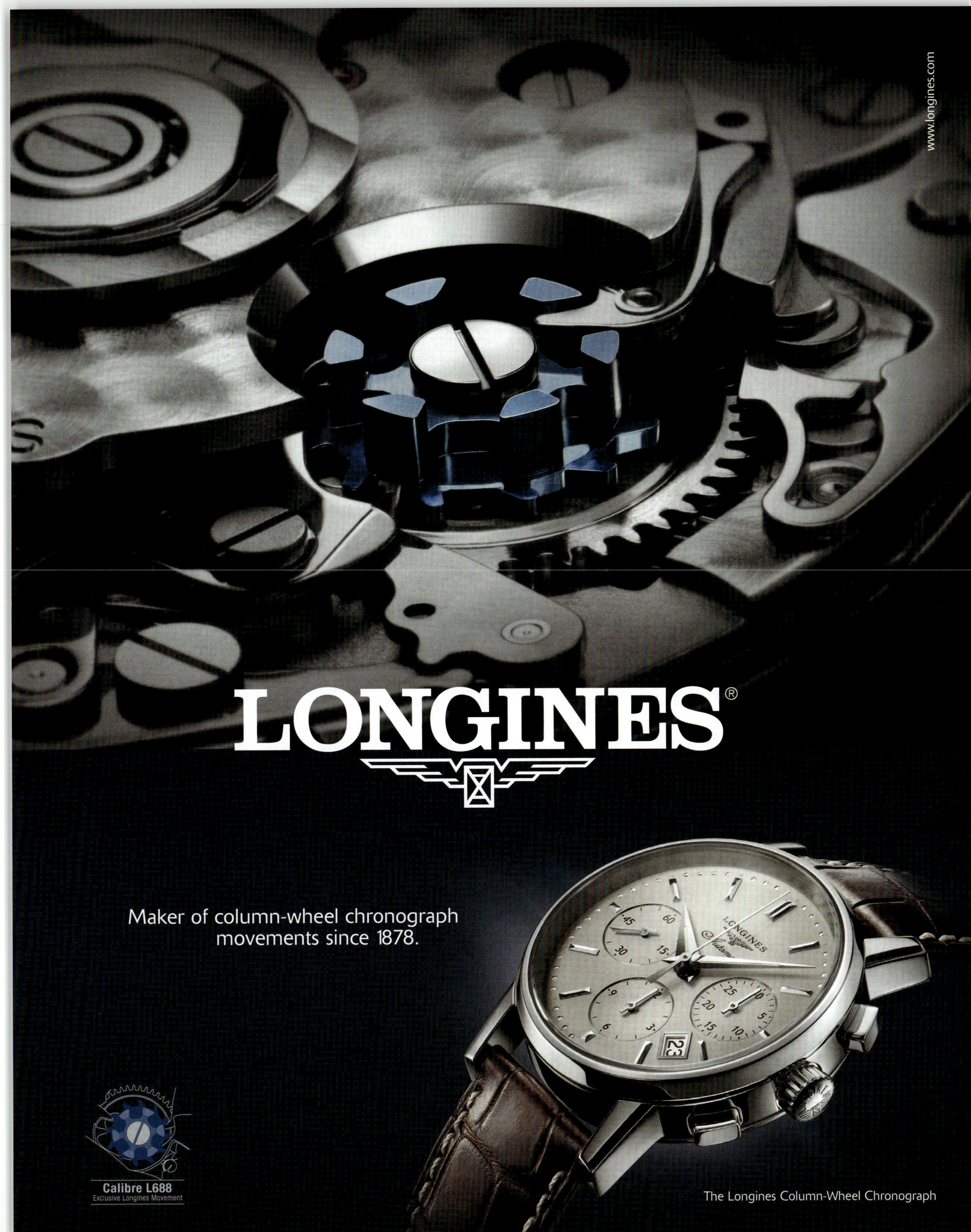
www.longines.com
LONGINES®
Maker of column-wheel chronograph
movements since 1878.
Calibre L688
Exclusive Longines Movement
The Longines Column-Wheel Chronograph

Index

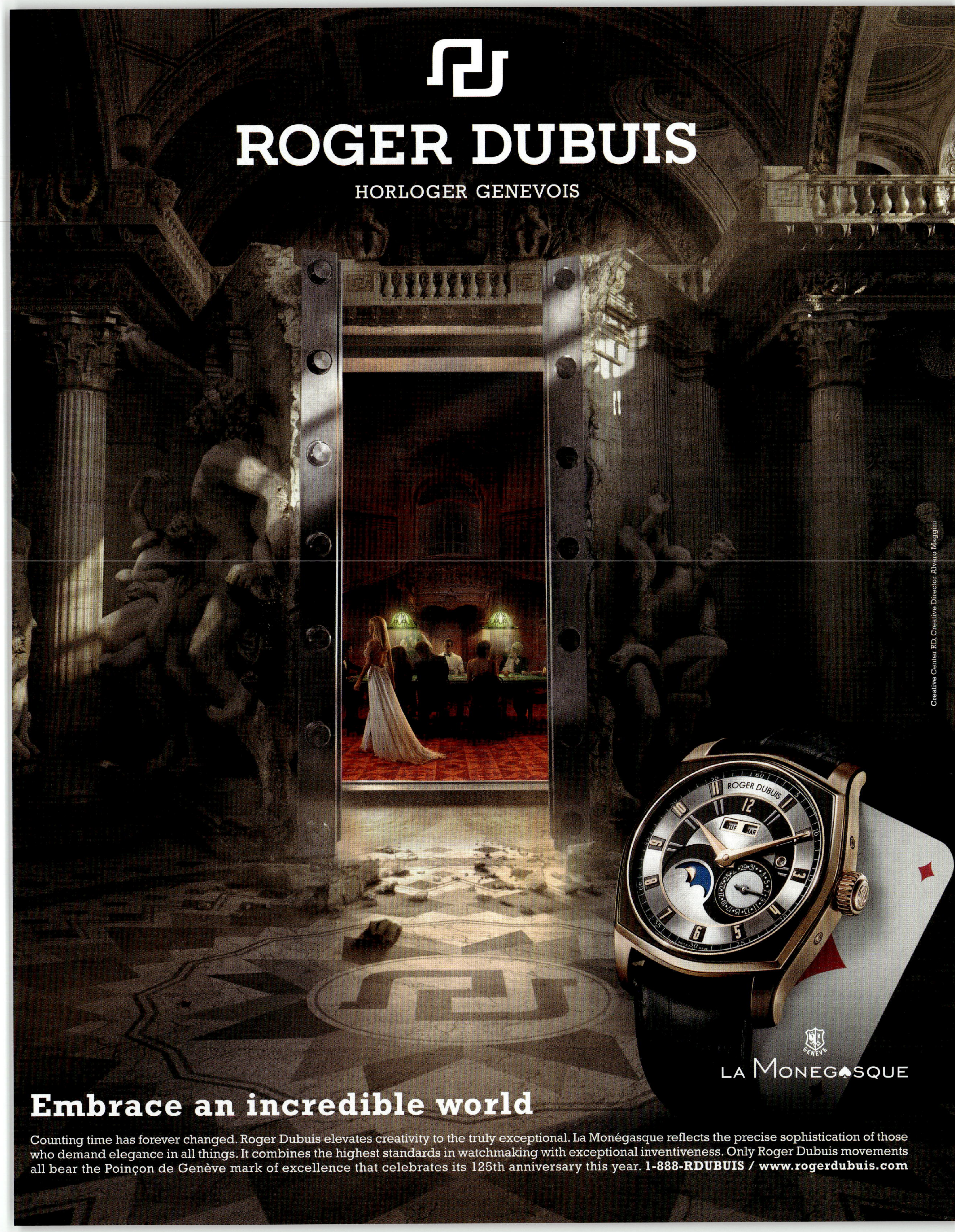

ROGER DUBUIS
HORLOGER GENEVOIS
LA MONEGASQUE
Embrace an incredible world
Counting time has forever changed. Roger Dubuis elevates creativity to the truly exceptional. La Monégasque reflects the precise sophistication of those who demand elegance in all things. It combines the highest standards in watchmaking with exceptional inventiveness. Only Roger Dubuis movements all bear the Poinçon de Genève mark of excellence that celebrates its 125th anniversary this year. 1-888-RDUBUIS / www.rogerdubuis.com
Creative Center RD, Creative Director Alvaro Maggini

Index

«TIME SPACE»
QUANTIEME PERPETUEL
GUY ELLIA
Arije Paris Arije Cannes Arije Saint-Jean-Cap-Ferrat
Doux Joaillier Courchevel Zegg & Cerlati Monaco Doux Joaillier Saint Tropez
Carat & Time Saint Barthelemy Avakian Geneva Hubner Vienna Arije London Piantelli London
Diamond Time Athens Steltman Den Haag Lydion Mucevher Antalya Azal Dubaï
Harvey Nichols Dubaï Louvre Moscow Crystal Kiev Sincere Kuala Lumpur
Sincere Singapore Cellini New York Westime Los Angeles
www.guyellia.com

« REPETITION MINUTE ZEPHYR »

Titanium TI 04 AAD
REPETITION MINUTES ZEPHYR
PARIS
LOS ANGELES
POWER RESERVE INDICATOR
12 pieces only
GUY ELLIA
SWISS MADE
GUY ELLIA
Arije **Paris** Arije **Cannes** Arije **Saint-Jean-Cap-Ferrat**
Doux Joaillier **Courchevel** Zegg & Cerlati **Monaco** Doux Joaillier **Saint Tropez**
Carat & Time **Saint Barthelemy** Avakian **Geneva** Hubner **Vienna** Arije **London** Piantelli **London**
Diamond Time **Athens** Steltman **Den Haag** Lydion Mucevher **Antalya** Azal **Dubaï**
Harvey Nichols **Dubaï** Louvre **Moscow** Crystal **Kiev** Sincere **Kuala Lumpur**
Sincere **Singapore** Cellini **New York** Westime **Los Angeles**
www.guyellia.com

Alarms

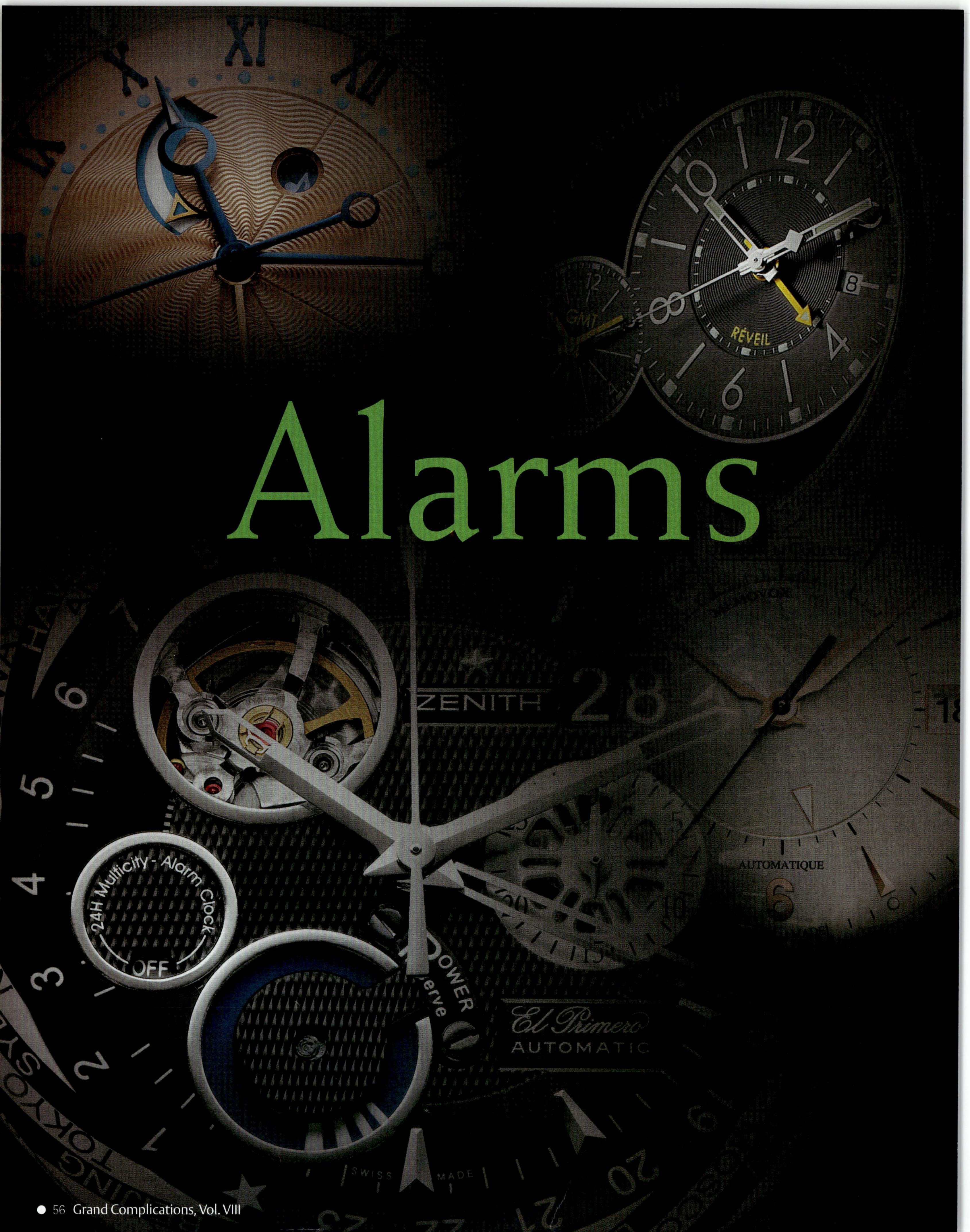
RÉVEIL
GMT
ZENITH
24H Multicity - Alarm Clock
OFF
POWER
Reserve
El Primero
AUTOMATIC
AUTOMATIQUE
SWISS MADE

CLOSE-UP ON ALARM WATCHES

Whether waking a sleeper, reminding the wearer of an appointment, signaling that the parking meter is about to run out, or indicating to a diver that it is time to begin swimming to the surface, the alarm is undoubtedly one of the most useful functions that a wristwatch has to offer. It is also one of the oldest complications, maybe even the oldest, if we consider the very first medieval mechanisms designed to wake monks when it was time for prayers.

Very much in vogue in the 1950s and 60s, the mechanical alarm watch seemed to have been permanently dethroned by electronic alarms, digital radio alarm clocks and cellular phones.

However, the truth is far different. Today, the alarm clock is waking up! For several years, we have been seeing many mechanical watches that give pride of place to this audible complication—including among the most exclusive brands and high-end models.

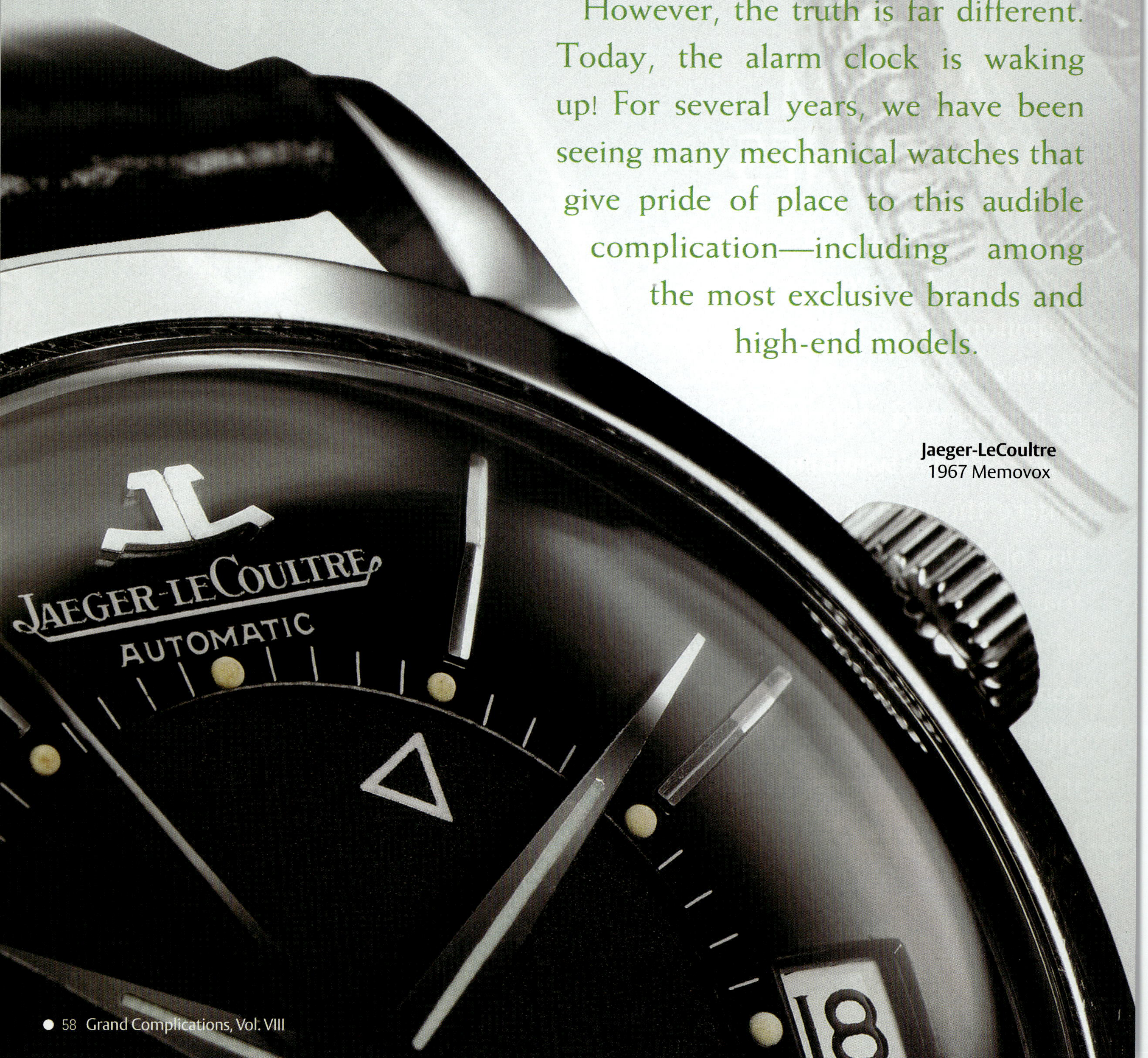

Jaeger-LeCoultre
1967 Memovox

Stimulated by this challenge, watchmakers apply themselves to developing new technical solutions to enhance the user friendliness and the quality of the sound. The choice broadens to include watches equipped with chiming mechanisms or "soft" alarms meant to discreetly remind the wearer of a private moment. The alarm is often accompanied by other useful complications such as a chronograph or a calendar—and especially the multiple time zone display, another traveler's friend currently experiencing an upswing in popularity. Moreover, audible alarm devices are increasingly used in robust diving watches.

It is this rich universe that we invite you to discover, with a brief history of alarm watches, a look at the way they function, as well as the panorama of dominant trends taking shape in today's production.

Eterna
1914 wristwatch alarm

A BRIEF HISTORY OF ALARM WATCHES

The alarm watch is undoubtedly the oldest horological complication. In fact, it seems that in the 13th century, and even earlier, Western monasteries were equipped with audible mechanisms—sometimes called *horologia nocturna* or *horologia excitatoria*—intended to awaken monks so they could say morning prayers at the prescribed hour. Even though at this point in time, the average man in the street or in the fields concerned himself very little with precision (minute and seconds hands would not appear until much later), monastic discipline was much more punctilious about the punctuality of prayers and religious services.

In the 15th century, table clocks were often equipped with an alarm mechanism that sounded on a small bell. This type of instrument would enjoy such high consideration that in 1601, the rules of the Corporation des Horlogers de Genève would demand that whoever wished to earn the certification of "maître" or master-watchmaker must produce a small clock with a morning alarm. The 16th century saw the appearance of pocket alarm watches with openworked casebacks to enhance the acoustics of the sound. Watchmakers also proposed diverse flights of fancy, such as the ring with a miniature alarm watch belonging to Elizabeth I of England, equipped with a silent alarm that discreetly "tapped" the queen's finger to remind her of an important time. In the 17th century, watchmakers also created oversized "carriage watches," with mechanisms to wake passengers in time to make their connections.

The first wristwatch alarm was presented by the Swiss firm Eterna in 1914, based on a patent from 1908. Its single barrel powers both the movement and the alarm, and the alarm time is set with the help of a rotating bezel. The hinged caseback optimizes the acoustics of the strike. In 1930, the same company presented an alarm wristwatch with eight days of power reserve. In 1920, Zenith also created an alarm movement that was equipped with two barrels wound by a single crown with two pushbuttons: one for setting the time, and one for setting the alarm. But these first mechanisms were not yet perfected. The alarm's vibrations tended to interfere with the watch, and the sound was not strong enough to wake a sound sleeper.

Jaeger-LeCoultre
1956 Calibre 815

Jaeger-LeCoultre
Calibre 956

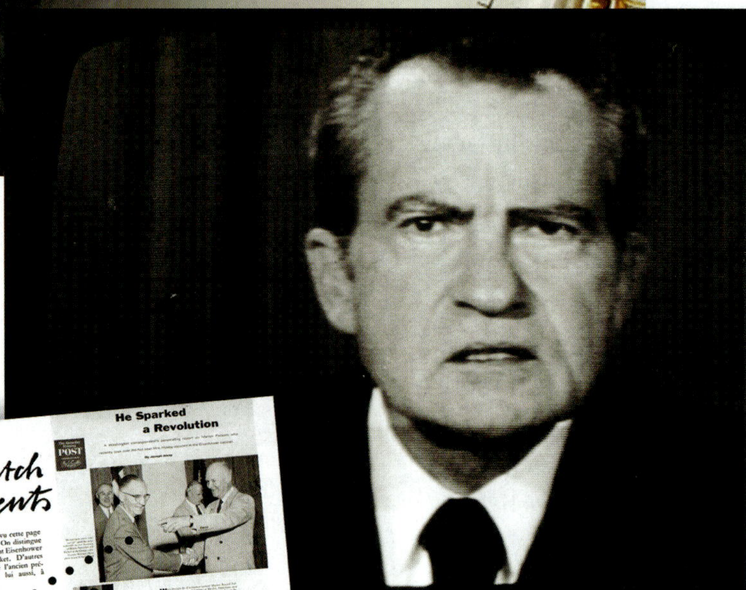

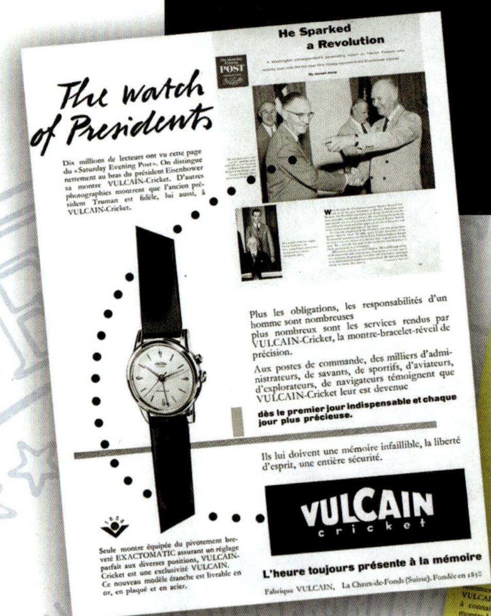

The world would have to wait until 1947, when Vulcain launched the first truly functional alarm wristwatch. The famous Cricket manual-winding movement possessed two barrels, one for the movement, the other for the alarm, which had a strike lasting almost 25 seconds. Thanks to a system with a pin fixed on a membrane and a double caseback pierced with holes, it emitted a strident sound capable of dragging the soundest sleeper from the arms of Morpheus. The Vulcain Cricket appealed to everyone: the masses, businessmen, travelers, but also the most powerful men in the world—Truman, Eisenhower, Johnson and Nixon—which earned it the nickname "The Presidents' Watch."

In the 1950s, the mechanical alarm watch experienced its golden age. Many watch brands were interested in this newly popular domain. In 1950, the firm Laco unveiled its Lanco-Fon, with a small window at 12 o'clock showing at a glance if the alarm function was engaged, and a single crown at 3 o'clock for setting the time and the alarm. The same year, Jaeger-LeCoultre presented its famous Memovox, with a domed caseback enabling two kinds of alarm: the first, to wake up in the morning, is louder, while the other, for meetings during the day, is more discreet. Here's the trick: the hammer directly strikes the caseback with a perforated cover and while the watch is being worn, the cover in contact with the wrist muffles the sound. This Memovox is equipped with two crowns, one for civil time, the other for the alarm, and the alarm time is set with the help of a mobile disc in the dial center bearing a small arrow.

The year 1955 saw the birth of two movements that would equip the alarm watches of numerous brands: the Venus 230 caliber, equipped with a single barrel, and the Alertic movement from A. Schild.

The second half of the 1950s also witnessed a multiplication of technical innovations, including the first alarm watch with double sonority (quiet/loud). In 1956, Jaeger-LeCoultre presented the first automatic-winding alarm watch. Two years later, the company unveiled the Memovox Parking, contemporary with the appearance of the first parking meters, as well as the Memovox Worldtimer, with a central disc bearing the names of 12 cities. In 1959, the Memovox Deep Sea was released, a model designed for scuba diving, an activity that was enjoying a surge in popularity.

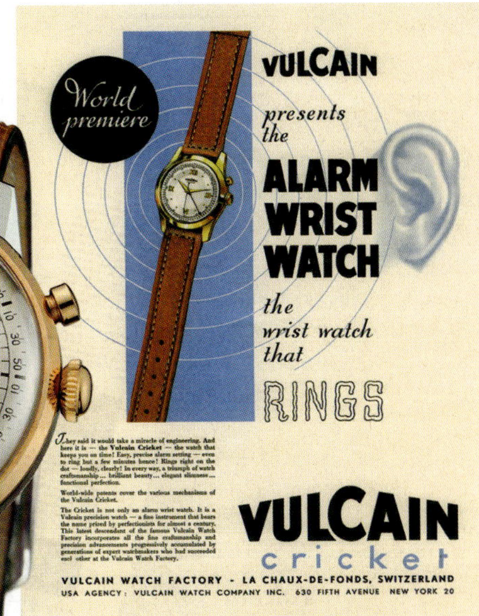

Vulcain
1947 Cricket

Jaeger-LeCoultre
1950 First Memovox
with Caliber 489

Jaeger-LeCoultre
1965 Memovox
Tribute to Polaris

Jaeger-LeCoultre
1960 Memovox
Worldtime

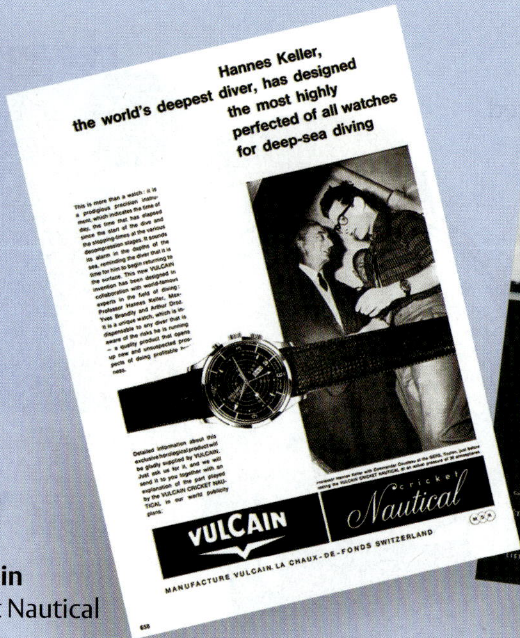

Vulcain
1961 Cricket Nautical

Jaeger-LeCoultre
1969-1970 Memovox ad

Vulcain, the other leading light of the alarm function, was not resting on its laurels. In 1958, the house launched the Cricket Golden Voice, designed for women. In 1961 came the Cricket Nautical, water resistant to 300 meters, with an alarm perfectly audible underwater and a dial displaying decompression stages.

However, in the 1970s, the tidal wave of quartz movements and radio alarm clocks seemed to sign the death warrant for mechanical alarm watches, now mere outdated curiosities. The renaissance of mechanical watchmaking, at the end of the 1980s, signaled the grand return of the wristwatch alarm. The brand Revue Thommen—then linked with Vulcain—took on the project of rereleasing the most famous Cricket models. In 1989, Jaeger-LeCoultre came out with the first alarm wristwatch with perpetual calendar: the famous Grand Réveil. In 1994, the company launched the Master Réveil, descendant of the Memovox, followed more recently by many models with alarm systems. In 1997, Fortis presented the first automatic chronograph equipped with an integrated alarm function, with a double barrel and a chime shaped like a tuning fork that sounded for up to 25 seconds.

In 2002, Vulcain awoke from its slumber, determined to make the most of its rich heritage, which it did by developing the Cricket movement and adding other complications to it, such as the simultaneous display of several time zones. In 2008, the company released the Cricket V-21 caliber, the first manual-winding version. This movement, composed of 257 parts, is equipped with a rotor mounted on ceramic ball bearings and a double barrel: one for the movement, the other for the alarm. Like its predecessor, it is equipped with the Exactomatic system—patented by Vulcain—assuring a more regular functioning when the watch is worn.

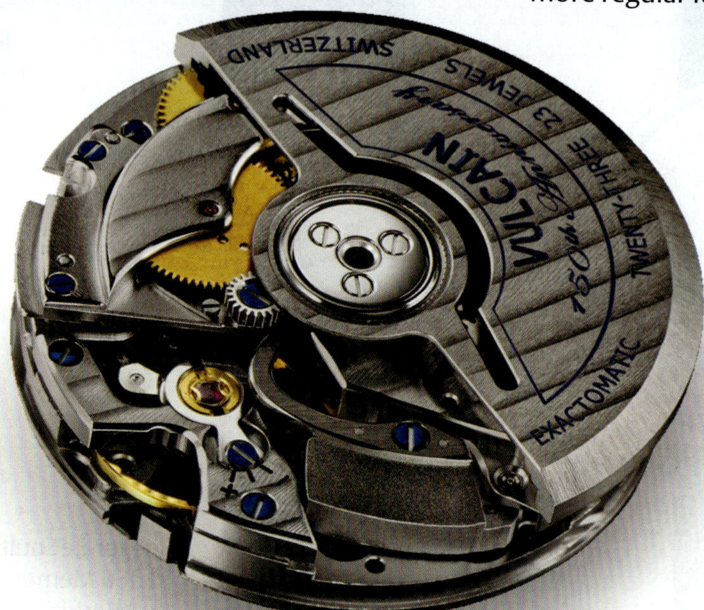

Vulcain
2008 Cricket V-21

However, Vulcain and Jaeger-LeCoultre are not the only players in the world of the alarm watch. For several years, this grand classic of horology has made a clear comeback, thanks to some of the biggest names in the industry. Technical enhancements abound, as do variations on display systems and designs—all of which are clear signs that this complication will be making itself heard for some time to come!

Jaeger-LeCoultre
2011 Master Memovox International

TECHNIQUE

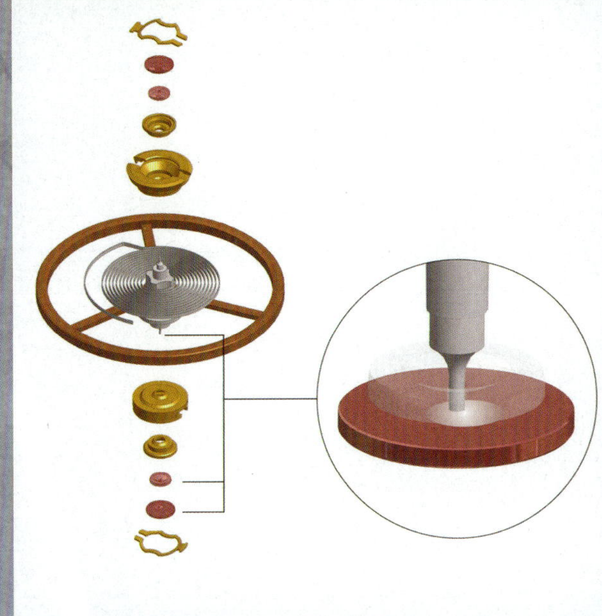

HOW DOES IT WORK?

The alarm watch mechanism comprises two parts, one for setting the time, the other to activate the alarm strike. As a rule, it uses its own barrel (energy storage), separate from the barrel that powers the movement.

Alarm wristwatches most often distinguish themselves by the presence of an additional crown, which allows the wearer to both reset the spring of the striking mechanism and set the alarm.

Certain models also boast a small display on the dial indicating if the alarm is engaged or not.

The sound is produced by a small hammer that strikes a piece of metal. This metal piece could be a membrane with a pin, a kind of bell set into the case middle, or a gong (a steel wire wrapped around the movement), as in minute repeaters. Gongs produce a less powerful sound than the other two solutions. The alarm sounds until the striking work barrel is completely wound down.

Rereleasing the Classics

The history of the alarm watch has its stars, its legends, its flagship models. Riding the wave of enthusiasm for all things vintage, several famous brands have recently rereleased certain classic pieces, adapting them to modern standards of size and technical sophistication.

Tudor, *Heritage Advisor*

Launched in 2011, the Heritage Advisor from Tudor draws inspiration from a 1957 model. It is equipped with an alarm module developed by the brand. The ON/OFF window at 9 o'clock indicates if the alarm function is engaged and the alarm's power reserve is displayed on a disc at 3 o'clock.

Jaeger-LeCoultre, *Master Memovox*

In 1956, Jaeger-LeCoultre made history by launching the first automatic watch with an alarm function. The manufacture paid homage to this iconic model in 2010 by creating the Master Memovox, with caliber 956 integrating the latest technical developments of the manufacture.

Jaeger-LeCoultre, *Master Memovox International*

Jaeger-LeCoultre celebrated the 1958 launch of the Memovox Worldtimer (also known as Memovox "Heures Internationales") by creating the Master Memovox International. The dial's central disc, which allows the wearer to set the alarm time, is adorned with the names of 24 cities, representing the 24 time zones.

Vulcain, *50s Presidents' Watch*

Tribute to the famous "Presidents' Watch," the 50s Presidents' Watch from Vulcain—launched in 2010—combines a design inspired by a 1950s model with the modern performance of the automatic-winding alarm caliber Cricket V-21.

Variations on a Theme

In its most classic version, the alarm watch stands out by its small additional hand or the central disc for regulating the alarm. But the choice is ever-expanding, with multiple variations on the display mode or the style (classic, sporty, modern)—whose partially openworked dials reveal the mechanisms within. On the technical side, the alarm sometimes accompanies other useful complications, such as the chronograph or the much sought after perpetual calendar.

Oris, *Artelier Alarm*

Oris—known for its small alarm clocks in the 1940s—now offers an elegant, classic wristwatch named Artelier Alarm, with an alarm chime specially developed by the brand.

Alfex, *Pazzola Giant Alarm*

In 2009, the brand from Tessin, Switzerland, Alfex, celebrated its 60th anniversary by presenting the Pazzola Giant Alarm. One technical and aesthetic innovation: setting the alarm is done via a disc placed under the dial, positioned in relation to a red marker at 6 o'clock.

Vulcain, *Anniversary Heart Automatique Calendrier*
Launched for Vulcain's 150th anniversary in 2008, the Anniversary Heart is distinguished by its openworked, semi-transparent dial revealing the movement. It is available in several versions, with manual or automatic winding.

Vulcain, *Golden Heart*
Due to its partially skeletonized dial, Vulcain's Golden Heart allows the wearer to admire the complex architecture of the manufacture's Cricket movement, with its anthracite coating and carefully executed finishings.

Jaeger-LeCoultre

Master Grand Réveil

A rare, even unique, example of an alarm watch with perpetual calendar, the Master Grand Réveil from Jaeger-LeCoultre can be set to either chime or vibrate. The alarm mechanism includes a barrel and lever independent from the principal movement, as well as a hammer that makes a gong suspended in the caseback vibrate.

Jaeger-LeCoultre
AMVOX1 R-Alarm

Born from the partnership between Jaeger-LeCoultre and Aston Martin, the AMVOX1 R-Alarm stands out for its sporty aesthetic that recalls automobile gauges. The alarm is set with a small hand on a minute track at the center of the dial.

Alarms one Can Set in Advance

On a traditional alarm watch, the alarm can only be set 12 hours in advance, i.e. in the evening for the next morning. To increase comfort, several brands have developed mechanisms that can set the alarm 24 hours ahead of time—or even a month in advance. Certain systems also set the alarm to the minute.

Glashütte Original, *Senator Diary*

The German brand Glashütte Original, a branch of the Swatch Group, innovated with its 2010 presentation of the Senator Diary, the first alarm watch programmable for up to 30 days in advance. The crown at 10 o'clock and the pushbutton at 8 o'clock allow the wearer to determine the date and time of the alarm to within a quarter of an hour.

Harry Winston, *Project Z6*

Harry Winston has put its name to a highly original reinterpretation of the alarm watch in its limited edition Project Z6. The small off-center dial at 4 o'clock allows the wearer to set the hour and minute of the alarm up to 24 hours in advance, using two discs and a day/night indicator. The rectangular gong, cast in one piece, guarantees optimal acoustics.

Ulysse Nardin,
Sonata Silicium Limited Edition

Launched in 2007, the Sonata Silicium Limited Edition from Ulysse Nardin is distinguished by several technical innovations. Using two cams (one for all 24 hours, the other for the minutes), the alarm mechanism—equipped with a cathedral chime—can be programmed with great precision up to 24 hours in advance.

Musical Alarms

Moving away from more strident sounds, certain brands prefer to charm the ear by equipping their alarm watches with "cathedral" chimes worthy of the most beautiful minute repeaters (see chapter on Minute Repeaters and Sonneries), or even the kind of precious mechanisms that play entire tunes, as do music boxes. These dulcet tones soften the harsh reality of waking up—or remind the wearer with a few notes of an important meeting during the day.

Breguet, *Réveil Musical*

Masterpiece of haute horology, Breguet's Réveil Musical possesses a patented mechanism inspired by music boxes, with the cylinder replaced by a disc with pins. During the melody, which lasts about 20 seconds, the dial completes a full rotation. The automatic caliber is equipped with a silicon escapement.

Vulcain, *Imperial Gong*
The first wristwatch with an alarm and a tourbillon, Vulcain's Imperial Gong—launched in 2005—also stands out for its cathedral chime, worthy of the most beautiful minute repeaters.

Pierre DeRoche, *TNT RendezVous*
Released in 2011, the TNT RendezVous from Pierre DeRoche is not designed to wake a slumberer. It prefers to discreetly signal a moment chosen in advance by a series of double chimes. Its two hammers strike two "cathedral" gongs partially visible through the dial.

Travel Alarms

What is more useful than an alarm while one is traveling? Inspired by this rhetorical question, watchmakers are increasingly combining the alarm function with a second time zone or "world time" display or (see chapter on Multiple Time Zones and GMTs). The most sophisticated models stand out due to their alarm mechanism that is always linked to the local time.

Vulcain, *Revolution GMT Automatic*

The Revolution GMT Automatic from Vulcain associates an automatic-winding alarm movement with a world-time display. The ring indicating the 24 reference cities for the 24 time zones can be set using a crown at 4 o'clock.

Vulcain, *Revolution Dual Time Automatic*

On the Revolution Dual Time Automatic from Vulcain, equipped with the alarm caliber Cricket V-21, the time of the second time zone can be set with the help of a screw-down crown situated at 4 o'clock.

Blancpain
Léman "Anniversary 1735-2005" GMT Alarm

On the Léman "Anniversary 1735-2005" GMT Alarm from Blancpain, the alarm is indexed to the local time display, indicated by the large hour and minute hands. Another practical innovation: the automatic-winding mechanism allows the wearer to charge the power reserve and the alarm simultaneously.

Blancpain, *L-evolution Alarm GMT*

In 2009, Blancpain introduced a model named L-evolution Alarm GMT, with a new manufacture movement featuring two barrels (one for the watch, one for the alarm), simultaneously charged by an automatic-winding system, as well as an alarm hand linked to the local time.

Breguet, *Le Réveil du Tsar*

The Réveil du Tsar, from Breguet, possesses an alarm mechanism indexed to the local time, with an alarm engagement indicator in a small window at 12 o'clock. The hours/minutes subdial, at 3 o'clock, allows the wearer to set the alarm with to-the-minute precision.

Zenith, *Grande Class Traveller Répétition Minutes El Primero*

The Grande Class Traveller Répétition Minutes El Primero from Zenith (see also the chapter on Multi-Complications) presents, among other functions, an alarm with strike or vibrate mode, as well as two power reserve indicators, one for the movement, the other for the strike.

Zenith, *Class Traveller Multicity Alarm*

The Class Traveller Multicity Alarm from Zenith associates the famous automatic-winding El Primero chronograph movement with an alarm and a world time display. It is equipped with two barrels, the first for the alarm, the second for the model's other functions.

Officine Panerai, *Radiomir GMT Alarm*

The Radiomir GMT Alarm from Officine Panerai combines a digital display of a second time zone at 6 o'clock with an alarm indicated by a central hand. The two functions are controlled by a crown located on the right side of the case featuring the brand's characteristic cushion shape.

Jaeger-LeCoultre
Master Compressor Extreme W-Alarm

The Master Compressor Extreme W-Alarm from Jaeger-LeCoultre, with a world time function, presents several patented innovations in its alarm mechanism, which is equipped with a gong wrapped around the movement. The time of the alarm can be precisely selected using a double disc with hours and minutes in a window at 9 o'clock.

Underwater Sounds

An ever-increasing number of diving watches are equipped with an alarm, and more and more alarm watches are getting their sea legs. This might seem like an odd alliance, as the ocean depths are not ideal for spending the night, or even for a small nap. But here the alarm is used to remind the wearer of a precise moment, notably the end of the dive time—and it doesn't hurt that sound carries much better underwater than in open air.

Vulcain, *Nautical*
In a rerelease of the 1961 model, the Nautical from Vulcain—water resistant to 300m—stands out for its alarm that is audible underwater, its central rotating dial displaying decompression stages and its triple-backed case, which serves as a resonance chamber for the chime.

Vulcain, *Diver X-Treme Automatic*

Vulcain has developed several watches that combine an alarm with underwater capability, such as the Diver X-Treme Automatic, with a case that is water resistant to 100m, audible underwater strike, rotating 60-minute bezel to calculate the dive time and an ultra-readable dial highlighted with luminescent indexes.

Breguet, *Marine Royale*

Breguet has released its sporty Marine Royale collection in an alarm model water resistant to 300m, with a modern aesthetic that combines rubber and rose gold.

Jaeger-LeCoultre
Memovox Tribute to Deep Sea

In homage to Memovox Deep Sea, the first Jaeger-LeCoultre diving watch, released in 1959, the Memovox Tribute to Deep Sea is powered by the automatic Memovox 956 caliber, with hours, minutes, seconds and alarm. The caseback reprises the timepiece's original design of a frogman surrounded by bubbles.

Jaeger-LeCoultre
Master Compressor Diving Alarm Navy SEALs

Jaeger-LeCoultre celebrated its partnership with the elite combat swimmers through the 2009 launch of the Master Compressor Diving Alarm Navy SEALs, a limited edition with a grade 5 titanium case, a ceramic bezel and water resistance to 300m.

Electronic Multi-Function Models

Of course, there are many quartz wristwatches equipped with an alarm, at all price points. However, there are a few that serve as true multi-function instruments, providing their users with numerous useful functions.

Seiko, *Sportura SNAD23-2*
On this Sportura SNAD23-2 from Seiko, the 1/5-of-a-second chronograph is complemented by an alarm that the wearer can set with a small analog hour/minute dial at 6 o'clock.

Tissot, *Sailing-Touch*
On the Sailing-Touch from Tissot, the wearer need only touch the crystal to display one of the numerous useful functions for under the sea: relative pressure, regatta countdown clock, chronograph with tachometer, compass, tide calculator, perpetual calendar, dual time zone—not to mention two alarms linked to the main time zone.

Breitling, *Chronospace*
Designed as an instrument for pilots, the Breitling Chronospace features a second time zone with independent alarm alongside several other eminently useful functions (1/100-of-a-second chronograph with split times, alarm, countdown clock, GMT, perpetual calendar).

TechnoMarine, *UF6 Magnum*,

Water resistant to 200m, the three-dimensional dial of this UF6 Magnum from TechnoMarine features a window for the date and a second time zone 24-hour display, as well as an alarm function that the wearer can set with an additional central hand.

The New Alarm Clocks

Highly fashionable from the 1940s to the '60s, small mechanical alarm clocks have mostly given way to quartz alarm clocks, radio alarms and cellular telephones. However, certain brands have restarted—or never halted—production of these clocks, in models that can be extremely high end. In the quartz arena, aside from the vast choice of inexpensive alarms available in just about any retail store, a diverse selection of more sophisticated creations play with design in a highly original way.

L'Epée, *Gorge à Complications*
Descendant of a famous French manufacture for travel clocks, the brand L'Epée—purchased in 2008 by the Swiss company Swiza—offers varied models of small high-end mechanical alarm clocks. The selection includes the Gorge, with carrousel, striking mechanism, repeater, alarm, day, date, moonphase and an eight-day power reserve.

Victorinox Swiss Army
Travel Alarm 1884 Limited Edition

Equipped with a quartz movement, the Travel Alarm 1884 Limited Edition alarm clock, from Victorinox Swiss Army, is inspired by the design of the famous Swiss Army knives and their characteristic opening and closing system.

Louis Vuitton, *Tambour XXL Réveil Quartz*

Inspired by the design of the Tambour wristwatches, this Tambour XXL Réveil Quartz travel alarm clock from Louis Vuitton also boasts a second time zone hours/ minutes display. The fold-out support is adorned with the famous monogram characteristic of the brand.

BREGUET

MARINE ROYALE – REF. 5847BB

The Marine Royale is powered by an automatic-winding 519R caliber that boasts a 45-hour power reserve. The dial displays hours, minutes, seconds, date at 6:00, the alarm power reserve between 9:00 and 11:00 and the alarm on/off indicator at 12:00. The 45mm 18K white-gold case possesses many notable characteristics, including a unidirectional rotating bezel with luminous markers, a wave-shaped ratchet at 3:00 to ensure the bezel's one-way rotation, a hand-guilloché sapphire crystal caseback, and rubber-covered alarm on/off pushbutton at 8:00. The 18K gold silvered dial also features hand-guilloché decoration, as well as a chapter ring with applied blued Roman numerals and luminous dots for nighttime readability.

BREGUET

REVEIL MUSICAL – REF. 7800BA

Breguet presents the melodious Réveil Musical. This alarm watch is powered by an automatic-winding 777M caliber housed within an 18K yellow-gold 48mm case. Endowed with a straight-line lever escapement, Breguet balance wheel and overcoil, and 55 jewels, the piece also possesses a dial that features a guilloché rotating bridge with platinum effects and blued-steel hands. Musical notes adorn the caseband. The Réveil Musical is also available in a white-gold case.

GLASHÜTTE ORIGINAL

SENATOR DIARY ROSE GOLD – REF. 100.13.01.01.04

The Senator Diary is beautifully balanced, with two crowns positioned directly opposite each other on either side of the rose-gold case, each accompanied by a pushbutton. The crown and pushbutton on the right operate the panorama date display at 3:00. Rose-gold hour, minute and sweep seconds hands enhance the elegance of the design. The Caliber 100-13 automatic movement boasts beautifully finished components, including a three-quarter plate with Glashütte ribbing, polished steel components, beveled edges and blued screws. The date indicator on the diary alarm subdial is in blue, as is the small arrow indicating the diary alarm time aperture at 6:00.

GLASHÜTTE ORIGINAL

SENATOR DIARY WHITE GOLD – REF. 100-13-04-04-04

This white-gold Senator Diary timepiece uses the darkness of its galvanized ruthenium dial as a counter-balance to the sheen of its case. Intuitively operated, the Glashütte Original 100-13 self-winding caliber permits the setting of an alarm up to 30 days in advance, even beyond the end of the current calendar month. Adjusted with a pushbutton at 8:00 and crown at 10:00, the innovative complication communicates with the running time, so that any correction of the date is transmitted to the appointment mechanism, removing the need for secondary modification. With the addition of a third spring barrel to the 600-component movement, the alarm remains wound even when the watch has exceeded its 55-hour power reserve.

JAEGER-LECOULTRE

MASTER MEMOVOX INTERNATIONAL – REF. 141.84.71

Released as a tribute to the historic 1958 model, the Master Memovox International also shows the world time zones on its central alarm disc, which is inscribed with the names of 24 cities. Each represents a different time zone, which allows the traveller to instantly tell the time anywhere in the world, a feature that nicely complements the indispensable alarm function. Powered by the automatic-winding Jaeger-LeCoultre 956, the Master Memovox International is housed in a stainless steel case that is water resistant to 50m.

ZENITH

GRANDE CLASS TRAVELLER REPETITION MINUTES EL PRIMERO

The El Primero 4031 caliber makes a solid argument for recognition as one of the most remarkable movements ever created. With a frequency of 36,000 vph, this bi-directionally self-winding mechanism features a minute repeater, alarm function with vibrating alert or buzzer, large date, triple power reserve indication for running time, minute repeater, alarm and dual time zone function. With its incredible range of complications, this watch boasts not only the optimal legibility of an ingenious design, but also a power reserve of 50 hours.

Multi-Complications

With hundreds of components, and a process of development and production that can take up to ten years of intensive efforts, ultra-complicated watches represent the quintessence of the watchmaking art. They are to haute horology what Formula 1 is to the automobile: the supreme demonstration of technical expertise—and the best testing ground for innovations that will later grace models with more mass appeal. Produced in extremely limited editions, and sometimes as one-of-a-kind pieces, these models serve as showcases for the most prestigious manufacturers—a way of declaring their consummate savoir-faire or commemorating an historical milestone. Alongside these unique productions and tours de force, horologers also offer a beautiful selection of multi-complicated watches, which include fewer functions and a keener focus on ease of use, functionality and readability. These pieces are a real feast for collectors and aficionados of rare pieces.

Philippe Merk

CEO of Audemars Piguet

"The design codes of the Royal Oak will lean toward finesse and elegance"

Wolfgang Sickenberg

Director of Sales, Audemars Piguet

Audemars Piguet celebrates, in 2012, the 40th anniversary of its emblematic model, the Royal Oak. Presented in 1972 at BaselWorld, its avant-garde design drove many to forecast a shipwreck. Forty years later, the Royal Oak has become a global legend! The celebration that awaits will bring several surprises: upon reaching the age of reason, the Royal Oak will, in 2012, be more demure and more strictly horological.

Appointed as the head of Audemars Piguet in January of 2009, Philippe Merk already has the brand under his skin. Supported by his right-hand man Wolfgang Sickenberg, he has a very clear vision for the oldest family-owned watchmaking house: to expand its unique horological expertise in every collection. On the eve of a transitional year—the 40th birthday of the Royal Oak—the two men are committed to showcasing the virtues of the Manufacture's timepieces, as well as the men and women who develop them, thereby providing a more complete understanding of the house.

EXTRA-THIN ROYAL OAK

ROYAL OAK AUTOMATIC

If you had to explain to a novice, in a few words, what Audemars Piguet means, what would you tell him?

Philippe Merk: It is the oldest watch manufacturer still owned by the founding family (or families in this case). This temporal dimension is essential, since it gives us genuine legitimacy in our field. Audemars Piguet is also a spirit of independence, free from all trends and fashions: the expertise that we have developed over the centuries will still be relevant in the coming centuries. Audemars Piguet is all of this: tradition, but also innovation. It's a fantastic driving force!

And if you had to explain Audemars Piguet to an economist?

PM: The group consists of 1,100 people, of which 800 are in Switzerland. We produce 30,000 watches annually with sales in excess of 500 million Swiss francs.

How are the sales of Audemars Piguet divided between regions?

Wolfgang Sickenberg: Our balance is quite nice: 35% in Europe, 40% in Asia, 20% in the Americas, while the Middle East makes up the remainder. This is a situation that works well for us; we are a globally appreciated brand.

Is China important to you at this time?

WS: Greater China, with Hong Kong and Taiwan, as well as Singapore and Korea, where a lot of Chinese people reside, represent a large portion of our worldwide sales. Once we take into account the Chinese who buy in Europe, this becomes our leading clientele.

It seems today that demand is insatiable…

WS: One must be careful: certain countries are clearly overheating; others work well because they are supported by an international clientele—such as Switzerland. We must continue to be present everywhere, to be close to the client.

Despite all of this, are you expecting, in terms of production, to see significant growth this year?

PM: We were relatively spared by the crisis, during which the collapse was not disastrous for us. Picking up from there was quite easy, again seeing positive growth in 2011.

WS: The difficulty is to be on time with the right quantity of the right product. At Audemars Piguet, we don't have a problem of quantity maximization, we simply need to maintain a stable balance: too many watches, and the value of the brand diminishes; too few, and the consumer, who is more demanding than ever, won't wait.

Is it easy to communicate the "substance" that a brand such as yours offers?

WS: It's important to give people the time to discover all the subtleties and details of a brand like Audemars Piguet. It is our responsibility to effectively communicate, to the marketplace, the differences between industrial results and hand-crafted finishing. With the euphoria that we have experienced over the last ten years, we may have forgotten to put that in the forefront. We have returned to these values with a complete marketing strategy that leans in that direction. It won't be the only axis, but it will be an important one.

Let's then discuss the Royal Oak, which celebrates its 40th anniversary in 2012...

PM: We have planned an itinerary of exhibitions that will travel to the world's key cities, as well as other activities in the form of slightly more local events that will find their way onto the program.

WS: The primary theme emphasis will be placed on Audemars Piguet, and within that, the 40 years of the Royal Oak, which has become a legendary icon in itself. The Royal Oak is almost as famous as Audemars Piguet. This is of course an enormous success, but we would like to give the brand renewed precedence over the timepiece.

Is the image of the Royal Oak too strong?

PM: Finding a better balance in our product portfolio is indeed one of our goals. We were obviously thrilled with reactions that followed the launch of the Millenary, with its very special and unusual shape. While we are able to produce such timepieces, we are equally convinced that with classical watches, we can do much more!

How do you integrate the very sporty Royal Oak within this strategy for the future?

PM: By further differentiating the Royal Oak and Royal Oak Offshore. The forthcoming design codes of the Royal Oak will lean more toward finesse and elegance.

WS: We would like to make the Royal Oak, not a classical watch, but a watchmaking classic. Fundamentally, it is a timepiece born from the sports world. Today however, in comparison to the Offshore, it has lost a bit of the extreme image that it had 40 years ago. We are therefore going to revise it so that it can regain its original aesthetic: same size, same logo placement, etc.

It's a return to authentic values...

PM: It's necessary. We must once again be inspired by the object!

WS: Audemars Piguet is fortunate to possess several platforms of communication: with the Offshore, we can move towards the future; with the Jules Audemars, we connect with tradition; the Millenary has a resolutely contemporary quality. We can be in the past, the present and the future. We aren't going to abandon timely relevance, the "success story" that we are enjoying today in the company of our ambassadors. We are simply going to restore the overall balance: less lifestyle and more horology. For example, we have invested a lot in our industrial capabilities these last few years, but we haven't highlighted this aspect as much as we should.

Audemars Piguet has stood out over the last few years by its audacity. Are you becoming less non-conformist?

WS: I wouldn't put it that way. We are going to better explore certain avenues, such as proprietary research by Audemars Piguet. The AP escapement, for example, which has perhaps not received all the recognition that it deserves: it was our desire to initially use it on a very small scale. But in the future, it is an extraordinary challenge to grow its production from around thirty to possibly 30,000! Now that is audacious!

TOURBILLON GMT ROYAL OAK CONCEPT

EQUATION OF TIME ROYAL OAK

Multi-Complications

Audemars Piguet,
Hand-Wound
Royal Oak Offshore
Tourbillon Chronograph

Patek Philippe
Leroy 01

Horology did not evolve in a purely linear fashion from simplest to most complicated timepieces. The minute display, which today seems one of the most basic functions, only became widespread at the end of the 17th century, with the invention of the regulating balance spring. However, some pocket watches already featured highly complex mechanisms by this point. As for the seconds display, it would not come along until another century later. Moreover, the history of horology is marked by several "setbacks," due to the shrinking size of the mechanisms. This is why the first portable clocks and pocket watches of the Renaissance were more rudimentary, technically, than the large astronomical clocks of the Middle Ages—and even the most sophisticated wristwatch today would not be able to display as many functions as an ultra-complicated pocket watch.

The first explicit mentions of mechanical clocks appear in the 14th century. Though we can reasonably assume that artisans began with simple mechanisms, the only clocks we know from that period are quite complex, such as the clock tower with the astronomical dial that Roger Stoke constructed for the Norwich cathedral between 1321 and 1325, and of course the "star" of the era, a marvel of its time, Giovanni de Dondi's astrarium in Padua, completed in 1364.

During the late Middle Ages and the Renaissance, the Church and political authorities encouraged and financed monumental clocks that boasted a large number of astronomical and astrological indications, equipped with audible strike systems that were often quite spectacular. Among the most famous examples are the astronomical clocks of the Lund cathedral, in Sweden (1380), the Saint-Etienne cathedral in Bourges, France (1424) and the Saint Mary of Rostock church in Germany (1472).

The first pocket watches, at the end of the 15th century, possessed only an hour hand. In the 16th century, artisans developed astronomical and astrological displays, then added more and more functions—alarm, calendar, strike in passing and on demand—as they competed to create watches that contained the largest number of complications.

The most famous example of this phenomenon is the Breguet Nº 160, better known as the "Marie-Antoinette," whose creation and history are shrouded in history. In 1783, Abraham-Louis Breguet, already a favorite of Louis XVI and his wife, received a commission from an officer of the queen's guards: to create a watch that would integrate all the complications and refinements of the time. Marie Antoinette, guillotined in 1793, would never see this beauty, as it was completed in 1827, under the direction of Breguet's son. This automatic-winding watch (referred to as a perpétuelle) contained within its gold case and rock crystal dial complications such as a minute repeater, complete perpetual calendar, equation of time, power reserve indicator, metallic thermometer, independent large seconds and small seconds hand—not to mention the many technical feats such as a double pare-chute, a gold balance spring and several components in sapphire crystal. The Marie-Antoinette passed through several hands, and was stolen from a Jerusalem museum in 1983. The company Breguet created an identical reproduction of the timepiece, but in the autumn of 2007, the original suddenly reappeared in the museum's collections under mysterious circumstances.

In 1925, the New York banker Henry Graves, Jr. commissioned Patek Philippe to create for him the most complicated watch ever. Comprised of over 900 components, this double-sided pocket watch includes 24 complications, including a grand strike on four gongs and alarm on a fifth gong. The title of "the world's most complicated watch" was long disputed between the Graves and another horological masterpiece, the Leroy 01 (1904). Its double-sided case contains 20 complications related to time measurement—equation of time, chronograph, the sky above the Northern and Southern Hemispheres, grand strike, etc.—and five non-horological functions: hygrometer, thermometer, barometer, altimeter and compass. This inclusion has given rise to a dispute between those who grant it 25 complications and those—partisans for the Graves—who contest that it has "only" 20.

In 1989, Patek Philippe put an end to the quarrel with its Calibre 89. With 33 complications and 1,728 components, this timepiece is today the most complicated portable watch in the world, though describing it as "portable" might be a stretch—at 88.2mm across and 41.07mm thick, weighing over 2 pounds, the Calibre 89 is not exactly a pocket or fob watch.

The advent of the wristwatch in the early 20th century obliged watchmakers to restrict their ambitions a bit for complicated pieces, given the smaller volume of the wristwatch's case. However, it also inspired them to come up with treasures of ingenuity to miniaturize existing complications and combine them in exceptional pieces. Today, the biggest names in the industry compete to create "the most complicated watch in the world," aided in their quest by computer software that allows for possibilities still unimaginable a few decades ago. In March of last year, Marc Alexandre Hayek unveiled the prototype of a Breguet wristwatch offering 35 different functions on the piece's two faces. Named Hommage à Nicolas G. Hayek Ref. 7887, this piece has what it takes to become "the most complicated wristwatch in the world." Stay tuned…

Patek Philippe
Graves

Pocket Records

Though pocket watches have been largely replaced by wristwatches, their larger cases provides horologers with a versatile field of experimentation when it comes to gathering as many complications as possible within the same timepiece. However, without shooting for the Guinness Book of World Records, larger horologers as well as artisans have recently offered extremely sophisticated pocket watches.

Breguet
Modern Reproduction of the Marie-Antoinette
In 2008, Breguet presented an identical reproduction of the famous ultra-complicated Marie-Antoinette watch (1827), one of the most impressive achievements of its history, housed in a box carved from the queen's favorite oak at Versailles.

Patek Philippe, *Calibre 89*
With 33 complications and a 1,728-piece movement, the Calibre 89 from Patek Philippe is to this day the most complicated portable watch in the history of horology. Besides the complete roster of "classic" complications (tourbillon, calendar, chronograph, strike, astronomical complications, etc.), it presents a few extremely rare functions such as the "secular" perpetual calendar (see chapter on Calendar watches), as well as a display of the date upon which Easter will next fall. It is also equipped with a celestial map that depicts the Milky Way and 2,800 stars of the Northern Hemisphere, as well as their relative size. Its development and production required nine years.

Patek Philippe, *Star Caliber 2000*

The double-sided pocket watch Star Caliber 2000, from Patek Philippe, associates 21 complications. Dedicated to our sun, the obverse dial displays functions including a running equation of time, times of sunrise and sunset, and a 24-hour day/night indication. The second dial, on the reverse side, pays tribute to the night sky with a map featuring the moon and stars, a moonphase display and a golden ellipse outlining the part of the sky visible from the selected observation site.

Breguet, *N° 5*

The N° 5 from Breguet, a replica of an older watch, associates automatic winding, 60-hour power reserve, moonphase display and a quarter repeater whose hammer strikes the inside of the case instead of a gong.

Vincent Bérard, *Quatre Saisons Carrosse*

Artisan watchmaker Vincent Bérard has chosen to reinvent the carriage watch with the Quatre Saisons Carrosse. This handmade piece combines a perpetual calendar, quarter repeater, a system of automatons on the dial, a power reserve indicator and a thermometer.

Audemars Piguet

Grande Complication Savonnette

Within its yellow-gold case cover, the Grande Complication Savonnette (hunter-type watch) from Audemars Piguet unites a perpetual calendar, minute repeater and split-seconds chronograph.

Exploits on the Wrist

The race to produce "the most complicated watch in the world" is in full swing. To stand out from the crowd, the most high-end watchmakers come up with feats of ingenuity, reinventing the base mechanisms that support the complications, most of which were invented and perfected before the 19th century. The time has come for new constructions, in new materials, with new interpretations that playfully overturn long-established traditions.

Hybris Mechanica
à Grande Sonnerie

Hybris Mechanica à Gyrotourbillon

Reverso à Tryptique Hybris Mechanica

Jaeger-LeCoultre, *Hybris Mechanica*

The 2009 Hybris Mechanica trilogy from Jaeger-LeCoultre displays a total of 55 complications, some of which are found on more than one model. The Hybris Mechanica a Gyrotourbillon is an homage to the quintessence of the mechanical measure of time, thanks to its "spherical tourbillon" (see chapter on Tourbillons), completed by a perpetual calendar with four retrograde hands and an equation of time function that can be adjusted according to one's location. The Hybris Mechanica à Tryptique comes up with an unusual take on the famous Reverso reversible case, originally created in 1931. The watch boasts three faces, for three dimensions of time. On the front of the case is civil time, with a new detent escapement system and a titanium tourbillon; the back shows sidereal time, with a sky map, Zodiac calendar, equation of time and times of sunrise and sunset; while the watch cradle displays perpetual time, with a complete calendar—making a grand total of 18 complications on this exceptional timepiece. As for the Hybris Mechanica à Grande Sonnerie, it contains no fewer than 26 complications, with a 1,300-piece movement that powers a flying tourbillon, perpetual calendar with retrograde hands and a strike/minute repeater mechanism with numerous patented innovations.

Patek Philippe, *Sky Moon Tourbillon*

The most complicated Patek Philippe wristwatch, the double-sided Sky Moon Tourbillon (2001) combines 12 complications, including a minute repeater with cathedral gongs, a perpetual calendar with retrograde date hand and a tourbillon. The dial on the reverse side presents a mobile map of the sky, reproducing—with extreme precision—the visible movement of the stars and the moon, as well as the moonphases.

Franck Muller, *Aeternitas Mega 4*

The Aeternitas Mega 4 model from Franck Muller houses, within its elegant tonneau-shaped case, 15 complications, including grand and small strike, minute repeater with Westminster chime, secular calendar with retrograde date, equation of time, large tourbillon, split-seconds chronograph and two additional time zones.

Vacheron Constantin, *Tour de l'Ile*

In 2005, Vacheron Constantin celebrated its 250th anniversary by creating the ultra-complicated model called Tour de l'Ile. This double-sided timepiece contains in its 834-piece movement no fewer than 16 complications, including a minute repeater, tourbillon, indications of the moonphase and age of the moon, perpetual calendar, equation of time, times of sunrise and sunset, and a map of the night sky.

Varied Triumphs

The horological superstars whose complications can be counted on the fingers of two, three, four, even five or six hands should not make us forget all the creations that—though they have achieved more modest recognition—are exceptional triumphs in their own right. A "grand complication," in the watch world, is created when a watch contains three or four supplementary functions—especially if each of those functions belongs to one of the traditional domains of haute horology (audible indications, calendars, chronographs, tourbillons, etc.).

Jean Dunand, *Grande Complication*

In 2005, the brand Jean Dunand—co-founded by Christophe Claret, the renowned constructor of complicated movements—presented a wristwatch called Grande Complication. This 827-piece timepiece includes, among other functions, a single-pusher split-seconds chronograph, tourbillon, minute/quarter/hour repeater and perpetual calendar with retrograde date and day indications.

IWC, *Portuguese Grand Complication*

The Portuguese Grand Complication from IWC offers a minute repeater and chronograph, as well as a perpetual calendar that indicates not only the date, day and month, but the year as well, via a four-digit display.

Cartier

Rotonde Grand Complication Skeleton

Issued in a limited edition of 30 pieces, Cartier's Rotonde Grand Complication Skeleton boasts a tourbillon, perpetual calendar, single-pusher chronograph and eight-day power reserve display—all within an entirely openworked, decorated 457-piece movement.

Zenith, *Grande Class Traveller Répétition Minutes El Primero*

Composed of 744 pieces, the movement that powers the Grande Class Traveller Répétition Minutes El Primero, from Zenith's 2005 releases, combines a minute repeater, alarm (with audible or vibration settings), a second time zone, a large date with instant jump and two power reserves, one for the watch, the other for the strike—not to mention, of course, the famous El Primero chronograph functions.

Vacheron Constantin
Patrimony Traditionnelle Calibre 2755

A worthy descendant of the prestigious Tour de l'Ile, released for the 250th anniversary of the brand, the Patrimony Traditionnelle Calibre 2755 from Vacheron Constantin brings together three major complications of the horological universe—minute repeater, tourbillon and perpetual calendar—in an elegant round case.

Patek Philippe, *Triple Complication Ref. 5208*

Unveiled in 2011, the new automatic Triple Complication Ref. 5208 wristwatch from Patek Philippe associates within its platinum case a minute repeater, single-pusher chronograph and instantaneous perpetual calendar with apertures. It also stands out for its escapement and balance spring in Silinvar®, a silicon derivative.

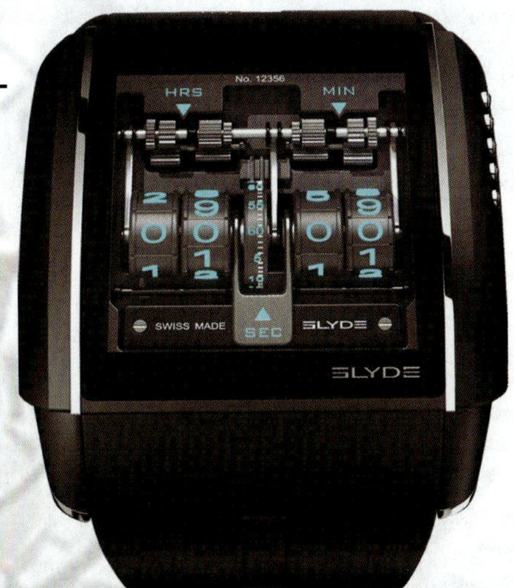

HD3, *Slyde*

An ultra-modern, ultra-geeky version of grand complications, the new electronic model Slyde from HD3 is distinguished by its curved tactile screen that displays the various indications (time, calendar, chronograph, countdown clock, moonphase, second time zone) in much the same way as a smartphone.

Christophe Claret
DualTow NightEagle

Christophe Claret scored a huge coup with its DualTow NightEagle, which features hour/minute displays on two belt drives inspired by treaded vehicles, a single-pusher planetary chronograph with strike and tourbillon, not to mention many other refinements and technical innovations.

Maîtres du Temps, *Chapter One*

Presented in 2008 in a tonneau-shaped case and rereleased in 2010 in a round version, Chapter One from Maîtres du Temps unites a single-pusher column-wheel chronograph, a retrograde second time zone display and retrograde date, as well as day and moonphase displays on two rollers at 6 o'clock and 12 o'clock.

Astronomical Watches

Astronomical complications are the very source of the art of horology, and they are part of the classic repertory of all ultra-complicated pieces. At the start of the third millennium, they are making a forceful comeback on highly sophisticated pieces that meld technical prowess and poetry. The major rising star is the map of the night sky.

IWC, *Portuguese Sidérale Scafusia*

The most complex watch ever created by IWC, the Portuguese Sidérale Scafusia displays on its double-sided case the solar time, sidereal time (that of the stars) and various other astronomical indications including a map of the night sky and times of sunrise and sunset—not to mention a constant-force tourbillon and perpetual calendar.

Van Cleef & Arpels
Midnight in Paris

The Midnight in Paris model by Van Cleef & Arpels reproduces on its aventurine dial the movement of the stars in the sky above Paris, the City of Light.

Louis Moinet, *Astralis*

Besides its astral tourbillon and split-seconds column-wheel chronograph, the new Astralis from Louis Moinet—a limited edition of just 12 pieces—stands out for its 24-hour planetary function, which successively displays four planets, each composed of an extremely rare meteorite.

Chopard, *L.U.C 150 All-in-One*

To celebrate its 150th anniversary, Chopard presented the L.U.C 150 All-in-One model. Possessing 516 components, the L.U.C 4TQE movement—certified as a chronometer and marked with the Geneva Seal—displays 14 complications (tourbillon, perpetual calendar, etc.) on the front and back of the watch, including, on the caseback, equation of time, power reserve, 24-hour day/night indication, times of sunrise and sunset and astronomical moonphase.

Ulysse Nardin, *Trilogy of Time*

Ulysse Nardin has demonstrated its commitment to the astronomical and astrological science of the Renaissance by creating an exceptional trio of timepieces called Trilogy of Time. The first piece, Astrolabium Galileo Galilei, depicts on its dial the functions of the astrolabium, a navigational tool that facilitated great discoveries. It indicates the respective positions of the sun, moon and stars as observed from the Earth. The Planetarium Copernicus continuously displays the month, Zodiac sign and astronomical positions of the planets in relation to the sun and the Earth using a dial composed of seven concentric rings. As for the Tellurium Johannes Kepler, with its cloisonné enamel dial representing the Earth as seen from above the North Pole, it displays times of sunrise and sunset (with areas of shadow and light), as well as solar and lunar eclipses.

Audemars Piguet, *Royal Oak Equation of Time*

Equipped with an equation of time system that takes longitude into account (see chapter on Equations of Time) the Royal Oak Equation of Time from Audemars Piguet is also one of the rare wristwatches to display times of sunrise and sunset utilizing three parameters: date, longitude and latitude.

Jaeger-LeCoultre

Master Grande Tradition Grande Complication

On the Master Grande Tradition Grande Complication from Jaeger-LeCoultre, the "orbital" flying tourbillon that serves as an hour hand indicates sidereal time, or time calculated by the stars. Civil time is indicated by a small sun turning around the periphery of the dial, and a Zodiac calendar indicates the position of the constellations as they appear throughout the year.

A. LANGE & SÖHNE

SAXONIA ANNUAL CALENDAR – REF. 330.026

An annual calendar complication is one of the most popular and sublimely useful functions in horology. A. Lange & Söhne has now added the first to the Saxonia family: the Saxonia Annual Calendar. This timepiece displays a large date, day of the week, and month. The moonphase display is so accurate that it only needs to be corrected by one day every 122 years, assuming the watch runs without interruption. The Saxonia Annual Calendar includes the self-winding SAX-O-MAT caliber with a 46-hour power reserve and a zero-reset hand-setting mechanism. The plates and bridges are made of untreated German silver and the balance cock is engraved by hand. The timepiece is available in a white- or pink-gold case with a diameter of 38.5mm.

AUDEMARS PIGUET

ROYAL OAK GRANDE COMPLICATION – REF. 25865BC.OO.1105BC.01

The Royal Oak Grande Complication is powered by the 2885 caliber, a self-winding movement of 13.5''', which features a split-seconds chronograph, a minute repeater and a perpetual calendar. Seconds are displayed in a subdial at 9:00. Housed in an 18K white-gold case, the movement beats at 19,800 vibrations per hour. The dial displays 12 indications, including day, date, month, leap years and moonphase. The movement is comprised of 654 pieces.

CHRISTOPHE CLARET

21 BLACKJACK – REF. MTR.BLJ08.000-021

A real miniature casino, the 21 Blackjack mixes grand complications with the world of gaming. In addition to transparency, relief, and the passage of time, Christophe Claret adds the sensory effects of blackjack, roulette and dice. The first game features a pair of miniature dice, which are located in a cage at the 4:00 position on the case middle that is visible through a sapphire crystal. On the back of the watch the winding rotor, which is visible through a sapphire crystal, serves as a roulette wheel. Once set in motion by one or two movements, the wheel turns for a few moments before stopping. Blackjack consists of drawing cards to equal or to come as close as possible to 21 points. On the lower part of the dial, between 3:00 and 9:00, the player's four cards appear in windows. Two are visible, the other two hidden by shutters. On the upper part of the dial are three additional windows for the dealer's cards, one of which is visible, the other two also hidden by shutters. Each time a shutter opens, a gong sounds whose mechanism is visible through a side window at 2 o'clock.

de GRISOGONO
GRANDE CHRONO N04

Framed by its generous 18K white-gold case, the uninhibited character of this timepiece sets an immediate tone of personality. A testament to de GRISOGONO's valiant rejection of convention, the dial's design finds poise in its decisively asymmetrical balance. The retrograde date calendar forms a clever twin arc around the radius of the central hour and minute hands, as if to inject horological geometry with a dose of modernity. While every digit of the dual-ring mechanism is visible at all times between 10:00 and 6:00, the day's date is clearly highlighted by a sapphire window with a white-gold case of its own at 3:00. The chronograph counters at 9:00 and 6:00 complete the controlled chaos of this expressive timepiece. As a final touch of exhibitionism, a window on the 9:00 side of the case offers a brilliant view of the automatic movement's steady heartbeat.

FRANCK MULLER
AETERNITAS III

One voyage of the eyes around the sun-stamped dial of the rose-gold Aeternitas III, and the overwhelming first impression turns to intelligible horological bliss. The open tourbillon escapement at 6:00 sets a tone of tasteful exhibition of technical virtuosity. The addition of a split-seconds chronograph and secondary time zone transforms this wristwatch into an elaborate timekeeping instrument. Just as the combination of modules and hands tells a story of innovative mechanical excellence, the majestic vision of the tourbillon cage reminds the owner of the distinguished heritage of traditional Swiss watchmaking.

FRANCK MULLER
AETERNITAS IV

While the hallmark 14mm tourbillon and light blue central hands perpetuate the spirit of this remarkable Franck Muller collection, the secular calendar of the Aeternitas IV recounts a narrative of its own. Set over 999 years and infinitely renewable, this demonstration of day, month, date, and moonphase possesses two additional sets of wheels to incorporate the Gregorian skipping of leap years once per century. The extremely accurate moonphase features a rate of accuracy 250 times greater than that of a traditional system. The retrograde date and power reserve at 12:00, as well as two secondary time zones, with 24-hour hands, on the left and right of the tourbillon, and an equation of time function that ensures exactitude when the watch is rewound after an indefinite period, complete a visionary calendar of eternal proportion.

FRANCK MULLER
AETERNITAS MEGA

Simply put: the most complicated wristwatch ever made! With 25 of this masterpiece's 36 complications visible to the wearer's amazement, the Aeternitas Mega may make its most impressive claim in the clarity with which its multitude of complexities are displayed. With an array of retrograde counters, a highly intricate single-pusher split-seconds chronograph, an extraordinary eternal perpetual calendar, the choice of grand or small strike of the Westminster Cathedral carillon, and two additional 24-hour time zones, to name a few of the 36 modules, this 1483-component magnum opus demonstrates the infinity of Franck Muller's daring vision of haute horology.

HUBLOT

CATHEDRAL MINUTE REPEATER CHRONO TOURBILLON – REF. 704.QX.1137.GR

This King Power masterpiece is a world first of monumental proportions. The innovative combination of a flying tourbillon, column-wheel chronograph, and minute repeater with two cathedral-type gongs, is a game-changing illustration of fusion between noble tradition and the modern spirit. Housed within a 48mm carbon fiber case, this groundbreaking timepiece boasts the impressive particularity of the skeletonized visibility of its three prized complications on the dial side.

IWC

PORTUGUESE GRAND COMPLICATION – REF. IW377402

Limited to 50 watches per year, the Portuguese Grand Complication combines a multiplicity of extraordinary horological feats within an 18K red-gold case. The warmth of the case and dark brown alligator leather strap, stitched with 18K red-gold threads, draws the eye to a cartographic silver-plated dial design that pays tribute to Vasco de Gama's navigational exploits. Along with a full perpetual calendar, programmed until the year 2499, and a small seconds subdial, this flagship masterpiece features a chronograph with central seconds hand, as well as 12-hour and 30-minute counters, a perpetual moonphase display, and a minute repeater. On the outside of the case, the crown, chronograph pushers and the repeater's sliding activator echo the brilliance of the dial's numerous red-gold appliqués. The theme of navigational exploration extends to the caseback, on which a sextant is engraved.

JAEGER-LECOULTRE

HYBRIS MECHANICA REVERSO GRANDE COMPLICATION A TRIPTYQUE 1 – REF. 232.64.20

The Reverso Grande Complication à Triptyque displays three dimensions of time—civil, sidereal and perpetual time—on three faces, pushing the boundaries of watchmaking possibility. The front side displays a tourbillon, while the back features a Zodiac calendar with an astronomical chart, an equation of time and sunrise and sunset times. The watch's third face is notable for its unusual position: a perpetual calendar in the Reverso carriage. The timepiece boasts a total of 18 functions and has six patents pending. The movement that drives all these functions is the manual-winding Jaeger-LeCoultre 175, housed within a platinum 950 case that measures 37.7x55x17.9mm.

JAEGER-LECOULTRE

MASTER GRANDE TRADITION GRANDE COMPLICATION – REF. 502.35.80

The Master Grande Tradition Grande Complication features three remarkable complications that combine refinement and elegance with the latest in technology: a minute repeater, flying tourbillon and Zodiac calendar with sidereal time. The tourbillon is exceptional in that it serves as an hour hand, indicating not solar time, but sidereal time, which is determined by the stars. The gong of the minute repeater is crafted from a special alloy and machined from a single piece, endowing it with an unusually rich sound. The Jaeger-LeCoultre 945 powers these complications, and the ensemble is housed in an 18K white-gold case.

JAEGER-LECOULTRE

MASTER GRANDE TRADITION TOURBILLON WITH PERPETUAL CALENDAR – REF. 500.24.2A

The first Jaeger-LeCoultre caliber to associate a tourbillon with a perpetual calendar comprises exactly 401 components. Its fascinatingly original conception is based on a split-level structure. The dial is divided between an upper part displaying the hours and minutes as well as the perpetual calendar indications, and a lower part on which a slight difference of level shows off the prominent tourbillon. The grade-5 titanium carriage is so light that the 78-part tourbillon escapement weighs a mere 0.28g! The perpetual calendar displays the date, day of the week and month, while automatically taking account of the length of the months and the leap-year cycle.

PATEK PHILIPPE

GRAND COMPLICATION – REF. 5073P

Adorned with 155 baguette-cut diamonds, of which 103 play their game of light on the platinum case's bezel, this Grand Complication model boasts the distinction of a self-winding movement. As the diamonds evoke the earth's immeasurable past, and the day, date, month, leap-year and moonphase indicators illustrate the future of time worth keeping, a cathedral-gong minute repeater reverberates a melody that revitalizes watchmaking's rich historical heritage. In addition to the comprehensive perpetual calendar, a 24-hour indicator, placed inside the day of the week circle at 9:00, puts the time of day in grander perspective.

PATEK PHILIPPE

GRAND COMPLICATION – REF. 5216R

An ergonomic slide piece on the side of the Grand Complication's rose-gold case reveals the melodious secret of this sophisticated perpetual calendar. As the opening of its halo-like horseshoe design is sealed by a moonphase with seconds subdial at 6:00, the pronounced retrograde date announces the innovative spirit of this timepiece. However, the calendar's clever integration of subtle apertures (for the day, month, and leap year) only tells a portion of the watch's story. Powered by the manually wound R TO 27 PS QR caliber, a minute repeater and tourbillon escapement save their manifestation for the intimate glance of the timepiece's owner. On the reverse of the silvery opaline dial with applied gold hour markers and rose-gold dauphine hands, the 506-component movement is on display through a sapphire crystal caseback.

PATEK PHILIPPE

TRIPLE COMPLICATION – REF. 5208P

Brilliantly contained within a 40mm platinum case, 12 perfectly arranged indications find their place on the Triple Complication's charcoal-gray sunburst dial. Joining the self-winding R CH 27 PS QI caliber's two-gong minute repeater, a single-pusher chronograph and instantaneous perpetual calendar make up the dynamic design of this sophisticated masterpiece. With its quadruple-aperture architecture, the perpetual calendar saves a particular spectacle for the turn of the New Year, when all four indicators—day, date, month and leap year in the seconds subdial at 3:00—switch with perfect synchronization.

URWERK

UR 110 TORPEDO

Within a functionally asymmetrical grade-5 titanium case, the Torpedo reaches the extremes of complexity to deliver time with effortless clarity. Ingeniously placed on the right side of the dial, so that time may be read without an adjustment of the sleeve, the graded minute scale is traversed by three torpedo-shaped satellites, whose astonishing sophistication spawns an unprecedented simplicity for reading the time. Mounted on three planetary gears, the three modules undergo a constant counteracting revolution, permitting them to stay perfectly parallel as they orbit the central carousel of the dial. During the active indicator's journey across the scale, the other two modules perform an additional vertical rotation, delivering the upcoming numeral to their visible top. When the minutes reach 60, the indicating responsibility is relayed to the subsequent torpedo, and the innovative ballet seamlessly continues its calculated performance.

VACHERON CONSTANTIN

OVERSEAS CHRONOGRAPH PERPETUAL CALENDAR – REF. 49020/000W-9656

Inspired by Vacheron Constantin's emblematic Maltese Cross, this dual-complication's titanium bezel draws the eye to a thoroughly expressive sunburst satin-brushed slate-gray dial. Using color contrast as a path to legibility, each subdial integrates two indications. While a white small seconds indicator complements the moonphase at 6:00, the principal dial, day of the week/12-hour counter at 9:00, and date/30-minute counter at 3:00, display the column-wheel chronograph's function via the bright contrast of yellow hands. In addition, a yellow numeral 4, within the 48-month subdial at 12:00, presents a clear view of the leap-year cycle. Powered by the self-winding 1136 QP caliber, this sporty and technically exceptional timepiece is housed within a stainless steel case with a soft iron cage, protecting it from magnetic fields.

VACHERON CONSTANTIN

PATRIMONY CONTEMPORAINE PERPETUAL CALENDAR – REF. 43175/000R-9687

On its silver-toned opaline dial with baton- and triangle-shaped 18K pink-gold hour markers, this elegant timepiece presents a perpetual calendar so effortless that the moonphase at 6:00 seems to conduct the entire time orchestra. Via a 4-year month dial at 12:00, Vacheron Constantin provides an optimally unambiguous display of the leap-year indicator residing in its interior. Contained within the 41mm 18K pink-gold case, the Geneva Seal-honored 112 QP self-winding movement provides a frequency of 19,800 vph, with a 40-hour power reserve. Turned over, the openworked back can be admired through a sapphire crystal.

VACHERON CONSTANTIN

PATRIMONY TRADITIONNELLE CALIBRE 2755 – REF. 80172/000R-9300

Combining the most exquisite innovations that watchmaking has to offer, this horological masterpiece tells, within its 44mm pink-gold case, not only the time, but also the history of fine watchmaking. Joining the fine snailed day of the week, month, and date counters, as well as a discreet leap-year window near 1:00, the exposed tourbillon, upon which seconds are driven, finds a noble home at 6:00 on this timepiece's silvered opaline dial. Yet this brilliant alliance is not all. Stamped with the Geneva Seal, the manually wound 2755 caliber integrates a minute repeater with Vacheron Constantin's innovative centripetal governor as a regulator of the chiming rate. The movement's 55-hour power reserve is indicated through the sapphire crystal caseback.

VACHERON CONSTANTIN

PATRIMONY TRADITIONNELLE CHRONOGRAPH PERPETUAL CALENDAR

REF. 47292/000P-9510

In an ingenious use of space, Vacheron Constantin turns a 43mm 950 platinum case into the frame for a masterful display of the multi-complication concept. Entrusted with a wealth of responsibilities, the 1141 QP manual caliber permits the harmonious integration of a chronograph with 30-minute counter at 3:00, into the design of the dial's perpetual calendar. By combining the date and moonphase into one intricately detailed section, and incorporating small apertures for the day of the week, month, and leap-year indications, Vacheron Constantin achieves the perfect legibility of a three-counter dial, completed by the small seconds at 9:00, and a 30-minute chronograph counter at 3:00. Worn on an alligator Mississippiensis strap that accentuates the deep gray of the watch face, this timepiece makes complicated look masterfully simple.

VACHERON CONSTANTIN

QUAI DE L'ILE DAY-DATE AND POWER-RESERVE – REF. 85050/000R-I0P29

The 264-component 2475 SC-1 automatic caliber of this watch provides an oscillation frequency of 28,800 vph and a power reserve of 40 hours. Framed by a cushion-shaped 18K pink-gold case, the timepiece's brushed dial features raised day of the week and date subdials, as well as a prominent and easy-to-read power reserve indicator. With an exhibition caseback, large pink-gold Arabic numerals, and three central hands displaying hours, minutes, and running seconds, this watch achieves perfect legibility within a luxurious context.

VACHERON CONSTANTIN

QUAI DE L'ILE RETROGRADE ANNUAL CALENDAR – REF. 86040/000R-I0P2R

This resolutely modern timepiece is powered by the new 2460 QRA self-winding caliber with a frequency of 28,800 vph. A unique display of sophisticated functions in a cushion-shaped pink-gold case and white-gold bezel make it a contemporary symbol of creative ingenuity. Being an annual calendar, the retrograde date at 3:00 needs only be adjusted once a year, to cope with the capricious month of February. In addition to the minimalist month subdial at 6:30, small seconds are indicated around the moonphase, leaving the watch uncluttered, and easily read. Equipped with a stop-seconds device for precise time setting, and a moonphase that requires a correction only once every 122 years, this timepiece is stamped with the Geneva Seal.

Tourbillons

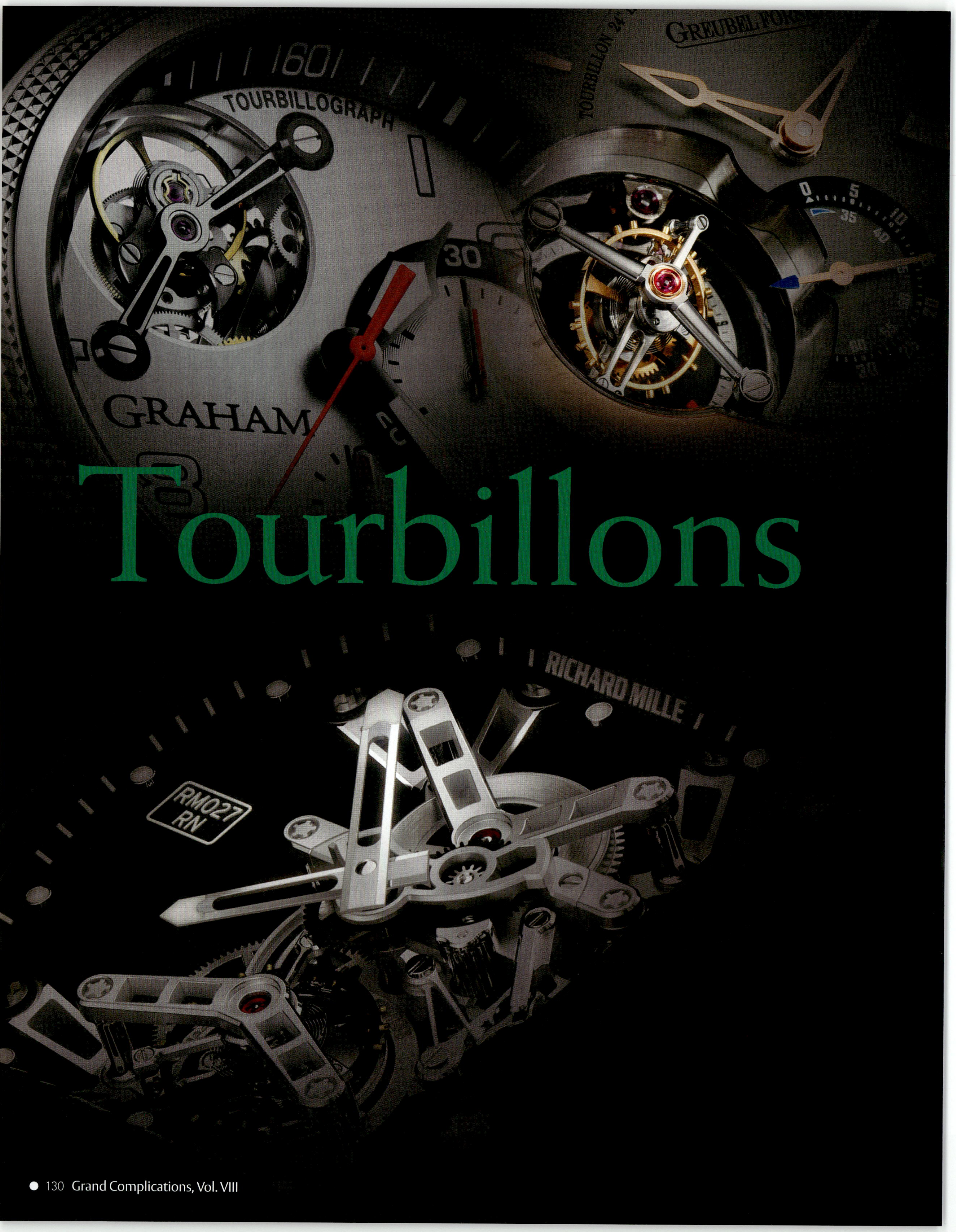

Created in the beginning of the 19th century to compensate for the functional irregularities due to the effect of gravity on pocket watches, the tourbillon might have been forgotten with the rise of wristwatches and later the quartz explosion. Far from it. With the triumphant return of mechanical horology in the 1980s, this ultra-sophisticated mechanism became the star of all complications. This unprecedented success has somewhat mitigated the complication's super-rare, exclusive qualities, but it has been matched by a technical revival. Many watchmakers have used the reinvention of this sophisticated mechanism to propose constructions more fitting to wristwatches—or to simply prove their unequalled virtuosity. This rise has been aided by the use of computer technology and high-tech materials. Central or off-centered tourbillons, flying tourbillons, tourbillons with double, triple or quadruple rotational axes, inclined tourbillons, multi-tourbillon movements—never has the "queen of complications" taken on so many different aesthetic and technical faces, to the great delight of horology aficionados.

"Our watches must be ready to face life on the front lines."

Richard Mille

CEO of Richard Mille

When it comes to adjusting strategic market distribution, widening his range or choosing partners, Richard Mille adopts a cautious attitude, consistently guided by a concern to take the watch beyond its traditional "horological ghetto." This approach is increasingly appreciated and imitated.

At the January 2011 Salon International de la Haute Horlogerie, Montblanc CEO Lutz Bethge made this telling statement when he visited the Richard Mille booth: "Here's a watchmaker who brings a breath of fresh air to the profession." Timepieces bearing the Richard Mille signature do indeed venture off the beaten track, yet without relinquishing one inch of the micro-mechanical culture that has made its way through the centuries and is pushed to extremes within the company. As Richard Mille likes to say: "My approach is somewhat original in that I'm not a watchmaker." And this despite the fact that after his business studies, he began his career in the Matra watchmaking division which was soon thereafter bought up by Seiko, and then worked for Mauboussin before fulfilling his yearning for independence. The latter has been strengthened by high-quality partnerships that for the past ten years have been engendering instantly recognizable products epitomizing the vision of a creative talent for whom horology has became a favorite playground. We took a chance to hear from the man himself.

How did the Richard Mille brand fare in the year 2011, with the time's welter of economic troubles to which the watch industry appears to be impervious?

Overall, the firm is doing well. As we speak, meaning mid-December 2011, my primary concern is for the end-of-year deliveries that will dictate my 2011 results. I still have part of the annual production stuck in the workshop awaiting certain components, and there are only two weeks left to dispatch them. Therein lies the paradox of watchmaking. When business is thriving for subcontractors, they tend not to deliver on time, and the same is true in downturn. That being said, the current year has been excellent for the brand, even in countries such as Japan, where we have achieved 50% growth. The same goes for North and South America, Asia and even Europe, which is up 17%. Not to mention China, which could absorb our entire production! As a precautionary measure, I am nonetheless determined to maintain a certain equilibrium by spreading sales reasonably on a scale of around one third for each of the three major geographical zones.

So 2011 was a great year?

As I mentioned earlier, everything will depend on the year-end deliveries. For the time being, the main bottleneck is in the area of cases, and the situation is not quite so bad for movements. Whatever happens, sales results will in any event be higher than in 2010—probably in the 90 to 100 million Swiss franc range. In a nutshell, exactly like every year and despite my efforts to plan efficiently, we are in a state of emergency that entails working overtime, including weekends.

RM 032

RAFAEL NADAL

BUBBA WATSON

PABLO MAC DONOUGH

Do you have any particular plans in terms of distribution?

We are taking it step by step in that area, according to opportunities that occur, because Richard Mille boutique openings are always done in partnership with local distributors. Among the brand's 100 points of sale, we have around 14 own-name boutiques that do excellent business. This being said, there are plans for Zurich and Milan, and possibly to extend our Paris boutique. We are also looking toward New York and Miami, as ever in keeping with our policy of loyalty to our partners.

So partnerships are clearly a strategic issue for Richard Mille?

Most definitely, and not just in terms of distribution and production. Our sports partners also play a very important role, as we are seeing with Rafael Nadal, Felipe Massa and Bubba Watson, as well as Argentinean champion Pablo Mac Donough, who has been named the world's best polo player and has just joined our team. The most important factor for us is that these elite sportsmen are able to wear our watches during competitions—which is why we aren't interested in soccer or basketball, for example. The watches dedicated to them, tailor-made in accordance with the stresses and strains they will endure in the practice of a given sport, must be ready to face life on the front lines. In this respect, these sportsmen are an integral part of the development process. By wearing these timepieces in extreme conditions, they help us find solutions to problems that may arise, because generally and almost inevitably, the first models break. We learn the lessons required to reach the final product. Moreover, this approach is also extremely useful in terms of after-sales service. It has helped us for example develop a new stem system with a dynamometric crown, an essential energy transmission component which, thanks to this new technique, serves to avoid any overwinding of the watch that might cause the stem to break or lead to excessive tension in the barrel. Within this context, we are presenting at the SIHH 2012 a model specifically made for Pablo Mac Donough, another truly astonishing watch.

Nonetheless, commercial aspects of sports results are not the ultimate goal—far from it! The personality of these sportspeople is equally important from our point of view. They must of course like watchmaking, but over and above that aspect, they are joining a family. We develop watches together and they are all actively involved. In a nutshell, we really have fun!

RM 053 PABLO MAC DONOUGH

RM 037

RM 033

You have just presented a new movement, self-winding Caliber CRMA1, the first in-house construction to emerge from your workshops in Les Breuleux. Is this kind of approach important?

It does indeed represent a new stage. The fact of having our own proprietary movement based on a set of technical specifications entirely in tune with corporate strategy contributes to establishing our know-how. But it is not a revolution, involving a goal of around 500 units per year. We will thus continue working with Audemars Piguet Renaud & Papi as well as with Vaucher Manufacture. We are also developing the production of our cases, which will open up whole new vistas. This being said, this Caliber CRMA1 is well designed and well finished. The latter aspect is particularly important to me when one considers that finishing is in fact the most complex and delicate part in building a timepiece.

What are you expecting in 2012?

We will continue to implement a determined strategy, while respecting our principles of due caution. This will in particular give rise to an increase in the number of references. In other words, we will extend our collections with more models, but fewer of each. To take an example: the RM011 is selling very well, but we are going to reduce quantities in comparison with other collections. I have also observed that each product's life cycle is getting shorter—a phenomenon that has been further sped up by the crisis in that the extreme high end of the market has found itself flooded in overly recurrent series. There are still as many clients in this segment, but in my opinion, once you get beyond 30 to 50 watches per model, it's time to move on. I realized this with the RM014 and RM015 models, of which several hundred were made. After two years, customers were clearly looking for something else. That's not a problem for me, because that's exactly what I love about watchmaking: the opportunity for constant reinvention. For the Rafael Nadal watch, I therefore stopped at 50 watches, even though I had enough orders to triple that figure.

There is however no question of satisfying such clients with Richard Mille models equipped with grande sonnerie mechanisms or a perpetual calendar. If for example, I place a tourbillon in my watches, this feature must not exceed 15% of the overall attraction it may exercise. The tourbillon is indeed a beautiful expression of the horological art, but it must not be a determining element. We must never fall into that trap. That is why I always say we must take watchmaking beyond its own ghetto. It must open up to the world, to architecture, to support and to people's lifestyles, while maintaining its inherent consistency. That is exactly the path chosen by Richard Mille.

RM 026

Jean-Claude Biver

Chairman of the Board of Hublot

Hublot has just presented a world-first scratchproof and stainless 18-karat yellow gold alloy—an innovation with "enormous" potential according to its dynamic Chairman of the Board, Jean-Claude Biver. Yet another outstanding accomplishment to his credit, after the Antikythera mechanism and the 360° partnership signed with Ferrari—and doubtless a healthy confidence booster for 2012.

Some said he would withdraw pretty fast after Hublot was bought up by the LVMH group. Almost four years later, not only is Jean-Claude still at the helm, but he is more energetic than ever. The production of his in-house-made UNICO movement should reach 10,000 units in 2012, and several other calibers are in the pipeline. On the distribution development side, he aims to focus on China, which currently accounts for only 3% of sales.

What kind of progress did you enjoy in 2011?

Over 30%—meaning growth well above that of Swiss exports as a whole. The total number of watches produced this year should be around 30,000.

How does 2012 look?

With American growth and the ongoing growth of the emerging markets, the year 2012 is liable to show a similar pattern to 2011. If we factor in development in Japan, there are several reasons to be optimistic about 2012. We naturally do not underestimate the economic significance of the political issues in Europe, but their outcome is hard to predict.

ANTIKYTHERA MECHANISM

UNICO MOVEMENT

"Our Magic Gold is the first innovation in gold since Tutankhamun"

OCEANOGRAPHIC 4000

Last year, you told us you were looking to open another 33 boutiques in China. How is this development coming on?

By the end of the year we will have nine boutiques or points of sale in China—which might give the impression that we are somewhat behind schedule. However, our delivery problems were so serious that it would have been tough to open other boutiques. Nonetheless, China will be a priority for 2012, and we hope to open an additional ten or so points of sale next year.

What percentage of your sales does China currently account for?

We achieved 3% of our sales in China in 2011. That's still 10 times less than our competitors, so there is huge growth potential in China for Hublot, which is why this country will become our top priority next year.

Does the international spread of sales suit you?

It currently suits us apart from two key weaknesses: China on the one hand, and Germany on the other. We will thus be making particular efforts in these two countries, as well as in Italy, where we are regaining direct control of our product distribution.

As far as the brand news is concerned, what were the highlights of 2011?

Definitely the exceptional creation of the Antikythera mechanism, which connects Hublot not only to the 17th century like all of watchmaking, but as far back as the 1st century BC. Another landmark introduction was Magic Gold, the first revolutionary gold alloy since Tutankhamun. It is an exclusive Hublot alloy developed in partnership with the Swiss Federal Institute of Technology Lausanne (EPFL), and which we introduced as a world-first: a gold that no longer be scratched or become discolored. Imagine a gold chain, ring or watch that, even after hundreds of years, would not bear even a single scratch. We produce this magic and unique gold alloy directly in the casting workshop of our own manufacture.

How do you see its potential?

The potential for our innovation and our license is simply enormous. It's a sensational revolution—the first since the Egyptians at the time of Tutankhamun invented the very first gold alloy. Not only is the potential enormous for 18-karat gold, but we have also filed the patent and the license for silver, platinum and aluminum—and in these three metals, the potential is even greater, particularly for silver and high-tech aluminum.

Which other item of news would you choose to pinpoint?

The 360-degree, five-year partnership signed with Ferrari! There too, we have innovated and entirely overturned the very concept of the partnership.

How does one become the partner of such a prestigious and sought-after brand as Ferrari?

Few brands have been very successful with Ferrari watches…

Why not?

In my view, it's because all the watch brands so far have focused on the franchise agreement and the right to make Ferrari watches, while completely neglecting—or not even considering—the major synergy opportunities stemming from the Ferrari brand. We thus did quite the opposite: we did not sign a franchise agreement, but instead a partnership contract. Moreover, we have become partner not of the Ferrari brand alone, but of the "Ferrari world," which is very different and much broader. We will consider Ferrari as a partner with which we are developing all kinds of synergies ranging from technology to events, along with Formula 1 and the automaker's dealer network, for example. Ferrari is our ambassador and we are its watchmaker. Together, we are going to develop products, new materials, new technologies, along with marketing, sports and promotional events. And finally, we will also make a watch with the Ferrari logo: not an entire collection, but a special watch to honor or celebrate an event such as the anniversary of a legendary car, a Formula 1 victory, etc.

Is this a long-awaited partnership?
Yes it is. We actually met Jean Todt in 2005, a time when he was serving as Chief Executive Officer of Ferrari and General Manager of the Racing Division. We had in fact designed the Big Bang for him. Since he hadn't selected us, we decided at the time—thankfully!—to simply incorporate the model within our collection and to name it Big Bang. Everyone is aware of the success it has enjoyed and the role it has played in the watch industry as a whole and for Hublot in particular.

BIG BANG FERRARI

What should one expect from this partnership, as much in economic terms as on a product level?
Five years is a minimum to build a relationship, an image, a collaboration, a partnership. Time will enable us to solidify, intensify, legitimize and optimize all the synergies shared by the two brands.

How are things progressing with the production of your Unico chronograph movement?
It is steadily rising and we hope to reach 10,000 movements by next year. That is really gratifying, especially since the movement is running really well and we've hardly experienced any growing pains. I believe we can be truly proud of this movement, which is both innovative and extraordinarily efficient.

What percentage of Hublot's chronographs does it currently equip?
Next year, we should be close to 50%, and in due course we can expect to equip 80% to 85% of our chronographs with the UNICO.

Marc A. Hayek

Member of the Executive Management Board of Swatch Group and CEO of Blancpain, Breguet and Jaquet Droz

Swatch Group is going from success to success and remains very confident about the year 2012. According to Marc A. Hayek, Member of the Executive Management Board of Swatch Group and CEO of Blancpain, Breguet and Jaquet Droz, demand currently stems from all price segments and is driving growth in production capacities.

"Overall, the Swatch Group is still struggling to meet demand, a situation currently experienced by a majority of Swiss watch brands. Although uncomfortable in itself, this situation gives me a lot of confidence for 2012," explains Hayek.

The year 2011 was indeed exceptional: it began at top speed and by July 2011, Swatch Group's turnover was 24.2% higher than 2010, already an exceptional year. Given the almost 20% rise in watch exports recorded during the second half of 2011, the Swatch Group was expecting an historic year—a remarkable result achieved despite the negative impact and penalizing effect of the strong Swiss franc and the increase in the price of precious materials.

CLASSIQUE HORA MUNDI
Breguet

"Each brand has its own personality corresponding to a different clientele"

CHRONOMETRY COMPETITION WINNER

This message from one of the key players in the watch industry deserves to be taken seriously. The virtual monopoly enjoyed by Nivarox, which supplies most brands with escapement modules—the crucial part of all mechanical movements—should for example suffice to evaluate its predominance.

But the Swatch Group also shines by the quality of its production. By way of example, ETA Caliber 2824-2 marketed under the Tissot label and part of the brand's standard production, won first prize in the "classic" category of the 2011 Chronométrie international timing competition, which is reputed for the severity of its testing procedure. Thus, in addition to high-volume production, the group also works to achieve optimal quality of its products—a fact that is indeed well known to and envied by the competition.

THREE MISSIONS

In addition to Blancpain, which he was already heading, Marc A. Hayek took the helm of Breguet and Jaquet Droz after the death of his grandfather, Nicolas G. Hayek, in June 2010. Also a member of the Swatch Group Board of Directors, he is thus responsible for the holding company's three prestigious brands, for which he has defined a clear-cut strategy. "Each has its own personality corresponding to a different clientele. This is in order to guarantee them maximum development potential and also to encourage competition between them. My role therefore consists in making each of them more efficient and more innovative. Nonetheless, they all share a common core: the mastery of mechanical watchmaking and undeniable savoir-faire. Breguet is thus distinguished by a French spirit, a more rigid yet impeccably reliable style, as well as strong historical roots through the destiny of the famous people who have worn Breguet watches—and above all by the name of its founder, who is unanimously considered the most brilliant horologer of all time. This is combined with a will to move forward, impelled by the strength of an ultra high-performing R&D department. My grandfather was a real visionary, and my conviction of this truth has been strengthened by the heritage he has left me in Breguet. Meanwhile, Blancpain embodies a youthful, sometimes sportier and less conventional spirit, as a strongly Swiss brand firmly embedded in the Joux Valley and brimming with projects. I have great trust in the team already in place with which I've been working for several years, and of which the various members will be shouldering increasing responsibility as time goes by. As far as Jaquet Droz is concerned, it represents the gateway to the luxury watch world. Now positioned below Breguet and Blancpain, it has undergone several adjustments in 2011, particularly in terms of its distribution and its catalog. These changes have indeed borne fruit, since sales exceeded my already high expectations. And 2012 will bring more surprises with the integration of playful mechanisms in the watches—a means of perpetuating the spirit of Jaquet Droz, creator of so many exceptional automatons."

MANUFACTURE BREGUET

X FATHOMS
Blancpain

Breguet has thus provided a privileged circle with a preview of an exceptional timepiece that is still being finalized. Named Hommage à Nicolas G. Hayek Ref. 7887, it is endowed with all the assets and qualities required to lay claim to the title of the world's most complicated wristwatch. Embodying a perfect balance between tradition and innovation, it has led to the filing of 26 patents representing 650 pages!

The major new launch at BaselWorld 2011 was the Classique Hora Mundi, designed to be the favorite companion for keen travelers. Equipped with a dual time zone display, it enables users to pre-record the time in two different parts of the world and to switch from one to the other at the press of a button at 8 o'clock. The date also automatically keeps step with the time changes. A moonphase indication rounds off the functions of a watch equipped with a silicon escapement to enhance its precision.

Blancpain caused a sensation in October 2011 by presenting its X Fathoms model at the Dubai Aquarium and Underwater Zoo. A worthy representative of the brand's famous diver's watch tradition, the model features a mechanical depth gauge capable of measuring depths of as much as 90m, with a separate display for the part ranging from 0 to 15m in depth. Accurate to within a +/- 30cm delta range inside this zone, it also has a five-minute retrograde counter for decompression stages. Its mechanical self-winding Caliber 9918B is also fitted with a silicon balance-spring as well as three barrels ensuring five days' autonomy.

Jaquet Droz's catalog has been significantly reshuffled. The major new feature was undoubtedly the launch of range-entry models with a steel case priced at less than 9,500 Swiss francs, such as the Grande Seconde. The new policy has already borne fruit, since the brand is having trouble keeping up with demand. Recently established in a brand-new building in the Eplatures district of La Chaux-de-Fonds, the brand has announced its support for an exhaustive exhibition dedicated to Pierre Jaquet-Droz, his son Henri-Louis and Jean-Frédéric Leschot, which is to take place in the three main towns of Canton Neuchâtel: Le Locle, La Chaux-de-Fonds and Neuchatel from April 28 to September 30, 2012.

GRANDE SECONDE QUANTIEME
Jaquet Droz

"When it comes to creating new models, my first aim is to design something that pleases me."

Franck Muller

President and CEO of Franck Muller

With a family history that includes a mother of Italian descent and a Swiss father, Franck Muller inherited both creative talent and rigorous exactitude. Immersed in the watchmaking world from childhood on, he learned the ropes of the industry at a very young age. He began by restoring watches, then devoted himself to the creation of one-of-a-kind timepieces. His meeting with Vartan Sirmakes in 1980 would lead to the birth of the Franck Muller brand and result in an idea of absolute excellence.

How and why did you become interested in watchmaking?
It was totally natural. I've always been interested in mechanical things in general, and that is why I decided to serve an apprenticeship in the field of precision mechanics.

Does your family have roots in watchmaking?
I come from a family of shopkeepers.

Has watchmaking changed much over the years? What new aspects do you hope to bring to the industry?
Watchmaking was really very different when I started. At the time, we didn't have computers and the other machines we use today. We had only impeccable manual dexterity helping us to create exceptional pieces.

What are the key moments that determined your path in the watchmaking industry?
All of the world premiers that I have created, especially the combination of tourbillons with other complications on a wristwatch.

What does it mean to create a new watch, or a new movement?
Above all, it brings great personal satisfaction to use your hands to work with inanimate material and give it life.

What do you look for when launching a new project?
I want to have fun and, if I can, do something that has never been done before. I love the idea of the impossible becoming possible.

GIGA TOURBILLON

You've created extremely complicated watches such as the Aeternitas, more playful ones such as the Long Island Crazy Hours and extraordinary ones such as the Mega Tourbillon. Where do you get your inspiration?

Inspiration comes from all over. I'm like a sponge, absorbing and synthesizing different sources of inspiration.

What are your most treasured creations, and why? Do you have any anecdotes about them?

When it comes to creating new models, my first aim is to design something that pleases me. My next creation is always the one that motivates me from day to day. To give you an anecdote, I came up with the idea for the Master Banker the day when a group of bankers visited the firm. Fascinated by the visit, one of the bankers said to me, "The watch we need doesn't exist." That piqued my curiosity. He was talking about a watch with a single movement and a single crown that indicated three time zones, with hours and minutes displayed. I later created this watch, which of course bears my name.

LADY TOURBILLON

Why do you have such affection for large Arabic numerals, vivid colors and cases with rounded shapes, such as the characteristic Franck Muller tonneau form?

When I started in this business, watches seemed very sad. The large Arabic numerals were quite natural for me, as I wanted to improve readability. I used colors because we don't live life in black and white, and added rounded shapes because a watch should be comfortable to wear as well as visually harmonious.

How do you see the haute horology of today?

It's a marvelous world, because new technology has made many things much easier—it's opened a lot of doors, creatively.

How has it evolved since you started out?

There's an enormous difference between my early years in the industry and the high-tech present day.

How do you feel about the changing role of the watch, from a time measurement instrument to a status symbol?

The watch has always been more than just an instrument, and it would be simplistic to describe it as such.

How have you handled the transition from watchmaker to co-owner of an international group that bears your name?
It's difficult, because it's one thing to be responsible for myself, and another to be responsible for thousands of families around the world.

What has the Franck Muller brand brought, and what does it continue to bring, to haute horology?
We could write a whole book about that! In brief: innovation, creativity, satisfaction and a thorough spring cleaning.

How would you describe the Franck Muller customer?
He or she is a leader in the field, whatever that field may be.

The Franck Muller Group owns production facilities in several countries outside of Switzerland. What is the reasoning behind this strategy?
These are minor facilities compared to the group as a whole, and very small compared to other major players in the Swiss watchmaking industry.

How do you see the announcement by Swatch Group that it will wind down selling movements and assemblages to other companies? How will the group respond to this change?
The Swatch Group is just bringing about a fair redistribution. It makes sense that watchmakers should reinvest a large part of their profits in independent production facilities.

What are Franck Muller Group's priorities at the present?
We're adapting to new markets that do not as yet have a deeply ingrained horological culture.

The Internet and social networks are increasingly part of our lives. Do you make use of them? What are their advantages and disadvantages?
Personally, I'm against using them, because the human touch remains essential for highly technological products such as watches. Personal contact can stand as a guarantee and offer expertise appropriate to customer service worthy of the name. However, we live in a technological era and we must adapt to this evolution, so we do use these tools.

INFINITY RONDE

Carlos Rosillo

CEO of Bell & Ross

Expanding The Mission

Many mechanical watchmaking advances made during the past century, particularly those related to durability and accuracy, were influenced by the needs of military personnel.

This ongoing evolution provides an endless wellspring of inspiration for Bell & Ross, says Carlos Rosillo, the company's CEO. "Military timepieces and military history have always inspired the design of Bell & Ross watches," he says. "Originally, our Vintage line was dedicated to reinterpreting pilot watches from the 1940s. We expanded that mission this year, going even further back in time, to the turn of the century."

Bell & Ross revisits the genesis of the modern military watch with the latest additions to its Vintage collection, the PW1 (Pocket Watch 1) and WW1 (Wrist Watch 1). "These watches represent the beginnings of the wristwatch—when pilots started to attach pocket watches to their wrists in order to aid them on their missions," Rosillo explains.

The brand evokes the pocket watches of the early 1900s with the Vintage PW1, but tempers its retro style with modern engineering. "It's for collectors who appreciate watches that reincarnate the past while reflecting the present," Rosillo observes.

Leaping forward 20 years, the Vintage WW1 explores the transitional period that took place during World War I, when aviators accelerated the watch's migration from the pocket to the wrist. Because wristwatches were only beginning to emerge in the '20s, Rosillo says it was common for a pilot to solder wire loops onto his pocket watch and use them to secure the timepiece to his wrist with a small strap. A key benefit of this makeshift arrangement was improved readability for the pilot. The watches in the WW1 collection all share a more comfortable version of those innovative case horns.

For the Vintage WW1's debut, Bell & Ross unveiled several models, including one with a large date, another with a power reserve display and a third that includes both complications.

VINTAGE PW1

VINTAGE WW1

WW1 MILITARY

WW1 HERITAGE

The WW1 Military and WW1 Heritage models are also part of the collection, but they sport a decidedly different look that displays the minutes and hours on separate indexes. "The design," Rosillo explains, "was inspired by the so-called navigation or observation watches used by military pilots to calculate their direction or speed."

More than just Bell & Ross's latest creation, the Vintage WW1's design is a fitting complement to the Vintage Original and Vintage Officers lines, which reference watches worn by aviators during the 1940s. Together, these watches capture key moments from the first generation of military watches.

One standout is the Vintage BR 126 Original. It combines several features prized by pilots, including a chronograph helpful for completing on-board navigational tasks and outstanding legibility, a key element of Bell & Ross' design code.

Rosillo reveals that plans are underway to develop the Vintage collection in the coming years. "Now that we've retraced the history of the military watch back to the pocket watch, we will begin to expand the WW1, Original and Officer lines with new complications, materials and designs."

In contrast to the Vintage collection's dedication to the past, Bell & Ross's Aviation collection is focused on the here and now. One of the most popular models from this line of square watches continues to be the BR01, which is easily spotted by its prodigious 46mm profile and its iconic design, which echoes the analog instrument panels found in modern cockpits.

The BR01's success gave rise to two variations—the 42mm BR03 and the 39mm BRS. Still, the original remains an important showcase for Bell & Ross's technical achievements. Among the most compelling examples is the BR01 Tourbillon.

Presented in a titanium case coated with a Diamond-Like Carbon (DLC) finish, the watch is powered by a distinctive tourbillon movement enhanced with an innovative indicator that shows when the mainspring is operating at peak performance levels. "One of our design principles is legibility, so we were the first watch brand to develop an easy-to-read precision indictor that is called a 'trust index,'" Rosillo says.

The company's expertise is not limited, however, to timepieces inspired exclusively by the aeronautical world. The company's dedication to legibility, reliability and functionality—which works so well at great heights—translates equally well to dark depths.

The BR02 collection of diving watches, like all Bell & Ross watches, faced a rigorous development process that relied heavily on input from professional users. Their advice, Rosillo says, led directly to one of the collection's key features. "They wanted a dive watch with an interior bezel, because it reduces the risk of accidentally hitting the bezel during a dive and losing track of the elapsed dive time."

At sea, in air and on land, Bell & Ross has explored the evolution of the military timepiece extensively. Even so, Rosillo says he feels like the journey is just beginning. "I can't say for sure what the future holds, but I'm not sure we'll ever reach the conclusion of this endeavor."

VINTAGE BR 126 ORIGINAL

BR 01 TOURBILLON

BR 02-94 STEEL

Tourbillons

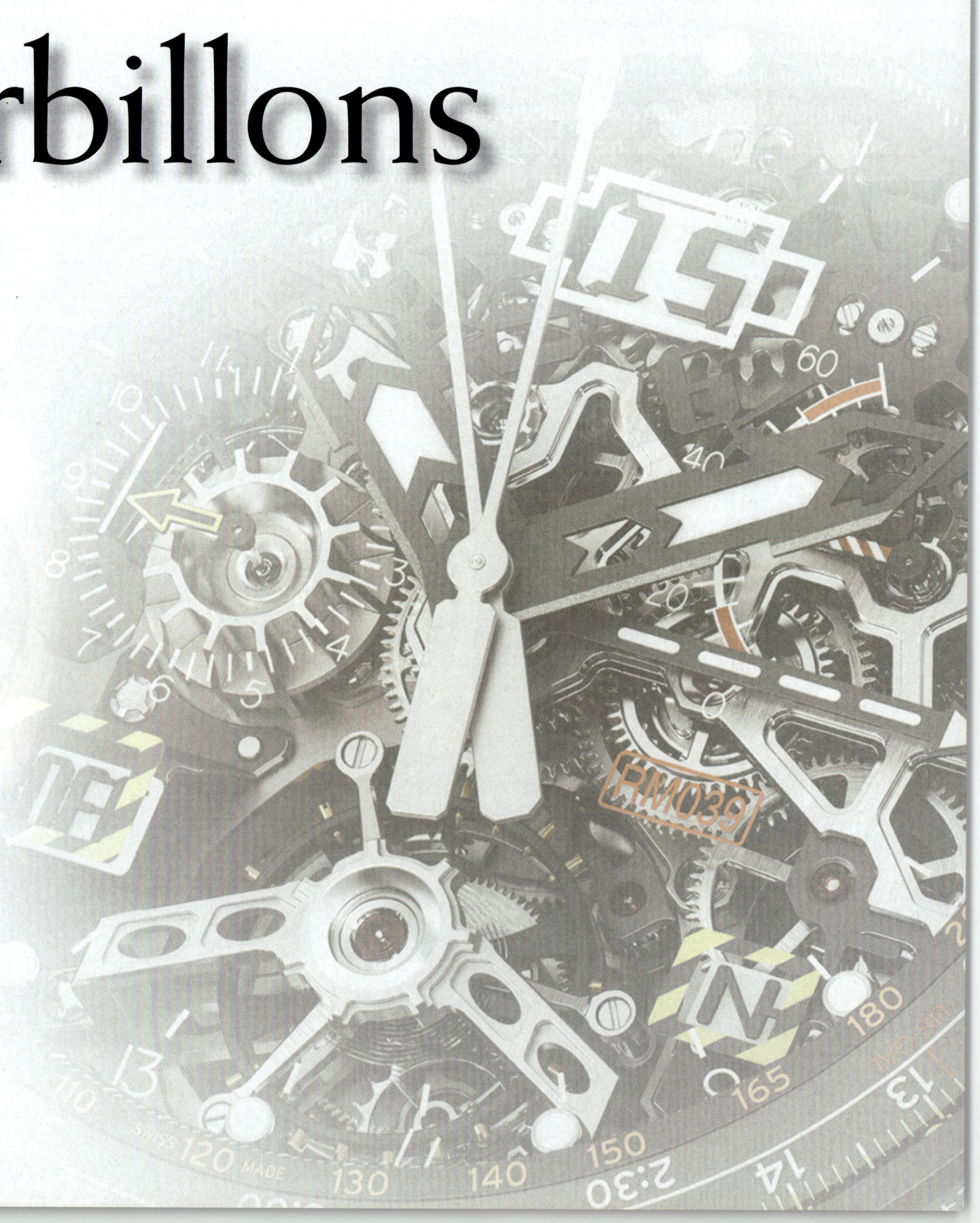

Richard Mille,
RM 039 E6B Aviator Tourbillon Chronograph

Pocket watches were usually carried in a special pouch or fob on a trouser belt, waistcoat or jacket—hence the name. Thus maintained in a vertical position for many hours, the mechanism—starting with the balance and the balance-spring, two necessary components for accuracy and precision—underwent the detrimental effects of gravity. To avoid such irregularities, the famous watchmaker Abraham-Louis Breguet (1747-1823)—one of the greatest horological geniuses of all time—had the idea of enclosing the “heart” of the watch (balance, balance-spring and escapement) within a small mobile carriage spinning on its axis within a predetermined time (generally one, four or six minutes). It was for this rotation that he chose to name his invention “tourbillon”—a term from astronomy synonymous with “planetary system” among 18th-century scientists. Breguet submitted the patent for his “watch compensating for all the inequalities that occur in the balance and balance-spring” on the 7th of Messidor in the 9th year of the Republican calendar—otherwise known as June 6, 1801. According to the house’s archives, 35 tourbillon watches were sold between 1805 and 1823, and throughout the 19th century the tourbillon remained an extremely rare complication, reserved for a few exceptional timepieces. The 20th-century triumph of the wristwatch could have brought about the disappearance of the tourbillon, as the complication loses much of its interest when the watch moves in all directions with the movement of the wearer’s wrist. However, the revival of mechanical horology in the 1980s propelled this mechanism into the firmament of horological complications by positing it as the nec plus ultra of Swiss savoir-faire, conferring upon any watchmaker entry into the ranks of the great. Since the turn of the millennium, the tourbillon has become wildly popular. Whereas only 670 tourbillons were produced between 1801 and 1986, today the global production stands at over 1,000 per year. Over 50 Swiss brands offer them among their collections, which is surprising when one considers that only a small handful of artisans are really capable of making this small magic carriage… Faced with this (relative) banalization, the major watch firms are determined to offer “in-house” tourbillons featuring new technical and aesthetic developments.

TECHNIQUE

HOW DOES IT WORK?

Placed horizontally, a watch's regulating organ (balance, balance-spring and escapement) is uniformly affected by the Earth's gravitational pull. However, when it is placed vertically (and to a lesser extent, in any position besides the horizontal), gravitational force causes certain fluctuations in its functioning and oscillations. These small accelerations and decelerations cause irregularities in the watch's functioning. The idea behind the tourbillon is to place the regulating organ in a small mobile carriage that completes one rotation in a given time, usually one minute. By successively adopting all possible positions, the carriage allows the small irregularities to cancel each other out. The tourbillon carriage is a tiny construction that may contain 70 components with a weight of less than 1g. This is why the production, assembly and setting of a tourbillon watch require exceptional expertise, reserved for the most elite watchmakers and incompatible with mass production.

TOURBILLONS AND PRECISION

The tourbillon was created for the pocket watch, which spends most of its time in a vertical position. It is less necessary on a wristwatch, when the daily movements of the wearer's wrist play the same role as the tourbillon in putting the regulating organ in a variety of positions. Some people go so far as to say that the tourbillon is completely useless in its classic form. To solve this problem, a new generation of tourbillons has arrived—with diverse variations on the manners, axes and speeds of rotation—that supposedly offers enhanced performances for wristwatches. Nonetheless, even though the tourbillon is not in itself synonymous with increased accuracy, the expertise necessary to create such a watch, and the extreme care involved in its production, are both guarantees of a watch that offers superior performance.

FLYING TOURBILLON

Normal tourbillons are supported by two bridges, one above the mechanism and the other below. "Flying" tourbillons are supported by only one, below the mechanism, which allows the watchmaker to give the construction a more ethereal and resolutely virtuoso appearance.

TOURBILLON AND KARUSSEL

Patented by the Danish Bonniksen in 1892, the karussel has the same ultimate goal as the tourbillon. However, it is distinguished (or could be distinguished—the experts do not all agree) by the double wheel train that links it to the barrel: the first provides the necessary energy for the functioning of the escapement, and the second controls the speed of the carriage's rotation.

A Reinvented Classic

With its mobile carriage spinning on its axis like a planet, the tourbillon provides a fascinating sight that most brands are keen to exhibit through the dial, traditionally through an aperture at 6 o'clock. But the ultra-sophisticated mechanism is now the object of numerous technical and aesthetic innovations, such as the use of new materials that offer enhanced lightness, or the search for unusual dial configurations.

Girard-Perregaux
1966 Tourbillon under a gold bridge

In 1889, Girard-Perregaux made horological history with its famous "tourbillon under three gold bridges." In 2011, the manufacture celebrated its 220th anniversary with a limited edition watch called 1966 Tourbillon under a gold bridge, featuring an original and elegant design.

A. Lange & Söhne
Richard Lange Tourbillon Pour le Mérite

Combining a tourbillon with fusee-and-chain transmission, the new Richard Lange Tourbillon Pour le Mérite from A. Lange & Söhne also stands out for its regulator-style display with hours at 4 o'clock, minutes at 12 o'clock and seconds on the tourbillon at 8 o'clock.

IWC, *Portuguese Tourbillon Hand-Wound*

In the new Portuguese Tourbillon Hand-Wound, the "whirlwind"—as the word translates—revolves on its axis at 9:00 on the dial, or, in nautical terms, at 270° west. The sight of the mechanical, cantilever-mounted minute tourbillon revolving around its own axis invariably attracts rapt attention from watch lovers.

Breguet, *Marine Tourbillon Chronograph 5837*

A worthy heir to the famous invention by Abraham-Louis Breguet, the Breguet Marine Tourbillon Chronograph associates a balance-spring, escapement wheel and lever in silicon with a tourbillon featuring a carriage partially made of titanium.

Jaeger-LeCoultre, *Master Compressor Extreme Lab*

Jaeger-LeCoultre sparked a real revolution with its Master Compressor Extreme Lab, the first mechanical watch to function accurately and reliably without lubrication. This exploit was made possible by a new balance geometry, new lightweight materials and a cutting-edge tourbillon equipped with a magnesium carriage.

Zenith, *El Primero Tourbillon*

Launched in 2010, the El Primero Tourbillon model from Zenith beats to the rhythm of the 36,000 vibrations per hour provided by the famous El Primero chronograph movement. Using a patented system, the date is displayed on the periphery of the tourbillon carriage, placed at 11 o'clock.

Patek Philippe
10-Day Tourbillon, Ref. 5101
Endowed with an exceptional power reserve of ten days, the 10-Day Tourbillon, from Patek Philippe is notable for its cambered Art Deco-style case. As with all its tourbillon watches, the manufacture prefers not to show the tourbillon from the dial side, for fear that sunlight might dry up the lubricating oils.

Bovet Fleurier
Amadeo Fleurier 44
7-Day Tourbillon
Reversed Hand-Fitting
Bovet Fleurier has adorned its Amadeo Fleurier 44 7-Day Tourbillon Reversed Hand-Fitting model with finely chased tourbillon bridges. The case is easily convertible into a wristwatch, table watch, pocket watch or pendant watch.

FP Journe, *Tourbillon Souverain*
The Tourbillon Souverain from FP Journe possesses a "remontoir d'égalité" (constant-force escapement) that regulates the energy of the barrels and provides a constant stream of power to the balance—which results in optimal time measurement.

Jaeger-LeCoultre, *Master Tourbillon*

Presented as the least expensive Swiss tourbillon on the market, the Master Tourbillon from Jaeger-LeCoultre possesses a high-frequency automatic movement, an additional time zone and a date display that jumps from the 15th to the 16th so as not to hide the titanium tourbillon carriage from view.

Montblanc
ExoTourbillon Chronographe

On its ExoTourbillon Chronographe, from the Villeret 1858 collection, Montblanc has placed the balance on the exterior of the tourbillon carriage. As the balance is larger, its amplitudes gain more precision, and the tourbillon carriage, freed from the weight of the balance, requires less energy for its rotation.

Graham London,
Tourbillograph Trackmaster Chromium

On the subject of more financially accessible tourbillons, Graham London has made a mark with its Tourbillograph Trackmaster Chromium, which entailed new production processes and earned two patents.

Room for Transparency

Certain brands have chosen to distill the tourbillon's magic with constructions whose heart is open, revealing the entire interior of the movement—masterpieces of skeletonization that push the frontiers of possibilities, or fascinating transparent stage-settings within which the mobile carriage seems to float weightlessly.

Chopard, *L.U.C Engine One Tourbillon*

The L.U.C 1TRM caliber that powers the L.U.C Engine One Tourbillon from Chopard is mounted on silent blocks that absorb shocks, just like automobile engines. This 28,000 vph movement has also been chronometer-certified by the COSC, a rare achievement for a tourbillon.

Richard Mille, *RM 027*

Weighing less than 20g, including the wristband, the RM 027 from Richard Mille—Rafael Nadal's watch—is one of the lightest timepieces ever devised. Its movement is in titanium and LITAL®, an avant-garde lithium alloy used in the aeronautic field.

Montblanc
Villeret Tourbillon Bi-Cylindrique

Introduced in 2011, the Villeret Tourbillon Bi-Cylindrique from Montblanc stands out for its architecture with openworked heart, double cylindrical balance-spring and its "mysterious hours" display that seems to float in the air thanks to the use of crystal discs.

Breguet, *Tradition Ref. 7047PT*

The Tradition Ref. 7047PT model from Breguet—equipped with a titanium balance and silicon balance spring—unveils a spectacular tourbillon mechanism with fusée-chain transmission that optimizes the movement's regularity.

Cartier
Rotonde Astrorégulateur

On its recent Rotonde Astrorégulateur, released in 2011, Cartier proposes an innovative alternative to the tourbillon by placing the regulating organ on the only element that remains constant in any vertical position: the rotor (oscillating weight), which is visible from the dial.

Corum, *Ti-Bridge Tourbillon*

On Corum's highly original Ti-Bridge Tourbillon, the flying tourbillon seems to float freely above the baguette movement, while the tourbillon carriage takes the shape of the brand's iconic key logo. The bottom plate and bridges are in ARCAP, a new copper and nickel alloy that is completely antimagnetic, and the case is in titanium.

Blancpain
L-Evolution One-Minute Flying Sapphire Carrousel

Blancpain has achieved a world first by reviving the carrousel (also known as the karussel), a mechanism that is close to the tourbillon (see "How Does It Work?"), and by incorporating it in several wristwatches, including the L-Evolution One-Minute Flying Sapphire Carrousel, with a tantalum case.

Omega
Skeleton Central Tourbillon Co-Axial Platinum

Omega pays tribute to the central tourbillon, one of the house's specialties, with the spectacular Skeleton Central Tourbillon Co-Axial Platinum, with a platinum carriage and a skeletonized movement that has been chronometer-certified by the COSC.

Piaget
Emperador Coussin Tourbillon Automatic Ultra-Thin

Equipped with a new manufacture movement of an exceptional thinness, the Emperador Coussin Tourbillon Automatic Ultra-Thin from Piaget stands out for its unusual geometry, with an off-center hours and minutes display, tourbillon carriage at 1:30 and a micro-rotor visible on the dial at 9 o'clock.

Ulysse Nardin, *Royal Blue Tourbillon*

On the Royal Blue Tourbillon by Ulysse Nardin, the sapphire bridges and bottom plate create the illusion that the mobile carriage is floating in mid-air. This transparent and magical architecture is highlighted by the setting of white diamonds and blue sapphires.

Hysek, *Furtif Tourbillon*

Hysek has wedded transparency and ultra-modern design in a new model called Furtif Tourbillon, with an in-house square movement that has been skeletonized by hand, a one-minute flying tourbillon and a titanium balance. It is available in a limited edition of 30 models.

Haldimann, *H8 Sculptura*

On its H8 Sculptura, Haldimann has eliminated the hour and minute indications, retaining only the fascinating spectacle of the central tourbillon floating in between two sapphire crystals. It is a true work of art, constructed entirely with traditional techniques.

The Third Dimension

Recent years have also witnessed the appearance of a new generation of tourbillons equipped with inclined carriages or several simultaneous rotational axes, and/or revolving at speeds that diverge from the traditional one minute (often 30 or 24 seconds). Besides their often spectacular appearance, these three-dimensional constructions are designed to be more suited to wristwatches, by multiplying the positions of the balance-spring within the case.

Greubel Forsey, *Double Tourbillon 30° Technique*

The esteemed tourbillon specialists Greubel Forsey have developed several innovative constructions that play on different angles and speeds of rotation—such as the Double Tourbillon 30° Technique, whose inner carriage rotates in one minute and outer carriage rotates in four minutes.

Greubel Forsey
Tourbillon 24 Secondes

On the Tourbillon 24 Secondes, the heart of Greubel Forsey's Invention Piece 3, the carriage—set at 25° and turning 2.5 times faster than an ordinary carriage—called for a new inclined gearing profile, as well as specific alloys.

Jaeger-LeCoultre, *Reverso Gyrotourbillon 2*

Based on a "spherical" tourbillon concept, the Reverso Gyrotourbillon 2 from Jaeger-LeCoultre presents two nested carriages. An outer carriage spins on its axis in 60 seconds, while the inner carriage, set at a 90° angle to the first, rotates in 18.75 seconds.

Girard-Perregaux

Bi-axial Tourbillon

The Bi-axial Tourbillon by Girard-Perregaux combines two concentric carriages, spinning on their respective axes in 45 seconds and one minute and fifteen seconds respectively. The two carriages weigh only 0.8g, and total over 110 components.

Panerai

Radiomir Tourbillon GMT Ceramica

On the Radiomir Tourbillon GMT Ceramica from Panerai, the carriage turns at a right angle to the oscillation axis of the balance, performing two turns per minute. Its in-house Caliber P.2005/S is also distinguished by a substantial six-day power reserve, achieved thanks to the energy from three barrels.

Concord, *C1 Quantum Gravity*

Concord created shock waves with its 2009 launch of the C1 Quantum Gravity, equipped with an unprecedented bi-axial tourbillon positioned vertically, i.e. almost outside the movement, and linked to the bottom plate by a series of cables reminiscent of suspension bridges.

Thomas Prescher, *Mysterious Automatic Double Axis Tourbillon*

On the Mysterious Automatic Double Axis Tourbillon from Thomas Prescher, only the tourbillon, the calendar, the oscillating weight and the drums serving as displays are visible. The movement is completely hidden by the bezel, in the left and right sides of the case. Placed on a rotation axis by means of a dedicated arm, the centered tourbillon turns on two axes.

Thomas Prescher
Triple Axis Tourbillon Regulator

On its Triple Axis Tourbillon Regulator, Thomas Prescher proposes a triple-axis flying tourbillon, supported on just one side—a real horological feat. The carriage rotating over one hour serves to indicate the minutes, while the hours and seconds can be read in two subdials.

Harry Winston
Histoire de Tourbillon 2

The new model Histoire de Tourbillon 2 from Harry Winston is equipped with a bi-axial flying tourbillon, with an outer carriage in titanium rotating over 120 seconds and an inner carriage inclined at a 10° angle turning over 40 seconds. The various indications—tourbillon paired with seconds at 9 o'clock, hours and day/night indication at 2 o'clock, minutes at 6 o'clock—are separated in off-centered subdials.

Zenith, *Christophe Colomb*

Zenith's Christophe Colomb explores an alternative path to the tourbillon by presenting an escapement mounted on gimbals, like marine chronometers, which allows it to maintain a horizontal position. The mechanism appears in a sapphire crystal bubble that crosses right through the movement.

Double Revolutions

A few innovative models offer a sophisticated system in which the tourbillon completes a rotation in one minute, while performing a complete turn of the dial in one hour—mirroring the double rotation of the Earth on its axis and around the sun. These are truly magical merry-go-rounds.

Piaget, *Polo Tourbillon Relatif Limelight Jazz*

The principle of a double revolution applies to Piaget's Polo Tourbillon Relatif Limelight Jazz. Suspended from the tip of the minute hand, the mobile flying tourbillon carriage appears to be disconnected from the movement driving it, creating a fine encounter between mechanical prowess and visual magic.

Jean Dunand, *Tourbillon Orbital*

On its Tourbillon Orbital, Jean Dunand offers a sophisticated system in which the tourbillon spins on its axis in one minute, while performing a complete turn of the dial in one hour.

Cartier, *Calibre Astrotourbillon*

The Calibre Astrotourbillon from Cartier presents an innovative construction with a central tourbillon placed above the movement. The elongated carriage spins around the dial in one minute, thus enabling the arrow-shaped balance to indicate the seconds.

Watches with Several Tourbillons

Another technical and aesthetic path explored by some watchmakers is the multiplication of tourbillons within a single watch. Horologers come up with double, even quadruple tourbillons, tied together by differential gear systems that average out the functioning of different regulating organs.

Roger Dubuis,
Excalibur Double Tourbillon Squelette

Boasting two flying tourbillons linked by a differential, the Excalibur Double Tourbillon Squelette model reveals all the technical sophistication and aesthetic refinement of its 292-component movement, graced by the prestigious Geneva Seal.

Harry Winston, *Histoire de Tourbillon 1*

The Histoire de Tourbillon 1 watch by Harry Winston is the first gem in a series of five extremely limited editions with just twenty models each, all devoted to the tourbillon complication. This inaugural piece features a case made from white gold and zalium, housing two ultra-light tourbillons set at a 25° angle and performing one rotation in 36 seconds.

Greubel Forsey, *Invention Piece 2*

A reinterpretation of its 2008 Quadruple tourbillon à différentiel, Greubel Forsey's Invention Piece 2 possesses two double tourbillon carriages (a first carriage executing a complete rotation in one minute, contained within a second carriage effecting a complete revolution in four minutes), linked by a spherical differential placed at the center of the timepiece.

Jacob & Co.
Napoleon Quadra Tourbillon

Crafted in titanium, the imposing Napoleon Quadra Tourbillon from Jacob & Co. features no fewer than four skeletonized tourbillons and four complete time zones with hour and minute displays.

Breguet, *Twin Rotating Tourbillons*

The Twin Rotating Tourbillons from Breguet boasts two independent tourbillons coupled by a differential gear and fixed to a bottom plate completing a full rotation in 12 hours. These two mechanisms mutually compensate for their infinitely small variations in rate in order to offer superior precision.

Ulysse Nardin
Freak Diavolo

The Freak Diavolo from Ulysse Nardin stands out for its highly original construction. The rotating movement within the case displays the hours and minutes without hands or a dial. The flying tourbillon, which completes a revolution in one minute, indicates the seconds. The escapement and balance spring are in silicon.

The Feminine Tourbillon

Celebrating the union of haute horology and haute jewelry, certain great names in the luxury business have also designed a few tourbillon watches specifically aimed at women.

Van Cleef & Arpels, *Midnight Tourbillon Nacre*

The superbly understated Midnight Tourbillon Nacre from Van Cleef & Arpels is available in a limited edition of 100 watches. The handcrafted mother-of-pearl dial reveals a tourbillon carriage that echoes the style of the Vendôme Column in Paris.

Chopard, *L.U.C Tourbillon Lady*

Chopard has innovated by dedicating to women a watch with a magnificent beating heart in the shape of an L.U.C in-house made movement, complete with tourbillon, nine-day power reserve, chronometer certification and the Geneva Seal. The case of the L.U.C Tourbillon Lady is entirely set with baguette-cut diamonds and the tourbillon bridge is adorned with a "C" for Chopard.

Audemars Piguet
Jules Audemars Ladies' Tourbillon Chronograph

The Jules Audemars Ladies' Tourbillon Chronograph from Audemars Piguet reveals its tourbillon on a mother-of-pearl dial that is set with pavé diamonds. The white-gold case sparkled with 251 brilliant-cut diamonds and 68 baguette-cut diamonds.

Parmigiani, *Kalpa XL Tourbillon Diamants*

The Kalpa XL Tourbillon Diamants offers a one-week power reserve and a carriage performing two rotations per minute. The tonneau-shaped case, inspired by the golden ratio, is adorned with a precious diamond pavé setting.

A. LANGE & SÖHNE

LANGE 1 TOURBILLON PERPETUAL CALENDAR – REF. 720.025

The Lange 1 Tourbillon Perpetual Calendar's self-winding L082.1 caliber is ingeniously fitted with a platinum centrifugal mass for exceptional winding efficiency. Thanks to an innovative rotating peripheral month ring that occupies a minimal amount of space, and an hour and minute circle off-centered on the solid silver rhodiumed dial, A. Lange & Söhne accomplishes a perpetual calendar of remarkable ease of use and legibility, despite its comprehensive constitution of moonphase, retrograde day, leap-year aperture and date. Admired intimately through the sapphire crystal caseback of this 41.9mm platinum masterpiece, the exquisite tourbillon is embellished with an extremely sophisticated black polished finish, and boasts a flawless diamond end stone as its radiant bearing.

A. LANGE & SÖHNE

RICHARD LANGE TOURBILLON POUR LE MERITE – REF. 760.032

The Richard Lange Tourbillon "Pour le Mérite" is powered by the manual-winding new hand-finished Lange manufacture L072.1 caliber. It incorporates a fusee-and-chain transmission as well as a tourbillon with a patented stop-seconds mechanism and a balance spring manufactured in-house. The 41.9mm case comes in platinum or rose gold with a 36-hour power reserve. Its dial features three intersecting circles for the time indicators. The largest dial indicates the minutes while the smaller subdials represent the seconds and hours. The watch includes a crocodile strap secured with a solid gold buckle. The Richard Lange Tourbillon "Pour le Mérite" in platinum is limited to 100 pieces.

AUDEMARS PIGUET

JULES AUDEMARS LARGE DATE TOURBILLON – REF. 26559OR.OO.D002CR.01

Home to Audemars Piguet's new 228-part 2909 caliber, this masterpiece showcases, via a stunning aperture at 6:00, a tourbillon that unarguably merits its prominent exhibition on the dial. The exposed heartbeat of the watch is balanced by the presence of an innovative large date at 12:00. The ingenious use of two superimposed dials, working in precise synchronization and without a separation of the tens and units, is crucial in permitting a date display of such magnitude. The Jules Audemars Large Date Tourbillon boasts a 72-hour power reserve, beats at a frequency of 21,600 vibrations per hour, and offers the choice of black or silver-toned dial, each of which is limited to 25 pieces.

AUDEMARS PIGUET

ROYAL OAK OFFSHORE HAND-WOUND TOURBILLON WITH CHRONOGRAPH

REF. 26288OF.OO.D002CR.01

The Royal Oak Offshore tourbillon chronograph, developed and crafted entirely by Audemars Piguet, houses the manual-winding 2912 caliber with two barrels, a tourbillon and a 10-day power reserve. The case is in 18K pink gold with a forged carbon bezel, black ceramic crown and pushers, assembly screws in polished steel and a glareproof sapphire crystal and caseback. The black dial is snailed and openworked at 6:00, 9:00 and 12:00, with applied luminescent gold numerals and hands.

BELL & ROSS

BR 01 TOURBILLON AIRBORNE

This limited edition of 20 pieces has a manual-winding mechanical movement and contains carbon-fiber bridges and plates and a black-gold tourbillon carriage. Hours can be read in a counter at 12:00, a trust index is positioned at 3:00, and the 120-hour power reserve indicator is at 9:00. A central hand displays the minutes. The three-dimensional dial has a black mesh-like design and is treated with a photoluminescent coating for nighttime reading. The 46x46mm case is titanium with a black DLC (Diamond-Like Carbon) coating. Water resistant to 100m, the watch features a shagreen strap.

BELL & ROSS

BR 01 TOURBILLON PHANTOM

Created in a limited edition of just 18 pieces, the BR 01 Tourbillon Phantom has a black carbon-fiber dial and is encased in titanium with DLC coating. It is powered by a mechanical manual-winding BR 01 Tourbillon with carbon-fiber mainplates and a black-gold tourbillon carriage. The hours are shown in a counter at 12:00, the trust index is positioned at 3:00, and the 120-hour power reserve indicator is at 9:00. A central hand displays the minutes. The indexes and hands are treated with a photoluminescent coating for nighttime reading. The watch is water resistant to 100m and is available on a rubber strap.

BELL & ROSS

BR 01 TOURBILLON PINK GOLD WITH ALUMINUM FIBER DIAL

The satin finish pink-gold case houses a manual-winding mechanical movement. The watch displays a trust index at 3:00, a 120-hour power reserve indicator at 9:00, an hour counter at 12:00 and a central minute hand. The BR 01 Tourbillon Aluminum Fiber Pink Gold features aluminum fiber mainplates and a tourbillon carriage in 5N gold. The dial is in aluminum fiber, with indexes and hands treated with a photoluminescent coating for nighttime reading. The case boasts a large 46x46mm measurement. Water resistant to 100m, the watch is available on a rubber or alligator strap. Limited edition of 20 pieces.

BELL & ROSS

BR 01 TOURBILLON PINK GOLD WITH CARBON FIBER DIAL

The BR 01 Tourbillon Pink Gold with Carbon Fiber Dial features a mechanical manual-winding movement that powers its various displays: minutes on a central hand, hours in a subdial at 12:00, a trust index at 3:00, and a 120-hour power reserve indicator at 9:00. The mainplates are carbon fiber and the tourbillon carriage is black gold. The hands and indexes feature photoluminescent coating for nighttime reading. The case, water resistant to 100m, is crafted in 18K pink gold and measures an extra-large 46x46mm. Limited edition of 20 pieces.

BELL & ROSS

BR MINUTEUR TOURBILLON PINK GOLD

This tourbillon is powered by a manual-winding mechanical movement and its bridges are in pink gold and anodized aluminum. The watch displays the hours, minutes, small seconds, a three-day power reserve indicator and a flyback function (2 counters: 60 minutes and 10 tenths of an hour), which features a zero-setting and quick reset. The case is in 18K pink gold and measures 44x50mm. The black dial possesses hands and indexes treated with a photoluminescent coating for nighttime reading. Water resistant to 50m, the watch is available on a rubber or alligator strap. Limited edition of 30 pieces.

BELL & ROSS

BR MINUTEUR TOURBILLON TITANIUM

This tourbillon is powered by a manual-winding mechanical movement and its bridges contain carbon-fiber mainplates and a black-gold tourbillon carriage. The watch displays the hours, minutes, small seconds, a three-day power reserve indicator and a flyback function (2 counters: 60 minutes and 10 tenths of an hour), which features a zero-setting and quick reset. The case is titanium with DLC coating and measures 44x50mm. The black dial possesses hands and indexes treated with a photoluminescent coating for nighttime reading. Water resistant to 50m, the watch is available on a rubber or alligator strap. Limited edition of 30 pieces.

BLANCPAIN

L-EVOLUTION TOURBILLON LARGE DATE – REF. 8822-15B30-53B

Beneath, and through, a dial that captivates with its inventive design, the automatic 4225G caliber reveals just enough to keep its owner in awe. With only two generous Roman numerals, at 3:00 and 9:00, this satin-brushed white-gold timepiece surrenders the spotlight to the movement's exposed complications. At 12:00, via a dynamic aperture, the movement's tourbillon brings a vibrating contrast to the dial's black atmosphere. At 6:00, surrounded by its exposed discs, the large date finds an unusual expression of modern watchmaking architecture. As a final creative touch, the power reserve is viewed, through a sapphire crystal caseback, on the finely decorated oscillating weight.

BREGUET

FUSEE TOURBILLON – REF. 7047PT

Breguet's Fusee Tourbillon boasts a manual-winding 596 caliber that possesses a 2.5Hz Breguet balance wheel in titanium with four adjusting screws in gold and a silicon balance-spring. The ensemble provides a 50-hour power reserve, and torque regularity throughout the operation of the timepiece is provided by the fusee-and-chain transmission. The 950 platinum 41mm case is water resistant to 30m. The Fusee Tourbillon shows off a one-minute tourbillon at 1:00 and a guilloché 18K gold subdial at 7:00 for the hours and minutes.

BREGUET

MARINE TOURBILLON PLATINUM – REF. 5837PT

Innovatively conceived with a balance spring, lever, and escape wheel, all made of silicon, and a carriage made of titanium, this timepiece's tourbillon possesses a light weight and exceptional shock and magnetism resistance, and needs no lubrication. Joining this complication on the silvered-gold dial, whose hand-engraved wave motif displays Breguet's mastery of the rose engine, is a chronograph with central seconds, 30-minute totalizer at 3:00, and 12-hour counter at 6:00. Oscillating beneath the intricately decorated watch face, within the 42mm platinum case, the hand-wound 554.4 caliber boasts a 50-hour power reserve.

BVLGARI

OCTO GRANDE SONNERIE TOURBILLON – REF. BGOW44BGLTBGS

The Octo Grande Sonnerie Tourbillon is the ultimate embodiment of horological complexity, especially since the automatic-winding movement that powers it is equipped with a tourbillon, retrograde hour display and power reserve indicators for the movement and striking mechanism. The four gongs are made from a special steel alloy, and are suspended between the movement and the inner surface of the case. Each one has a different length to produce its own specific sound, and each corresponds to a hammer that strikes a specific spot on the gong. The minute repeater mechanism is capable of both grand and small strike, as well as sounding the time in passing and on demand. Retrograde hours and a disc minute display complete this exceptional piece.

BVLGARI

TOURBILLON SAPPHIR – REF. BGGW53GLTBSK

The patented construction of the Tourbillon Sapphir takes on the task of the openwork concept with spectacular clarity. Secured from the outside by specially designed pillars, the sapphire crystal case middle is framed by a bezel and caseback in 18K white gold. The manual-winding GG 8000 caliber features a skeletonized tourbillon with sapphire bridges, and possesses a hefty power reserve of 70 hours. As the rhodium-plated hands with skeleton stems make their rounds, the owner is treated to an openworked display both serene and pleasantly modern.

CHANEL
J12 TOURBILLON

Innovation has always been at the heart of CHANEL. Its guiding principles have always remained the same: to go against the flow, subvert the role of the objects created and divert them from their normal use to bring them a new meaning and function. After transforming ceramic into a precious material and overturning the codes of timekeeping, CHANEL goes even further and brings ceramic to the very heart of its movement. The J12 Tourbillon is the first timepiece to feature a bottom-plate made of high-tech ceramic, with a 1/100 accuracy never before achieved in this material. It is the perfect blend of J12 high technology and one of the most respected watchmaking complications. Limited to 12 pieces, the J12 Tourbillon is equipped with the CHANEL 05-T2 manual-winding movement that provides a 100-hour power reserve. In 18K white gold and white high-tech ceramic, the timepiece is set with 46 baguette-cut diamonds (~4.55 cts).

CHANEL

PREMIERE FLYING TOURBILLON

CHANEL makes its first foray into the world of feminine mechanical complication watches with its Première Flying Tourbillon , which owes as much to its purity and poetry as to its complexity and virtuosity of construction. Almost secretly, the Flying Tourbillon beats within its stylized case in the form of a camellia, Mademoiselle Chanel's favorite flower. The absence of an upper bridge magnifies the Tourbillon's aesthetic—its frame becomes a micro-mechanical marvel in a three-dimensional assemblage of thin elements. This exceptional Tourbillon was developed in collaboration with Renaud & Papi Manufacturing (APRP SA), the high-end research and development wing of Audemars Piguet. Available in a limited edition of 20 pieces in 18K white gold, the Première Flying Tourbillon combines Haute Horlogerie and High Jewelry. The timepiece is set with 101 baguette-cut diamonds (~5.7 carats) and 127 brilliant-cut diamonds (~2 carats).

DEWITT

TWENTY-8-EIGHT REGULATOR A.S.W. HORIZONS – REF. T8.TA.002

Inspired by New York City's cutting-edge skylines, this 46mm 18K rose-gold timepiece gives the brilliance of the tourbillon an Art Deco makeover with a futuristic appeal. The imposing architecture of the four-column structure widens to embrace the open carriage, blending past and present in perfect harmony. While the sword-shaped hour and minute hands make their way around the subtle layers and transparencies of the dial, the deadbeat seconds hand, which is cleverly connected to the tourbillon carriage, ticks each second as a precise time interval. Incorporating a Straumann hairspring with Phillips curve and the patented Automatic Sequential Winding system, the watch's mechanical movement boasts a power reserve of 72 hours. As intricate and exciting as the dial, the sapphire crystal caseback, in conjunction with the use of a peripheral oscillating rotor, grants a vibrant view of the watch's spectacular Art Deco bridges and fascinating sliding-pinion deadbeat seconds lever.

DEWITT

TWENTY-8-EIGHT TOURBILLON – REF. T8.TH.006

Adorned on its flanks with DeWitt's imperial columns, the Twenty-8-Eight Tourbillon's 18K white-gold case features a crown decorated with a blackened-titanium "W" signature ring. Every finely crafted line of the timepiece's dial echoes the vivacious intricacies of the tourbillon carriage that breaks its plane. The DW8028 caliber that powers this watch is equipped with a variable-inertia balance and spiral with Breguet curve. As the smooth union of Roman and Arabic numerals give meaning to the openwork sword-shaped hands' revolutions, two curious "children" appliqués at 3:00 and 9:00 rise from the dial's two-tone sunray pattern and respond, in color, to the black semi-transparent carriage "grille."

DEWITT

X-WATCH "ONLY WATCH 2011 – CHARITY AUCTION MONACO"

For its third concept watch, DeWitt makes "reversible" the subject of momentous innovation. Activated by four pushbuttons around the grade-5 titanium case, the X-shaped bonnet cover spectacularly separates in its center to reveal this masterpiece's dual-personality interior. Once open, the case may be flipped over and locked again, at which point its ingenious design still permits perfect legibility of the watch's features. On the dial side, an elevated hourglass-shaped appliqué drives the eye to the mysterious tourbillon cage. On the chronograph side, the "Monaco-red" openworked dial features a highly sophisticated chronograph with gliding seconds disc, and a three-arm, three-level, 30-minute counter. Powered by a single exceptional movement driven by a peripheral oscillating rotor, both dials play off the shape of the bonnet by indicating the hours and minutes via openworked sword-shaped hands against retrograde scales on either side of the cover.

FRANCK MULLER
AETERNITAS I

The first in Franck Muller's five-model Aeternitas collection, this timepiece features an open tourbillon at 6:00 as the star of its finely crafted silver dial. The elegant white-gold curvex case gracefully frames the journey of the boldly contrasting blue hands around the black Arabic numerals. With an automatic-winding double-barrel movement that guarantees an eight-day power reserve, and a stunning 14mm tourbillon, this Aeternitas model dazzles with its balance of visual serenity and spectacular technical prowess.

FRANCK MULLER
AETERNITAS II

Adding an element of tasteful symmetry to the Aeternitas series, the power reserve indication at 12:00 presents a combined reading of the remaining energy in both days and hours. The sharp red hand of the gauge plays off the bright shade of the central hour-and-minute indicators to create a multi-colored ambience for the enchanting inner workings of the exposed 14mm tourbillon, in the lower tier of the dial. Meanwhile, the micro-rotor at 6:00 is visible through the watch's caseback, providing a supplementary treat to the connoisseur who wears this distinguished timepiece.

FREDERIQUE CONSTANT

FREDERIQUE CONSTANT MANUFACTURE GRAND FEU – REF. FC-980EGF4H9

Individually numbered and perfected with a silicon escapement, this 188-piece limited edition masterpiece's innovative self-winding FC-980 caliber boasts a perfect weight equilibrium within the 80-component tourbillon cage, thanks to the house's patented Smart Weight Balancing system. Adding to the shine of the 42mm 18K rose-gold case, the genuinely enameled dial achieves the depth of its luster via a rare and ancient process that demands the highest degree of expert craftsmanship. While the splendid one-minute tourbillon with running seconds is revealed on the lower half of the dial, a rose-gold and blued-steel day/night indicator, read off an Arabic numeral inner semicircle, ingeniously joins the black steel hour and minute hands. Completed with a sapphire crystal caseback and hand-stitched alligator leather strap, this exclusive timepiece exquisitely blends the brilliance of the past with the triumph of modern innovation.

GLASHÜTTE ORIGINAL

SENATOR MEISSEN TOURBILLON – REF. 94.11.01.01.04

Two world-famous Saxon inventions unite in the Senator Meissen Tourbillon: Meissen porcelain and the flying tourbillon. The timekeeper is a picture of stylish classicism in its 40mm rose-gold case, outfitted with exquisite technology. The passing of time is measured by traditionally blued hour and minute hands that glide across the surface of the wafer-thin, white Meissen porcelain dial. The painting of the dial alone requires eight hours to complete. Another significant challenge is posed by milling the cutaway needed to observe the flying tourbillon at the 6:00 on the 0.8mm-thick porcelain dial. The Senator Meissen Tourbillon is powered by the exquisitely finished automatic manufacture Caliber 94-11, which can be admired through the sapphire crystal caseback.

GRAHAM

SILVERSTONE TOURBILLOGRAPH FULL BLACK – REF. 2TSAB.B02A

The result of a four-year research and development program that has led to two patents, the Tourbillograph has made the traditional fragility of the tourbillon a thing of the past. Combining a reduced number of components, a double-bridge construction, and the use of iron-free elements, Graham-London equips this timepiece with a shockproof tourbillon that is highly insensitive to magnetism. With nearly every one of the watch's parts delicately blackened, the Silverstone Tourbillograph Full Black is a sophisticated column-wheel chronograph, which runs at a frequency of 28,800 vph, and is beautifully suited for both the elegance of the gala and the most extreme conditions that its owner may desire.

GUY ELLIA

TOURBILLON ZEPHYR

With a movement created by Swiss manufacture Christophe Claret, the Tourbillon Zephyr symbolizes transparency with excellence. Caliber GES 97 features a 110-hour power reserve and winding ring set with 36 baguette-cut diamonds (1.04 carats), or engine turning and one-minute tourbillon movement. The latter beats at 21,600 vph within an entirely hand-chamfered cage. The convex case with 950 platinum sides has a transparent back cover and hearth engraving. Mounted on an alligator strap with a folding buckle, this model is also available in platinum and titanium.

GUY ELLIA

TOURBILLON MAGISTERE TITANIUM

Designer Guy Ellia presents the titanium version of his famous skeletonized mysterious-winding tourbillon. The Time Square Tourbillon Magistère's Caliber TGE 97 was created by Swiss manufacturer Christophe Claret and features a 110-hour power reserve, one-minute tourbillon, and a titanium bottom plate and bridges. The movement beats at 21,600 vph within an entirely hand-chamfered cage.

GUY ELLIA

TOURBILLON MAGISTERE II

Guy Ellia has renewed its collaboration with Christophe Claret to present their latest timepiece enhanced with a tourbillon escapement: the Tourbillon Magistère II. Inside its distinctive case, an elongated rectangle (44.2x36.7mm), the skeleton movement features mysterious winding and features an "invisible" dial, whose main hands display the hours and minutes while seeming to float in space. In fact, the technical genius of this watch, produced in a limited edition of 12 pieces for each version, lies in the inversion of its bridges compared to a classic tourbillon timepiece. Hence the location of the winding crown at 6:00 and the use of the crown positioned at 12:00, while maintaining pressure on the security pushbutton at 10:00 to set the time. This piece is for lovers of fine watchmaking in search of the unusual.

HUBLOT

BIG BANG VENDOME TOURBILLON – REF. 305.PX.0009.GR

Within a 44mm case made of 18K red gold, this Big Bang grand complication houses the entirely built in-house, manual-winding HUB 6003 tourbillon movement. This deceptively sophisticated timepiece features an hour and minute indicator at 12:00, and tourbillon cage at 6:00, upon which the seconds are displayed. The dial's architecture, a testament to the house's philosophy of visual simplicity, provides the perfect canvas for this genuine exhibition of technical sophistication.

JACOB & CO.

CRYSTAL TOURBILLON – REF. CR2

The Crystal Tourbillon is powered by the manual-winding Jacob & Co 7 Caliber, skeletonized and set with 1.6 carats of baguette-cut diamonds. The tourbillon movement can be seen through both the transparent dial and the exhibition caseback. The 47mm case, crafted in 18K white gold, is set with 17.48 carats of baguette-cut diamonds. Mounted on a satin strap, the watch also bears 2.22 carats of baguette-cut diamonds on its buckle.

JACOB & CO.

RAINBOW TOURBILLON – REF. R1WGDC

In the pursuit of sophistication, innovation, and perfection in the field of fine watchmaking, Jacob & Co visualized the combination of a tourbillon device with the multiple time zone concept. The resulting world-class product was the Rainbow Tourbillon, the first timepiece to marry these two features in a limited edition collection. The specific time zone varies by style, with the timepiece covering between 12 and 24 time zones in addition to the primary time zone of the wearer. The 24-jewel movement operates at a frequency of 21,600 vph, with a 120-hour power reserve. The movement is a mechanical manual-winding tourbillon device visible through the dial and the exhibition caseback. The limited edition series of 47.5mm timepieces with 11.72 carats of diamonds on the case will feature 18 pieces produced in each metal: white, yellow and rose gold.

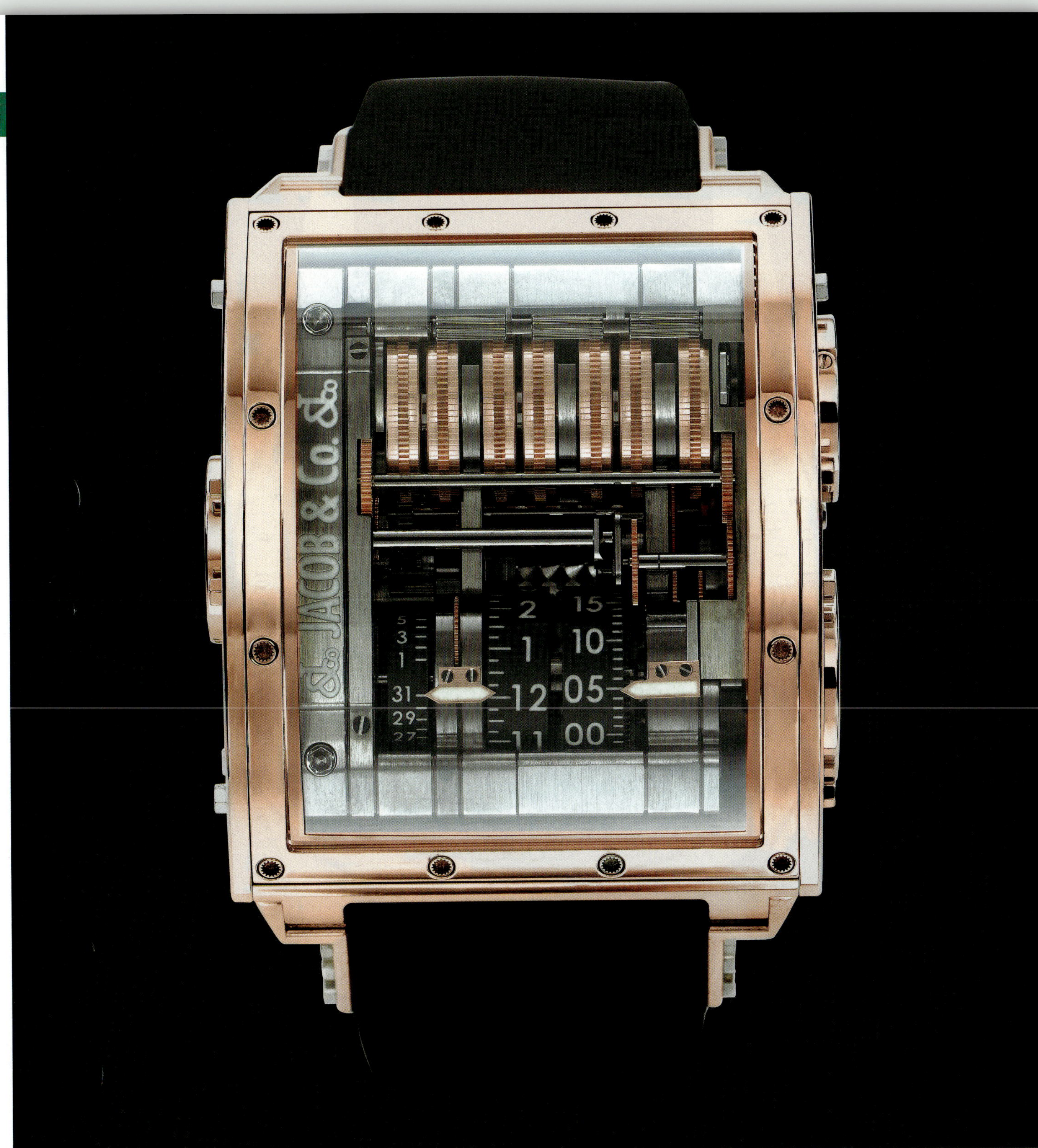

JACOB & CO.
THE QUENTTIN – REF. QUENRG

The Quenttin is the most technically advanced in the Jacob & Co family and arguably throughout the timepiece world. This limited edition, Swiss made, technically sophisticated instrument melds movement and state-of-the-art craftsmanship. The Quenttin, housing a vertical mechanical movement with manual-winding escapement, has the first ever 31-day power reserve supplied by the energy of seven spring barrels. Due to the unique configuration of this revolutionary tourbillon, the hours, minutes and power reserve are indicated by vertical discs assembled coaxially. Only 135 pieces of this innovative timepiece will be created; 99 pieces in white gold, 18 pieces in 18K rose gold and 18 pieces in magnesium.

JAEGER-LECOULTRE
MASTER TOURBILLON – REF. 165.24.20

The Master Tourbillon shows off its namesake complication in a classic display at 6:00, which finds an echo at 12:00 in a small second time zone indication. A red-tipped hand slowly sweeps around the dial to indicate the date—slowly, that is, until it swiftly makes the transition from 15 to 16, so as not to obstruct the tourbillon. All of this is driven by the automatic-winding Jaeger-LeCoultre 978 caliber, which possesses 302 components and 33 jewels. The silvered, sunray-brushed dial is adorned with gilt Arabic numerals and hour markers that match the piece's 18K pink-gold case, which is water resistant to 50m.

PANERAI

LUMINOR 1950 TOURBILLON GMT TITANIO, 47MM – REF. PAM00306

The Luminor 1950 Tourbillon GMT in titanium is powered by the Panerai P.2005 movement with tourbillon, representing the sophistication of Officine Panerai's manufacturing skill. Not only does the cage make a full rotation in 30 seconds instead of every minute, it is also the only existing tourbillon to place the rotating balance wheel inside a cage that is perpendicular to the base of the movement. This unusual feature better compensates for any positional inaccuracies the watch may assume while being worn on the wrist. Made up of 239 components and featuring a six-day power reserve, this structurally complex and highly innovative hand-wound movement is revealed through the sapphire crystal caseback and stealthily indicated by the luminescent dot at 9:00. This piece is water resistant to 10 bar (100m).

PANERAI

RADIOMIR TOURBILLON GMT CERAMICA, 48 MM – REF. PAM00348

As part of Officine Panerai's dual-timepiece tribute to the 400th anniversary of Galileo Galilei's discovery of the four moons of Jupiter, the manufacturer set about creating the Radiomir Tourbillon GMT Ceramica, also known to Panerai fans as "Lo Scienziato." The main novelty of Lo Scienziato is its skeletal structure, made of a fine mesh that supports both the external band (which has small ecru luminescent Arabic numerals and hour markers) and subdials showing small seconds, tourbillon movement and AM/PM. The second time zone is indicated by a third central hand. The watch is powered by the 277-component Panerai P.2005/S movement, which is characterized by its tourbillon that rotates perpendicularly to the balance axis and completes two rotations per minute to guarantee greater precision. The case itself is made of a zirconium oxide ceramic, an exceptionally hard, corrosion-resistant material, and is water resistant to 10 bar (100m), qualifying it as a true traditional Radiomir. This tribute to the Florentine astronomer is available in a limited edition of 30 pieces.

PATEK PHILIPPE

10 DAY TOURBILLON – REF. 5101R

The new Ref. 5150R runs accurately for 240 hours when fully wound, as indicated by the power reserve indicator at 12:00. In this extraordinary 28-20/222 manufacture movement, Patek Philippe has implemented yet another rare mechanism: a tourbillon escapement. The device consists of 72 individual parts that together weigh a scant 0.3g. All steel parts of the filigreed cage are meticulously finished by hand. Despite its considerable length of more than 5cm, the anatomically curved 18K rose-gold case gently hugs the wrist. The sapphire crystal caseback reveals the meticulously decorated plate and bridges, the intricate tourbillon, and the jewels held in gold chatons.

PIAGET

ALTIPLANO TOURBILLON GOUSSET IN WHITE GOLD – REF. G0A32063

Piaget now revives the tourbillon pocket watch, interpreted in a highly contemporary square form characteristic of the brand, that of the Altiplano collection. The 40mm white-gold case houses the Piaget mechanical hand-wound Calibre 600P, the world's thinnest tourbillon movement at just 3.5mm thick. Admirably reflecting the mastery inherent to the manufacture, the carriage of this tourbillon—visible through a dial opening at 9:00—is made of 42 parts and weighs a mere 0.2g. Like all vintage Piaget models, the caseback is engraved with the brand's coat of arms. To provide a variety of manners of wearing it, this refined and elegant watch comes with a white-gold chain as well as a leather cordlet.

PIAGET

PIAGET EMPERADOR COUSSIN TOURBILLON AUTOMATIC ULTRA-THIN – REF. G0A36041

Derived from Piaget's 600P and 1208P calibers—the world's thinnest hand-wound tourbillon movement and the world's thinnest self-winding movement with a micro-rotor—the house's 1208P caliber earns this avant-garde timepiece the title of world's thinnest self-winding tourbillon. Measuring a mere 10.4mm in thickness, this new interpretation of Piaget's aesthetic codes possesses an architecture as spectacular as the exposed movement that powers the watch's heartbeat. Through a laser-engraved sapphire crystal, the wearer may admire an offset gold micro-rotor and imposing tourbillon cage, offering a veritable third dimension to a dial that features a delicate laser-guilloché craftsmanship and beautifully tapered hour markers that point to the off-centered hour and minute hands at 5:00.

PIAGET

PIAGET EMPERADOR TOURBILLON – REF. G0A32246

This watch hides two timepieces: the first one contains a small quartz movement under a dial of inlaid white mother-of-pearl, set in a module that drops down when closed. But a new surprise lies in the discovery of a second watch—the world's thinnest version of a tourbillon (Calibre Piaget 600P) highlighted in a diamond-rimmed dial, baguette hour markers and a center of Polynesian mother-of-pearl as well as a power reserve indicator in inlaid colored mother-of-pearl. The case, encrusted with 589 brilliant-cut diamonds (approximately 2.9 carats) and 207 baguette-cut diamonds (approximately 32.9 carats) each cut and set by hand, extends to a black alligator leather bracelet.

PIAGET

PIAGET EMPERADOR TOURBILLON SKELETON – REF. G0A29108

Equipped with the mechanical manual-winding Piaget 600P shaped caliber, this Piaget Emperador tourbillon symbolizes the alchemist's blend that Piaget achieves once again between haute horology and haute jewelry. Piaget has developed the world's thinnest tourbillon, a mere 3.5mm thick, and has chosen a flying version placed at 12:00 for aesthetic reasons. The shaped caliber's lower side is graced with the extreme refinement of a sunray guilloché decorative motif comprising 60 divisions representing 60 seconds. This movement has a power reserve of approximately 40 hours and beats at a cadence of 21,600 vph.

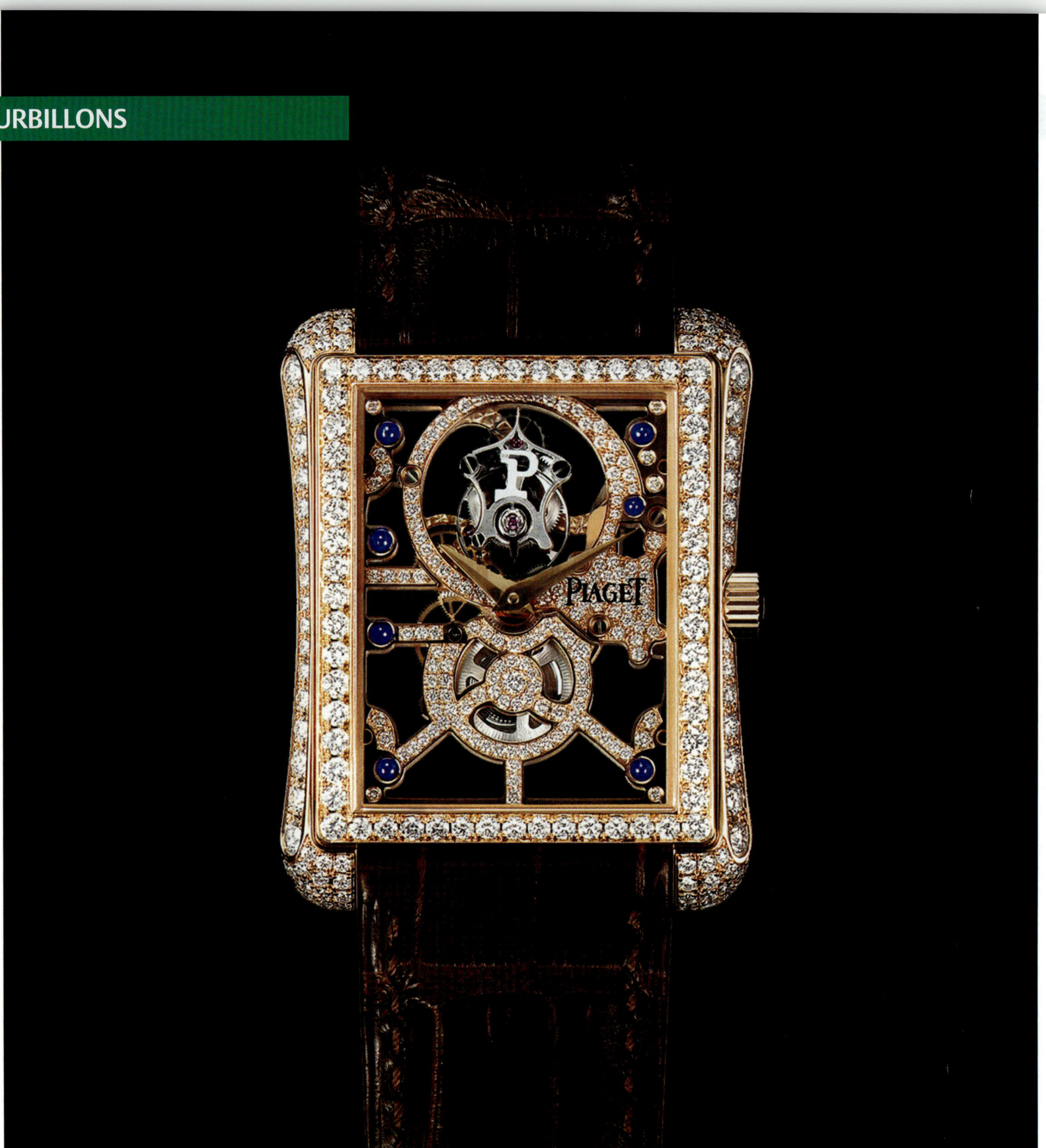

PIAGET

PIAGET EMPERADOR TOURBILLON SKELETON GEMSET – REF. G0A31047

This Emperador Tourbillon symbolizes the alchemist's blend that Piaget achieves once again between haute horology and haute joaillerie. Piaget has developed the world's thinnest tourbillon, at a mere 3.5mm thick, and has chosen a flying version placed at 12:00 for aesthetic reasons. One hundred fifty-nine round diamonds totaling approximately 2 carats and 7 sapphire cabochons (0.2 carat) adorn this exceptional caliber, whose lower side is graced with the extreme refinement of a sunray guilloché decorative motif comprising 60 divisions, which correspond to 60 seconds. This hand-wound movement has a power reserve of approximately 40 hours and beats at a cadence of 21,600 vph.

PIAGET

PIAGET POLO GEMSET TOURBILLON RELATIF – REF. G0A32148

The Piaget Polo Gemset Tourbillon Relatif, a huge success and exclusive to Piaget, features a rotating mobile carriage apparently disembodied from the movement at the end of the minute hand. This watch houses the Calibre 608P, a mechanical manual-winding flying tourbillon movement beating at a frequency of 21,600 vph and endowed with a 72-hour power reserve. Development took three years and watchmakers needed almost a week to assemble each piece. The case is covered with brilliant-cut and baguette diamonds, each cut and set by hand. Each numbered piece sparkles with 731 diamonds weighing a total 19.3 carats. Setting them in sequence took around 200 hours.

PIAGET

PIAGET POLO TOURBILLON IN PINK GOLD – REF. G0A36111

One thousand, one hundred and ninety-six diamonds of mesmerizing depth adorn the entirety of this masterful combination of sublime jewelry and haute horology. This remarkable composition of baguette-cut and brilliant-cut gemstones, positioned vertically and horizontally, give this timepiece an allure of royal divinity. A testament to Piaget's watchmaking perfectionism, the Polo Tourbillon's 44mm 18K pink-gold case houses the 600P mechanical caliber, which, at 3.5mm thick, boasts the honor of world's thinnest flying tourbillon movement ever made.

PIAGET

PIAGET POLO TOURBILLON IN WHITE GOLD – REF. G0A30111

A wonderful rendition of an iconic timepiece, this Piaget Polo Tourbillon is equipped with the shaped 600P caliber. The mechanical manual-winding movement consists of 24 jewels and offers 40 hours of power reserve; the bridges of the tourbillon are created in titanium. The case is crafted in 18K white gold and set with fancy-cut diamonds.

PIAGET

PIAGET POLO TOURBILLON RELATIF ENAMEL PERSONALISED – REF. G0A33045

This creation evokes the black and white colors of a classic New York evening. The Polo Tourbillon Relatif combines the complexity of a Piaget 608P flying tourbillon movement with the extreme sophistication of a stunningly beautiful enameled and chased décor. The Calibre 608P is housed within an 18K white-gold champlevé enameled case. The outlines of the city's twelve highest skyscrapers are engraved on an 18K white-gold dial, illuminated by the contrasts with black enamel surrounding them. Moreover, the black enameled side of the case is engraved with the most famous landmarks, and the crown of the model bears a symbol representing New York.

PIAGET

PIAGET POLO TOURBILLON RELATIF IN PINK GOLD – REF. G0A35124

Suspended from one end of the minute hand, the flying tourbillon carriage appears to be disconnected from the base movement driving it. The hours are read off a central disc, while the tourbillon carriage is swept along in the rotation of the minute hand. Expressing the magic of perfect equilibrium, the Piaget Polo Tourbillon Relatif marks off time to the rhythm of the new proprietary Calibre 608P, a mechanical manual-winding flying tourbillon movement. Composed of 42 parts, the carriage—which spins on its axis once per minute, in addition to the hourly rotation around the dial—weighs a mere 0.2g! Within a 45mm black and 18K rose-gold case, the tourbillon movement, Piaget Calibre 608P, beats at a frequency of 21,600 vph and is endowed with a 72-hour power reserve.

PIAGET

PIAGET POLO TOURBILLON RELATIF IN WHITE GOLD – REF. G0A31123

Suspended from one end of the minute hand, the flying tourbillon carriage appears to be disconnected from the base movement driving it. The hours are read off a central disc, while the tourbillon carriage is swept along in the rotation of the minute hand. Expressing the magic of perfect equilibrium, the Piaget Polo Tourbillon Relatif marks off time to the rhythm of the new proprietary Calibre 608P, a mechanical hand-wound flying tourbillon movement. Composed of 42 parts, the carriage—which spins on its axis once per minute, in addition to the hourly rotation around the dial—weighs a mere 0.2g! The tourbillon movement, Piaget Calibre 608P, beats at a frequency of 21,600 vph (3 Hz) and is endowed with a 72-hour power reserve.

REBELLION TIMEPIECES

REB-5 TOURBILLON

Within the modular construction of its high-powered case—available in red gold, titanium or black titanium DLC—the REB-5 Tourbillon astonishes its owner with a dial that is nothing more, or rather nothing less, than the top of its intricately finished open movement. While the one-minute tourbillon ensures a high-precision regulation of the effects of gravity, the details of the watch's exposed micro-mechanics leave little doubt as to the character of the timepiece. Drilled and engineered to evoke the wheels and brake discs of a high-performance sports car, the twin mainspring barrels provide an exceptional seven-day power reserve for this manual-winding horological engine, which is exclusively limited to 12 pieces per year. With its spectacular exhibition caseback and revealing side window, the REB-5 Tourbillon thankfully leaves little to the imagination.

RICHARD MILLE

RM 017 EXTRA FLAT TOURBILLON

A world premiere for 2011, with a total thickness comprising a mere 8.7mm, the new RM017 with its manual-winding movement with circa 70 hours power reserve is amongst the thinnest tourbillon constructions ever created. The RM017 uses a movement baseplate in grade 2 titanium, treated with a black PVD coating. The wearer activates the separate functions of winding, neutral and hand-setting via a special pusher in the crown for. The RM017 combines cutting-edge technology with elegance and exceptional lines, useful functionality and unmistakable recognition: the RM 017 Extra Flat Tourbillon typifies everything that Richard Mille Watches stands for.

RICHARD MILLE

RM 021 TOURBILLON 'AERODYNE'

Continuing the expansion and application of truly unique materials to watchmaking, the RM 021 Tourbillon 'Aerodyne' is the first watch created with a composite baseplate utilizing a titanium exterior framework in combination with honeycombed orthorhombic titanium alumide and carbon nanofiber. This material was originally the subject of research by NASA for application as a core material of supersonic aircraft wings. This new tourbillion provides hours, minutes, indicators for power reserve (circa 70 hours), torque indicator and function indicator for winding, neutral, and hand-setting operations. The PVD-treated variable inertia balance wheel with overcoil spring and ceramic endstone for the tourbillon cage offers optimal chronometric results and excellent long-term wear capability.

RICHARD MILLE
RM 052 SKULL TOURBILLON

Over the centuries, the skull has become the emblem of rebellion and insubordination, its previously macabre associations having been usurped by those of freedom and nonconformity. The RM 052 Skull Tourbillon visualizes these precepts in timekeeping. The baseplate and bridges take the form of a skull sculpted from grade-5 titanium; indeed, the tourbillon movement itself is built inside these front and back skull plates. The upper and lower jaws hold the ruby of the tourbillon cage and the back of the skull is actually the movement's center bridge. The entire movement is connected to the case by four bridges that are inspired by the crossed bones from pirate ship's flags. The new case design, with its opened flanks, continues this visual allegory to the human skeleton.

RICHARD MILLE

RM 053 TOURBILLON PABLO MAC DONOUGH

Carrying the name of polo champion Pablo Mac Donough, the limited edition RM053 is built for one of the toughest sports played today. This new polo watch has been built to deal with forces far different from the norms found in other sports disciplines. With a totally new armored and sculpted case design with two raised arcs, the viewing windows are tilted at an angle of 30°, ideal when seen from the rider's saddle position. The seconds run with the tourbillon cage on the left viewing window and on the right the hours and minutes are shown. The highly compact, totally new tourbillon movement design utilizes a highly skeletonized baseplate and bridges with a compact going train-winding barrel arrangement. Since the movement itself is ultra light and tightly unified, it is less susceptible to the centrifugal and centripetal forces generated during a game.

ROGER DUBUIS

EXCALIBUR AUTOMATIC FLYING TOURBILLON – REF. EX45-520-20-00/0ER01/B

This highly expressive white-gold timepiece offers a double insight into the intricate inner workings of its sophisticated RD520 automatic movement with 60-hour power reserve. The large white transferred Roman numerals set a dynamic structural tone on the charcoal satin sunburst background. On the left side of the dial, the magic happens. In addition to the black onyx plates, and flying tourbillon with small seconds at 7:30, Roger Dubuis delivers, at 10:00, a highly detailed micro-rotor aperture, turning this dial into a thorough, and splendid, exhibition of the watch's heartbeat.

ROGER DUBUIS

EXCALIBUR DOUBLE FLYING TOURBILLON – REF. EX45-01-50-00/09R01/B

By developing a double tourbillon with differential, Roger Dubuis takes a pioneering step in precision and reliability. Housed within a 45mm pink-gold case that echoes the sheen of the double tourbillon ring, this innovative timepiece's 413-piece RD01 caliber complements the two one-minute tourbillons with the ingenious touches of jumping hours and retrograde dragging minutes. In two clever maneuvers to improve legibility, the transferred Roman numerals X through II appear on the dial's inner circle, surrounded by the engraved Arabic numerals of the retrograde minute circle. Completing the dynamic design of this high-performance timepiece, the Excalibur Double Flying Tourbillon features a 48-hour power reserve display on its caseback, and is worn on a hand-stitched black alligator strap.

ROGER DUBUIS

EXCALIBUR MINUTE REPEATER TOURBILLON – REF. EX45-08-50-00/VER00/B

Cleverly activated by a turning of the bezel, this extraordinary minute repeater with centrifugal dissipator boasts the rare distinction of an automatic-winding mechanical movement. But such was not enough for Roger Dubuis. Transporting this timepiece into the realm of pure horological magnificence, the Genevan watchmaker incorporates a flying one-minute tourbillon into its RD08 caliber, making the 45mm pink-gold case the guardian of an unquestionable masterpiece. Revealing a glimpse of the watch's heartbeat, the dial features a dual composition of charcoal gray and sapphire crystal, along with engraved Roman numerals. Fitted with a double platinum micro-rotor, flying tourbillon and minute repeater, it comes as no surprise that this wristwatch is honored with the distinguished Geneva Seal.

ROGER DUBUIS

EXCALIBUR SKELETON DOUBLE FLYING TOURBILLON – REF. EX45-01SQ-20-00/0E000/B

As though the extraordinary creation of a double flying tourbillon with differential weren't enough, Roger Dubuis bares the thrill of this timepiece's structure with a skeleton design of the 319-component RD01SQ caliber. Carefully adjusted in six positions, this revealing masterpiece boasts two one-minute tourbillons, each with a frequency of 21,600 vph. Within the 45mm white-gold case and charcoal gray flange, the owner is treated to the intricacy of detail of the Roger Dubuis manufacture. This skeletal triumph of modern haute horology is secured to the wrist by a fully adjustable hand-stitched black alligator strap with white-gold folding buckle.

ROGER DUBUIS

EXCALIBUR SKELETON FLYING TOURBILLON – REF. EX45-505SQ-20-00/0E000/B

Playing off the suspended effect of the flying tourbillon at 7:30, the Excalibur Skeleton Flying Tourbillon presents a seemingly weightless appeal through the audacious geometry of its transparent design. Surrounding the exposed mechanism, the charcoal gray flange, with red minute-circle transfers and charcoal gray hour-marker screws, is framed by a 45mm case made of gleaming white gold. Despite its minimalist approach, this timepiece boasts a power reserve of 60 hours. The Excalibur Skeleton Flying Tourbillon beats at a rate of 21,600 vph and is worn on a hand-stitched alligator strap.

ROGER DUBUIS

LA MONEGASQUE FLYING TOURBILLON – REF. MG44-540-80-00/03R01/B

Through the rhodium-plated aperture at 7:30, the golden tone of the gravity-defying flying tourbillon oscillates in powerful contrast to the assertive shimmer of the 42mm platinum case. With its off-centered positioning, the one-minute tourbillon shares its spotlight with the snailed silver power reserve at 4:00 and large date at 12:00 on the silver satin sunburst dial center. On the charcoal satin exterior, discreet Arabic numerals confirm the gray brilliance of this emblematic expression of haute horology. The RD540 that powers this timepiece grants it a power reserve of 60 hours. The Monegasque Flying Tourbillon is worn on a hand-stitched black alligator leather strap.

STÜHRLING ORIGINAL

KING'S COURT TOURBILLON – REF. SW-01

Declaring its royal personality with a solid 18K yellow-gold case and leaf-shaped hands, this timepiece provides an impressive throne for its meticulously embellished movement with 72 hours of autonomy. Powering the hour and minute indicators' voyage around the intricate specially pressed dial, the watch's 26-jewel mechanical double-barrel tourbillon movement is fully decorated with Côtes Circulaires and blued steel screws. While the sapphire crystal presents a regal view of the dial-side time indications and tourbillon aperture at 6:00, the screw-down exhibition caseback's transparency lets the timepiece's owner admire its internal distinction while adorning his wrist with a 22mm-wide genuine crocodile leather strap. The King's Court Tourbillon is limited to 14 pieces.

STÜHRLING ORIGINAL

MIRAGE TOURBILLON – REF. 243

Injecting classical watchmaking with a dose of intrigue, the Mirage Tourbillon's 18-jewel, ST-93351 tourbillon movement beats with a frequency of 28,800 vph. Deeply engraved "vines" curve and contort to frame the 6:00 customized tourbillon assembly, whose inclusion of a symbolic "S" figure adorns the timepiece with a nod to the brand. The 41mm solid stainless steel case is decorated brilliantly with a coin-edge beveled bezel and hosts a 22mm-wide genuine crocodile strap. The limited edition Mirage Tourbillon is hand-assembled in Switzerland and consists of 300 total units (125 silver tone, 75 gold tone, 100 rose tone).

STÜHRLING ORIGINAL

PHANTOM TOURBILLON – REF. 153

The combination of a ceramic case and bracelet with a carbon-fiber dial brilliantly showcases the timepiece's genuine tourbillon movement. A new exploit in versatility for Stührling Original's tourbillon models, the Phantom's sleek design provides a clean demeanor that fits perfectly as an elegant dress piece or dynamic sport timekeeper. The 47mm ceramic case with sapphire crystal houses the ST-93301 caliber, an 18-jewel tourbillon movement that beats at 28,800 vph and features a custom tourbillon assembly accented with a triple "S" design, denoting the first initial of the manufacture's name. Entirely hand-assembled in Switzerland, the Phantom Tourbillon is presented as a 400-unit limited edition (320 black, 80 white).

STÜHRLING ORIGINAL
SOVEREIGN TOURBILLON – REF. 127D

With its distinctive placement of the crown at 12:00, the Sovereign Tourbillon makes its mark as one of Stuhrling Original's signature designs. This hand-wound masterpiece boasts the ST-93961 caliber tourbillon movement with four subdials segmenting the watch's complications, which stand out beautifully with the bright blue tone of their indicating hands. While the small 24-hour counter at 12:00 is mirrored in dimension by the power reserve indicator at 6:00, the tourbillon at 9:00 prominently echoes the off-centered hour and minute dial with Arabic numerals at 3:00. The skeletonized movement is decorated with deeply engraved scrollwork, beats at 28,800 vph, and is protected by a sapphire crystal. The 46mm Emperor-style case is constructed of 316L stainless steel and is secured to the wrist via a 24mm-wide genuine crocodile strap. Provided as a limited edition of 150 pieces (50 silver tone, 50 gold tone, and 50 rose tone), the Sovereign Tourbillon is completely hand-assembled in Switzerland.

VACHERON CONSTANTIN
PATRIMONY TRADITIONNELLE 14-DAY TOURBILLON

The first Vacheron Constantin timepiece to meet the newly appointed criteria of the Geneva Seal, this horological symbol of purity combines refined tradition with modern savoir-faire. Using four barrels, mounted in pairs, that unwind simultaneously, the hand-wound 2260 tourbillon caliber endows this timepiece with an exceptional two weeks of power reserve. Visually, the 42mm pink-gold case luxuriously sets the stage for the silver-toned opaline dial, upon which the intricately finished tourbillon, with small seconds at 6:00, and power reserve indicator at 12:00, alludes to the architecture of several of the brand's celebrated 20th-century pocket watches.

ZENITH

EL PRIMERO TOURBILLON – REF. 03.2050.4035/21.C630

Zenith's El Primero Tourbillon is distinguished by its chronograph with central seconds hand, 30-minute counter at 3:00 and 12-hour counter at 6:00. The El Primero 4035 D automatic-winding movement, whose oscillating weight bears a Côtes de Genève decoration, beats within the stainless steel 44mm case, which is water resistant to 100m. The dial features rhodium-faceted hands and indexes treated with SuperLumiNova SLN C1. The tourbillon at 11:00, which makes one turn per minute, displays small seconds on and date around the carriage. Completed with an alligator leather strap with stainless steel triple-folding buckle, the El Primero Tourbillon is available in a limited edition of 250 pieces.

Chronographs, Split-Seconds and Flyback Chronographs

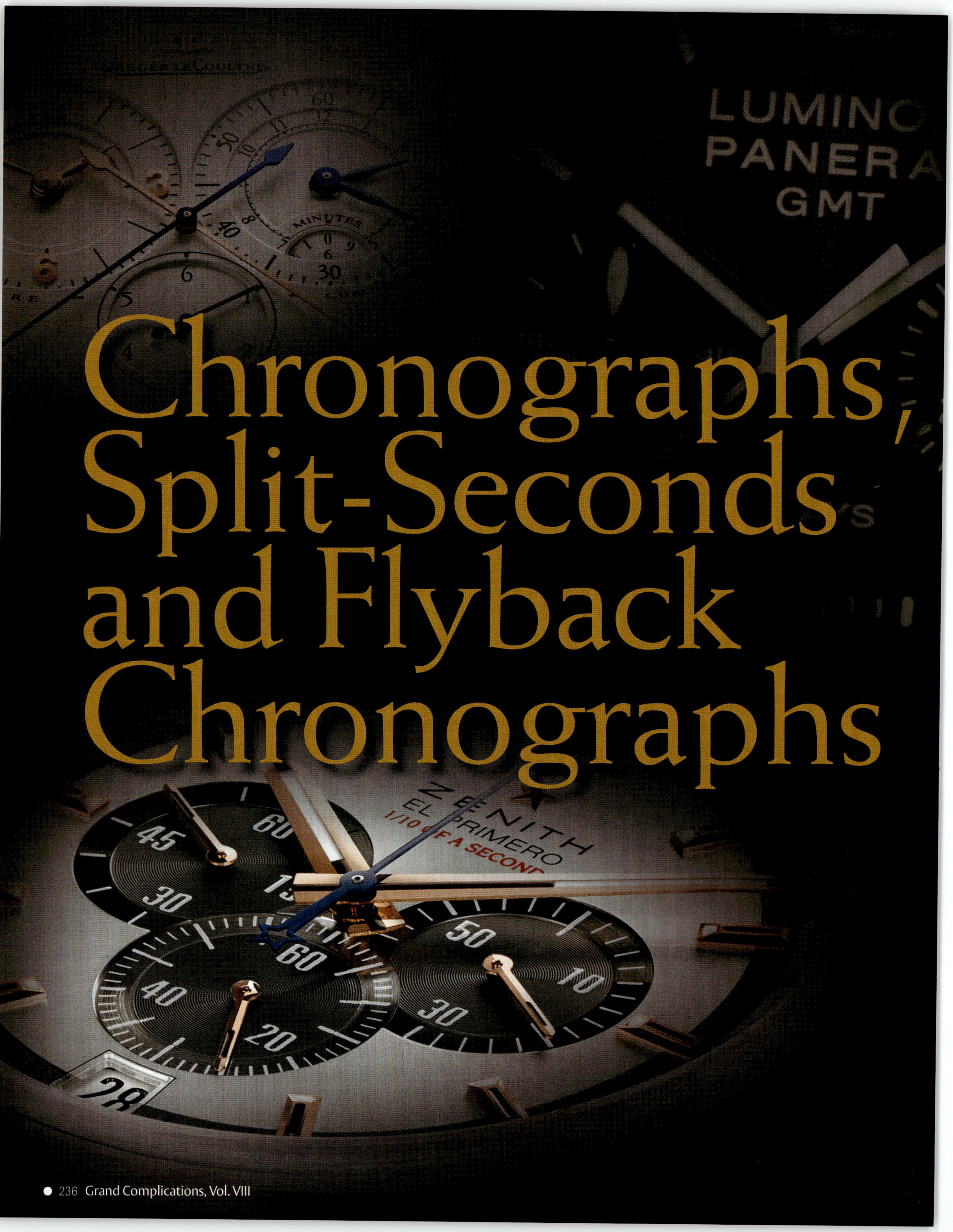

The chronograph celebrated its 190th birthday in 2011. First appearing in 1821, this mechanism, which allows its user to calculate the time passed, is actually, if one excludes multiple time zone watches, the youngest of the classic complications—and the perfect emblem of the modern age. Today, the chronograph is one of horology's stars, essential in any self-respecting collection. This success can be explained by its practical utility, but also by its sporty and technical appeal, which reflects a dynamic lifestyle. To respond to this infatuation, brands are continually inventing innovations in terms of design, materials, mechanisms and performance. It is also increasingly common for brands to create their own mechanical chronograph movement—a way for the owner to possess a timepiece with an exclusive "motor."

Juan-Carlos Torres

CEO of Vacheron Constantin

"Human quality can be both seen and felt in a watch."

Masterfully guided by Juan-Carlos Torres, Vacheron Constantin is experiencing remarkable success, notably in the United States and China. To cope with this strong demand, the brand is substantially investing in production facilities and projects a doubling of its workforce, a decision that matches the manufacture's philosophy of combining strong human resources with audacious innovation.

"Vacheron Constantin has grown strongly, everywhere," notes Juan-Carlos Torres, the brand's CEO. This growth has entailed an impressive increase of 55% in the United States, along with a Chinese market to which "our entire production could be devoted if we so wished. This is why we have decided to maintain the existing product and production strategy, while increasing our means," explains Torres.

To keep pace with its current success, the manufacture is making considerable investments this year in its production sites of Plan-les-Ouates and Le Brassus, in Switzerland's Vallée du Joux in the Jura Mountains. The objective? To increase the number of watches produced annually from 19,000 to 33,000, all the while preserving and further nurturing the very essence of the brand.

In parallel, Vacheron Constantin will strengthen its distribution network in several markets, including by opening proprietary boutiques in Macau, Seoul, Paris, Taiwan, Los Angeles and São Paulo, as well as a fourth store in Hong Kong.

PATRIMONY
TRADITIONNELLE
CHRONOGRAPH

SYMBOLIQUE DES LAQUES

"I DON'T ADD MACHINES, I ADD WORKSHOPS"

To increase the capacity of production, Torres does not follow the path of excessive industrialization. He instead builds on the foundations of the success and the reputation of this ancient manufacture, founded in Geneva in 1755: namely, its strong attachment to ancestral techniques, particularly hand craftsmanship. "The development strategy of hand-made crafts will be further reinforced," he points out, "because I don't add machines, I add workshops made up of professionals. This is why we are going to double our collective team in Switzerland in the years to come, rather than undertake excessive mechanization of production." These human skills are duly fostered at each level, as the manufacture is equally committed to its internal training program and is accordingly doubling its number of apprentices.

The future of the manufacture is already clearly expressed in the models presented in 2011, representing a tribute to the horological arts. At the heart of the Vacheron Constantin workshops, a Métiers d'Art unit that brings together virtuoso exponents of their crafts, is a gathering of artisans gifted with talents that are both remarkable in themselves and extremely rare. There, Vacheron Constantin perpetuates traditional expertise through dedicated collections, such as the Masques series of 2007, and the Symbolique des Laques line introduced in 2010. The brand also achieved a world first for the Only Watch charity auction held in September 2011. The dial of the Colombes watch features the alliance of four separate decorative techniques: engraving, guilloché, gem setting, and enameling. This timepiece, inspired by M.C. Escher's technique of repetition of forms, heralded the birth of a new collection: Métiers d'Art – Perspectives d'Art. In doing so, the manufacture innovated by developing a new style of guillochage. Beyond the repeating motifs, the craftsman creates veritable drawings, which are all miniature works of art.

Uniting these same competencies, the one-of-a-kind Métiers d'Art – Chagall & l'Opéra de Paris piece flirted with the limits of achievability, as the engraver needed fairy-like fingers to sculpt the gold while preserving the dial's grand feu enameling miniature artwork.

In 2011, Vacheron Constantin additionally unveiled two pieces that are part of its Atelier Cabinotiers project, launched in 2006 and never before seen in the field of horology. Devoted to the creation of custom-built, one-of-a-kind pieces of exceptional craftsmanship, the project provides absolute exclusivity and complete personalization. A single hand, for example, revolves around the Philosophia's dial! And as if to free its owner from the frenzied race for precision, only the hours are displayed. If needed, a minute repeater comprising three gongs provides a precise indication of time. Representing the ultimate complication, a tourbillon sets the final touch to this masterpiece…

Vladimir, the second one-off piece born in the Atelier Cabinotiers, marries high-flying technique and artistic craftsmanship, with the hand-decoration of each of the movement's 891 components, and the bas-relief engraving adorning the case. The heart of the watch houses 17 complications, making it, following four years of development, one of the most complicated watches on the market.

TRADITION, THE ROOT OF TECHNICAL INNOVATION

Building on past achievements to propel them even farther is the trademark of Vacheron Constantin. As early as 1930, the House, in collaboration with Louis Cottier, became one of the earliest manufactures to develop watches with world-time displays. At last year's Salon International de la Haute Horologie, the brand unveiled the Patrimony Traditionnelle Heures du Monde. Thirty-seven time zones, including half zones and even quarter zones, are displayed on the dial. This timepiece is the only one to date to boast such a complete and comprehensive display, a prowess that notably earned it the second prize of *Montres Passion* magazine's Watch of the Year competition. Endowed with a rich heritage, Vacheron Constantin proves its willingness to reinterpret tradition through the glorious spectrum of technical innovation.

The year 2012 began with the presentation of the exceptional Patrimony Traditionnelle 14-Day Tourbillon, featuring an impressive record-setting power reserve for this complication, combined with the absolute purity of a round and sober case. In fact, the new Vacheron Constantin 2260 caliber beating at the heart of the Patrimony Traditionnelle 14-Day Tourbillon is simply unrivaled in the industry. And that isn't all: this new arrival in the Patrimony Traditionnelle line is the first Vacheron Constantin timepiece to be officially recognized as meeting the new criteria of the Geneva Seal, thereby already making it a collector's piece.

UPDATING THE GENEVA SEAL FOR THE GOOD OF THE INDUSTRY

Vacheron Constantin also took part in redefining the criteria of the Geneva Seal. To celebrate the distinction's 125th anniversary, it was revised to become "more understandable and more attuned to customer expectations." The requirements are now applied not only to the movement, but also to the finished watch. Through its active participation in the new definition of the Geneva Seal, Vacheron Constantin has expressed its pronounced interest in our shared horological heritage and its determination to be a driving force in the pursuit of excellence.

In 2012, Vacheron Constantin's agenda is expressed through the consolidation of its lines and products, the enlargement of its offering, and the investments it is making, which encompass the production facilities of Plan-les-Ouates and Le Brassus, as well as human resources. Torres explains: "The necessary concern for these three elements is driven not by financial reasons, but most importantly by a need for quality!" The soul of Vacheron Constantin, linked to its expertise in hand-craftsmanship, is thus beating more vibrantly than ever. And if the timepieces may serve as stages for extraordinary complications and virtuosity, the brand well knows how to demonstrate an intelligent simplicity, while truly focusing on the long term.

PATRIMONY TRADITIONNELLE HEURES DU MONDE

Chronographs, Split-Seconds and Flyback Chronographs

IWC,
Portofino Chronograph

In 1821, Nicolas Rieussec

(then "watchmaker to the King") was tasked with timing a horse race on the Champs de Mars in Paris. He developed for the occasion a timepiece that he would patent the following year, under the name of "chronographe à seconde" (seconds chronograph). Accurate to one fifth of a second, this instrument was equipped with a tip that deposited a drop of ink on the dial at the beginning and at the end of each measurement. This invention would be perfected by Frederick Louis Fatton, who transformed it into a pocket chronograph with a fixed dial for Abraham-Louis Breguet. The year 1838 saw the invention of the split-seconds chronograph (see "How does it work?"), and the first system to reset the hands to zero came into being around mid-century. Now equipped with its three main functions (start, stop, reset), the chronograph would become very useful in several domains (science, technology, transportation, the military), and it is not by chance that its rise coincided with that of the industrial society and competitive athletics. During this period the chronograph would also gain several new scales for various measurements: tachometer (speed), telemeter (distance), pulsometer (pulse), etc.

The first wristwatch chronographs made their appearance in 1915. They were equipped, as were the pocket chronographs, with a single pushbutton for all three functions, usually housed in the crown. Breitling designed the now dominant chronograph configuration by adding the first independent pushbutton, and then in 1934, another one for resetting the chronograph. In 1937, the Dubois Dépraz manufacture presented a movement whose chronograph command operated using a cam system, less expensive and less difficult to produce than the traditional column wheel. The system would slowly be adopted by most brands.

In July of 1969, the Speedmaster, from Omega, would accompany American astronauts on their first visit to the moon. That year was also marked by the appearance of the first automatic chronograph movements. The movement developed by the Büren/Breitling/Heuer-Leonidas threesome in collaboration with Dubois Dépraz was a cam movement featuring a modular construction, with an off-centered microrotor (oscillating weight); the one from Zenith, the famous El Primero, was an integrated movement with a column wheel in its central rotor. Thanks to its frequency of 36,000 vibrations per hour, it was also the first chronograph movement capable of measuring times to one-tenth of a second.

The advent of quartz movements, which were much more precise, was nearly the deathblow for the mechanical chronograph, but the renaissance of mechanical horology in the late 1980s signaled its triumphant return. Let us remember that it is very rare for watch brands to design and produce their own chronograph movements. A large percentage of the chronographs on the market today house an ETA 7750 Valjoux movement, reworked to a greater or lesser degree and sold with differences in price that can be hard to justify... But the situation is beginning to change. The public, better informed on the subject than previously, is more than willing to pay a premium for a high-end chronograph, but on the condition that it is an exclusive movement—or at least somewhat original. The Swatch Group's announcement that it would stop selling ETA movements has also inspired competing brands to look for alternative solutions. For several years, we have been seeing an increase in the number of "in-house" chronographs featuring interesting innovations.

TECHNIQUE

HOW DOES IT WORK?

The chronograph functions using a complex system of levers, springs and wheels. The chronograph mechanism is "grafted" onto the movement's base. When the "start" pushbutton is pressed, the chronograph wheel joins the wheel for the seconds, and the hand starts ticking. When the chronograph is stopped, the chronograph wheel separates from that of the seconds, and the chronograph hand stops again. The reset function is effectuated by a system of a hammer on a spring and a "heart."

SPLIT-SECONDS CHRONOGRAPHS

Split-seconds chronographs are equipped with an additional seconds hand, which can be stopped independently to measure a "split" time or a reference time. They are recognizable by the additional pushbutton they bear. Activating the pushbutton is all that is needed for the split-seconds hand to catch up with the main chronograph hand, so that the two may continue running together.

COLUMN-WHEEL AND CAM MOVEMENTS

There are two kinds of chronographs with respect to the "control group" governing the start, stop and reset functions. The chronographs considered to be the most prestigious are equipped with a column-wheel, a complex organ that uses a system of slots and tabs to govern the movements of the levers. Most current mechanical chronographs are equipped with a cam system of simpler construction.

MODULAR AND INTEGRATED CONSTRUCTIONS

In modular constructions, the chronograph mechanism is totally independent of the base movement. It is mounted on an additional plaque affixed to the dial side of the movement. This solution allows the watchmaker to link a chronograph mechanism to an existing movement, without having to develop a new caliber. In integrated constructions, the chronograph components are placed directly on the movement, on the bridge side. Column-wheel chronograph movements are the result of integrated constructions.

FREQUENCY AND PRECISION

The precision of time measurement and display of a mechanical chronograph depend on the frequency of its regulating organ, i.e. the number of vibrations per hour (one oscillation equals two vibrations) of the balance-spring. The higher the frequency, the smaller units of time that can be measured.

Vibrations per hour	Frequency (in Hz)	Smallest measurable unit of time
18,000	2.5 Hz	1/5 of a second
21,600	3 Hz	1/6 of a second
28,800	4 Hz	1/8 of a second
36,000	5 Hz	1/10 of a second
360,000	50 Hz	1/100 of a second

FLYBACK FUNCTION

The flyback function allows the wearer to instantly start a new round of timing while the chronograph is already operating. For this, one need only activate the reset pushbutton, without stopping the hands first; all three chronograph hands will immediately return to zero to start another measurement.

JUMPING SECONDS

The term "jumping seconds" refers to a setup in which the second hand leaps around the dial in one second—usually in four or five smaller steps. This system is a way to measure and display times of one-fourth, one-fifth—even one-eighth or one-tenth of a second.

CHRONOGRAPH AND CHRONOMETER

The word "chronometer" is often used incorrectly to designate a chronograph, but they are two very different things. A chronometer is a watch whose movement has received an official certificate attesting to its extreme precision. This certificate is awarded by the COSC (Swiss Official Chronometer Testing Institute) after two weeks of very rigorous testing. A chronograph may be a certified chronometer, but it is by no means certain that any given chronometer will also be a chronograph.

A Reinvented Classicism

Chronographs have long been distinguished by their rather classic aesthetic, with three small symmetrically placed subdials. This traditional look has now been swept aside by many models that reinvent the ways in which we measure time. The chronograph universe has also been marked by the appearance of new materials that allow the watches to become lighter, more robust or more technically sophisticated, as well as shaking up aesthetic codes.

Chopard, *L.U.C Chrono One*

Chopard equipped its L.U.C Chrono One model with a certified chronometer in-house movement, which boasts a column wheel, vertical clutch, flyback function and 60-hour power reserve.

Omega, *Moonwatch Apollo 11 40th Anniversary Limited Edition*

The only watch to have been worn on the moon—hence its Moonwatch nickname—the famous Omega Speedmaster is presented in a version that stays true to the original, recognizable for its ultra-readable black dial and its tachometer.

Roger Dubuis
La Monégasque Chronograph

Equipped with a new movement produced entirely by the Roger Dubuis manufacture, La Monégasque Chronograph—launched in 2011—also stands out for its highly original case and the oversized counters on its dial.

Breitling, *Chronomat 01*

Breitling's flagship model, the Chronomat, received a new movement in 2009—an automatic chronograph movement entirely developed and produced in-house. Like all the brand's movements, it is a certified chronometer.

Piaget, *Polo FortyFive Chronograph*

Launched in 2009 to celebrate the 30th anniversary of the Polo line, Piaget's Polo FortyFive Chronograph—whose sporty look melds titanium, steel and rubber—houses a manufacture-made movement with an additional 24-hour time zone display and flyback function.

Montblanc, *Metamorphosis*

On the spectacular Metamorphosis from Montblanc, a bolt at 9 o'clock causes the hours/minutes/seconds/date dial to disappear as if by magic, making way for the chronograph's minute counter, as the central seconds hand becomes that of the chronograph function.

Zenith, *El Primero Striking 10th Chronograph*

Equipped with the famous El Primero automatic chronograph movement, Zenith's El Primero Striking 10th stands out for its jumping seconds hand that measures and displays times of one-tenth of a second.

Quinting, *Mysterious Chronograph*

To create the Mysterious Chronograph, which offers a magnificent take on transparency, Quinting developed a 237-component mechanical movement powered by four motors hidden within the circumference of the watch.

Rolex, *Cosmograph Daytona*

Created in 1963 for racecar drivers, Rolex's Cosmograph Daytona has become one of the most legendary chronograph models. It is equipped with a completely Rolex-made movement with an ultra-shock-resistant Parachron balance spring.

Tudor, *Grantour Chrono Flyback*

A tribute to automotive sport, the Grantour line from Tudor (Rolex's "little sister") welcomes a new Chrono Flyback model with a retro-chic look, whose flyback pushbutton at 2 o'clock is underlined in red.

Jaeger-LeCoultre, *AMVOX2 Chronograph Concept*

On its AMVOX2 Chronograph Concept watch, Jaeger-LeCoultre introduced a small revolution in terms of controls. The traditional pushbuttons were replaced by a system in which the case middle pivots around a horizontal axis from 9 to 3 o'clock. To start or stop the chronograph, one need only press gently on the upper half of the crystal; resetting is done by a push on the lower half.

Audemars Piguet
Millenary MC12
Tourbillon Chronograph

The Millenary MC12 Tourbillon Chronograph from Audemars Piguet combines high-tech materials (carbon mainplate, anodized aluminum bridges) with a daring automotive-inspired design.

Eberhard & Co., *Chrono 4 Géant*

Equipped with four horizontally aligned counters, the Chrono 4 Géant from Eberhard & Co. enjoyed a 2011 release in a titanium limited edition of just 1,887 pieces: an homage to the year in which the house was founded.

IWC, *Portofino Chronograph*

Released in 2011, the new Portofino Chronograph from IWC is notable for its sober, refined elegance, with 30-minute and 12-hour counters placed along a vertical axis, day-date display with a double aperture and old-fashioned pushbuttons.

Union Glashütte, *Averin Chronograph*

Within an imposing square case, the Averin Chronograph from Union Glashütte presents a highly original dial geometry, with date display via a three-pointed hand and chronograph counters arranged on a vertical axis.

Disc Displays

Varying the looks and methods of reading the time, watchmakers sometimes have a little fun by replacing the chronograph minutes hand (or even the hour or seconds counter hand) with an aperture and disc display—an excellent way to combine originality and readability.

Pierre DeRoche
GrandCliff TNT Penta
Equipped with an exclusive Dubois Dépraz movement, the GrandCliff TNT Penta uses five discs (hence its name) to display the large date and the small seconds as well as the 60-minute and 12-hour counters of the flyback chronograph.

TAG Heuer
Grand Carrera Chronograph Calibre 17 RS2
The Grand Carrera Chronograph Calibre 17 RS2 from TAG Heuer utilizes its Rotating System to present two disc-type indications: small seconds at 3 o'clock and chronograph minute counter at 9 o'clock.

Jaeger-LeCoultre
Master Compressor Extreme LAB 2
Designed to withstand even the most challenging conditions, the Jaeger-LeCoultre Master Compressor Extreme LAB 2 is distinguished by its patented digital counter and its very readable way of indicating the chronograph's jumping minutes.

Montblanc, *Nicolas Rieussec Open Date Silicium Escapement*

A tribute to the inventor of the first chronograph, the Nicolas Rieussec Open Date Silicium Escapement from Montblanc displays the chronograph minutes and seconds using two rotating discs equipped with fixed pointers.

Porsche Design, *P'6910 Indicator*

On the P'6910 Indicator chronograph from Porsche Design—with a resolutely automotive look—the hours and minutes of the chronograph function are displayed "digitally" with discs rotating past a double aperture at 3 o'clock.

Cartier, *Rotonde Central Chronograph*

On the Rotonde Central Chronograph from Cartier, the chronograph indications have the place of honor at the center of the dial, with a seconds hand and a counter that sweeps across an arc as a 30-minute totalizer.

The Fashion for Single Counters

Eschewing the system of two small separate counters for the minutes and the hours, a growing number of watchmakers are opting for a single counter that displays both indications. The goal is to enable simpler, quicker reading of longer time measurements, just as one might read the time on the central dial.

Jaeger-LeCoultre, *Duomètre à chronographe*

On the Duomètre à chronographe by Jaeger-LeCoultre, equipped with two independent mechanisms synchronized by the same regulating organ, the hour and minute counters are grouped together at 2:30, while a flying seconds hand at 6 o'clock allows measurements of one sixth of a second.

IWC

Portuguese Watch Club Chronograph

A new interpretation of an iconic IWC model, the Portuguese Watch Club Chronograph displays the chronograph's hours and minutes in a subdial at 12 o'clock. The chronograph also boasts a flyback function.

Omega

Speedmaster Moonwatch Co-Axial Chronograph

Worthy heir to the legendary "Moonwatch," the new Speedmaster Moonwatch Co-Axial Chronograph from Omega stands out for its single counter at 3 o'clock, as well as for the movement's exclusive co-axial escapement.

Patek Philippe,

Annual Calendar Chronograph Ref. 5960

The Annual Calendar Chronograph Ref. 5960 from Patek Philippe utilizes a vertical disc clutch system, which allows the watch to use the central hand for chronograph seconds and a single subdial for the minute and hour counters.

Pierre DeRoche, *SplitRock*

On its SplitRock, Pierre DeRoche emphasizes simplicity and ease of reading by proposing a chronograph with three concentric hour/minute/second hands, equipped with an exclusive Dubois Dépraz caliber.

Bulgari, *Endurer Chronosprint All Blacks*

A tribute to the renowned New Zealand rugby team, the Bulgari Endurer Chronosprint All Blacks boasts a striking, original design and a completely black dial featuring a large single-counter chronograph and Maori symbols.

Single-Pusher Chronographs

In terms of specialty constructions, we are seeing an increase in single-pusher, or monopusher, chronographs. These pieces feature a sophisticated arrangement: the sole pushbutton handles the start, stop and reset functions, in succession.

Corum,
Admiral's Cup Chronograph 44 Centro Mono-pusher
Launched in 2010 to celebrate the collection's 50th anniversary, the Admiral's Cup Chronograph 44 Centro Mono-pusher from Corum is distinguished by its highly readable system of a red-tipped central hand that acts as a minute counter for the chronograph.

Christophe Claret
DualTow NightEagle
The DualTow model from Christophe Claret, shown here in its NightEagle version, is especially notable for its planetary-gear system, which drives the hours, minutes and seconds, and limits the variations in amplitude of the balance spring, providing a much greater precision.

Blancpain
Villeret Single-Pusher Chronograph

Available in steel or red gold, the Villeret Single-Pusher Chronograph from Blancpain also displays a complete calendar—date indicated by a pointer, day, month and moonphase—upon its refined dial.

Jaquet Droz
Complication La Chaux-de-Fonds Chrono Monopusher

The Complication La Chaux-de-Fonds Chrono Monopusher from Jaquet Droz is notable for being the first timepiece of its kind equipped with an hour counter as well as an off-centered hour and minute indication.

Panerai
Luminor 1950 Chrono Monopulsante 8 Days GMT

Equipped with an in-house manual-winding caliber, the Luminor 1950 Chrono Monopulsante 8 Days GMT from Panerai comprises—as its multilingual name indicates—a single-pusher chronograph, a power reserve of eight days and a second time zone.

Montblanc
Grand Chronographe Régulateur

Montblanc confirms its rise through the ranks by unveiling the Grand Chronographe Régulateur, a single-pusher chronograph with an hour display at 12 o'clock and a large central minutes hand.

Split-Seconds Chronographs

Split-seconds chronographs possess an additional seconds hand that can be stopped to measure an intermediate or split time. This ultra-sophisticated clutch system is widely recognized as one of the most difficult complications to master—the equal of a tourbillon or a minute repeater—and the most prestigious brands are eager to offer it among their collections.

Panerai
Radiomir Regatta 1/8th Second
The split-seconds chronograph Radiomir Regatta 1/8th Second possesses two counters: one with a flying second that makes a complete one-second rotation in increments of one-eighth of a second, the other with a scale graduated in nautical knots that calculates the speed of a boat.

Patek Philippe, *Ladies First Split Second Chronograph Ref. 7059*
Patek Philippe paid tribute to women in 2011 with the launch of its Ladies First Split Second Chronograph Ref. 7059, a single-pusher split-seconds chronograph powered by an ultra-thin movement that also drives several men's models.

Bulgari, *Tourbillon Chrono Rattrapante*
The Tourbillon Chrono Rattrapante model from Bulgari associates two of the most sophisticated horological complications in a case with an instantly recognizable silhouette.

IWC,
Pilot's Watch Double Chronograph Edition Top Gun
On its Pilot's Watch Double Chronograph Edition Top Gun, dedicated to the famous pilot training program, IWC has lodged the split-seconds chronograph in a high-tech scratch-resistant ceramic case that contains an interior carriage in soft anti-magnetic iron.

A. Lange & Söhne
Tourbograph Pour le Mérite

On its Tourbograph Pour le Mérite, A. Lange & Söhne enhances a split-seconds chronograph with two of the most complex mechanisms ever designed to improve the movement's precision: a tourbillon and a fusee-chain transmission.

A. Lange & Söhne, *Double Split*

The German brand A. Lange & Söhne presents a new innovation with its Double Split, the first wristwatch chronograph with both a split-seconds mechanism and a split-minutes mechanism.

Hundredth-of-a-Second Timing

For many years, the display of time to one tenth of a second reigned as the supreme accomplishment for a mechanical chronograph. A few watchmakers have taken up the challenge, daring themselves to break the sound barrier and present chronographs able to measure and display one one-hundredth and even one one-thousandth of a second. It is an admirable technical advance, even though the inevitable reaction time and delay in activating the pushbutton limits the usefulness of such a function in the field.

TAG Heuer
Carrera Mikrograph 1/100th Second Chronograph

To display the hundredth of a second using a central hand, the Carrera Mikrograph 1/100th Second Chronograph from TAG Heuer is equipped with two escapement systems in the same movement, of which one balance-wheel (powering the chronograph) oscillates at a frequency of 360,000 vph.

TAG Heuer, *Mikrotimer Flying 1000*

The first mechanical chronograph capable of measuring and displaying thousandths of a second, the experimental Mikrotimer Flying 1000 from TAG Heuer is equipped, like the Carrera Mikrograph 1/100th Second Chronograph, with two escapement systems. The one for the chronograph beats at the phenomenal frequency of 3,600,000 vph, or 500Hz.

F.P. Journe, *Centigraphe Souveraine*

On the Centigraphe Souveraine from F.P. Journe, equipped with a single balance wheel beating at 21,600 vph, hundredths of a second are read off using a "flying" hand that makes a full rotation in one second. The associated tachometric scale can measure speeds of up to 360,000 km/h!

Regatta Chronographs

Models described as "regatta chronographs" possess a notable countdown system that marks off the last five or ten minutes before the race begins. With the growing popularity of sailing competitions such as the America's Cup, these models are getting new wind in their sails.

Rolex, *Oyster Perpetual Yacht-Master II*
Rolex has reaffirmed its place in the sailing world by launching the Oyster Perpetual Yacht-Master II, which boasts an ingenious bezel/crown/pushbutton system that follows the countdown using a large triangular hand.

Louis Vuitton
Tambour LV Cup Régate Noir
On the Tambour LV Cup Régate Noir from Louis Vuitton, the round apertures have been replaced by five trapezoidal cutouts that combine to form the silhouette of a spinnaker. This automatic chronograph is also equipped with a flyback function.

Glashütte Original, *PanoRetroGraph*
Though it is not a true regatta watch, the PanoRetroGraph from the German brand Glashütte Original stands out for its mechanical chronograph system that allows the wearer to count "up" as well as "down."

Time for Women

A sign of the times, and a notable trend at the beginning of the third millennium, a growing number of chronographs are designed exclusively for feminine wrists. These sporty, elegant watches are often adorned in soft colors and graced with finely finished dials featuring materials such as mother-of-pearl and diamonds, following the lead of more formal watches. These beauties meld technical excellence and aesthetic refinement.

Harry Winston
Premier Large Chronograph
Equipped with a sunray dial and a diamond setting on the bezel and lugs, the Premier Large Chronograph from Harry Winston unites a sophisticated technique with the characteristic refinement of Harry Winston jewelry.

Patek Philippe

Ladies First Chronograph Ref. 7071

Launched in 2009, the Ladies First Chronograph Ref. 7071 from Patek Philippe was the first watch to house the brand-new in-house chronograph caliber CH 29-535 PS, which is classically constructed; it has since appeared in a masculine model.

A. LANGE & SÖHNE

1815 CHRONOGRAPH – REF. 402.032

The 1815 Chronograph houses an A. Lange & Söhne manufactured manual-winding L951.5 movement complete with a hand-engraved balance cock. One of the highlights among the numerous technical features is the flyback function with precisely jumping minute counter, a device found only in very few chronographs. The two symmetrically positioned subsidiary dials for the seconds and 30-minute counter emphasize the balanced geometry and the classic style of the watch. The pink- or white-gold case measures 39.5mm and is fitted with antireflective sapphire crystal on the front and back. The dial is solid silver with blued steel hands. The hand-stitched crocodile strap is secured with a solid gold buckle.

A. LANGE & SÖHNE

DATOGRAPH UP & DOWN – REF. 405.035

The equilateral triangle design of the watch face, formed by two flyback chronograph counters at 4:00 and 7:00 and large date at 12:00, forms a harmonious aesthetic balance that contrasts with the black dial to offer optimal legibility. With its central chronograph seconds hand and precise jumping minute counter, the manually wound L951.6 manufacture caliber offers an unmistakable measure of an elapsed time interval. Framed by a 41mm platinum case, the Datograph Up & Down presents a 60-hour power reserve indicator at 6:00, whose red zone distinctly warns of a needed supply of fresh energy.

A. LANGE & SÖHNE
DOUBLE SPLIT – REF. 404.032

This model is powered by the manual-winding Lange L001.1 movement. The Double Split is a flyback chronograph with double rattrapante, controlled by classic column wheels. Included is a jumping chrono minute counter and rattrapante minute counter, flyback function with indication for hours, minutes, small seconds with stop seconds and power reserve indicator. The movement is encased in a 43mm rose-gold case with sapphire crystal on the front and caseback. The dial is two-tiered solid silver. The Double Split is also available in platinum.

AUDEMARS PIGUET

ROYAL OAK OFFSHORE CHRONOGRAPH – REF. 26400RO.OO.A002CA.01

The Royal Oak Offshore model involves far more than just a change of size; the entire aesthetic of the case has been reworked. The 44mm case middle is composed of two materials: ceramic and pink gold. The extreme reliability of the 3126/3840 movement provides excellent user-friendliness, particularly due to the instant jump and fast-adjusted date mechanism, along with a 60-hour power reserve and a stop seconds device when setting the time. The movement can be admired through the sapphire crystal caseback. Finally, the newly developed oscillating weight is crafted all of a piece from a block of 22K gold coated with an anthracite galvanic treatment.

AUDEMARS PIGUET

ROYAL OAK OFFSHORE SELFWINDING TOURBILLON CHRONOGRAPH

REF. 26550AU.OO.A002CA.01

A first glance at the Royal Oak Offshore Selfwinding Tourbillon exposes the perfect combination of a powerful design and mechanical finesse. The innovative 2897 caliber daringly brings together the mystical quality of the tourbillon and the functional precision of its high-end chronograph. Finally, while the case's blend of forged carbon, ceramic and rubber highlights the timepiece's robust quality, a peripherally mounted oscillating weight provides optimal visibility of the watch's intricate internal spectacle.

BVLGARI

ENDURER CHRONOSPRINT ALL BLACKS SPECIAL EDITION – REF. BRE56BSBVDCHS/AB

With its expressive dial decorated with a Maori tattoo pattern, this timepiece celebrates the values shared between Bulgari and the New Zealand Rugby legends. The mono-pusher activated chronosprint function of the automatic DR 1306 caliber operates within a dual-counter dial on the watch's lower half, as the patented large date display makes the upper half its home. The 56mm stainless steel case with black DLC treatment features a transparent caseback adorned with the 1905 All Blacks® logo, sealing this exceptional union of global excellence. Worn on a black rubber strap, this 28,800 vph timepiece takes the field with pride in the brilliance of its monochromatic symbolism.

BVLGARI

PAPILLON CHRONOGRAPH – REF. BRRP46C14GLCHP

Learning to read this elaborate multi-layered lacquered dial is half the pleasure of the Papillon Chronographe. Within the 46mm 18K pink-gold case, the automatic manufacture DR 2319 caliber is decorated with devoted intricacy. While the column-wheel chronograph itself offers a relatively traditional design for ideal legibility, the running time with which it is splendidly amalgamated is bursting with ingenuity. As the smooth jumping hour is read through a large white aperture, two retractable blue papillon hands, mounted on either side of the open central disc, cleverly execute the minutes indication on a half-circle graduated scale that fits delightfully within the sophisticated watch face.

CHRISTOPHE CLARET

DUALTOW NIGHTEAGLE – REF. MTR.CC20A.009

The DualTow, created to celebrate the 20th anniversary of the Claret manufacture, is a single-pusher planetary-gear chronograph with striking mechanism and tourbillon. The major innovation of this timepiece, issued in a limited series of just 68 unique and customizable watches, lies in its patented world premiere chronograph function. This remarkable chronograph operates 3 differential systems for the seconds, minutes and hours by means of 9 planetary gears all through a single pushbutton that simultaneously activates a gong for each change of function (start, stop and reset)! Its exceptional belt-type display indicating the hours and minutes bestows high-tech sophistication. The latest version, named the DualTow NightEagle, features a variety of inspirations including the ultra-secret world of stealth aircraft such as the American F-117 Night Hawk.

DIOR
CHIFFRE ROUGE A02

This new timepiece is a chronograph with a date marker and blue-toned dial matching its navy alligator strap. This timepiece, imagined by the Dior Homme Design Studio, is quintessentially masculine and is the perfect watchmaking re-transcription of the Dior Homme codes. The two universes relate the same man: manifestly modern, determined and impervious to the diktats of fashion. Its 38mm diameter revives the elegance of bygone timekeepers. This version comes in a limited edition of 200 and is like the Dior Homme fashion collections: subtle and chic.

GLASHÜTTE ORIGINAL

PANOMATICCOUNTER XL – REF. 96.01.02.02.04

The PanoMaticCounter XL presents its curiously fascinating counter complication in an elegant and effective manner. Red numerals appear on a black background in a double-digit window positioned at 9:00. The wearer activates the counter using three pushers positioned on the left side of the stainless steel case moving the count forward, backward, or resetting it to zero. Aligned along the vertical axis are the off-center hour and minute display in the lower half of the dial and, in the upper half, the large chronograph stop-seconds scale, raised above the black dial and flanked by the small seconds and 30-minute counters, whose zero points have been rotated 60° to guarantee optimum legibility. The PanoMaticCounter XL features the new Caliber 96-01, a classic column-wheel chronograph with flyback function, which is based on the award-winning Glashütte Original Caliber 95.

GLASHÜTTE ORIGINAL

SENATOR RATTRAPANTE – REF. 99.01.01.01.04

The Senator Rattrapante's domed, anti-reflective sapphire crystal reveals a look at its cleanly designed and structured dial, with all relevant details legible at a glance. The sweep hour and minute hands as well as the off-center stop seconds hand glide in shiny blue across the dial. Should the wearer activate the rattrapante function, the red split-seconds hand begins to chase after its blue counterpart. The dial also shows off the panorama date so characteristic of Glashütte Original at 4:00. Another remarkable characteristic of the Senator Rattrapante is its flyback function. The great advantage of this is that the wearer can take a differential time measurement, reading the result directly without needing to reset. This exclusive timepiece's manual-winding Caliber 99 ticks within a solid, completely polished 42mm rose-gold case.

GUY ELLIA

JUMBO CHRONO

The Jumbo Chrono, the first round men's watch created by Guy Ellia, is based on an interesting technological approach demonstrating that it is possible to combine aesthetic balance with masculine detail and a fine mechanical movement. The Jumbo Chrono boasts an exceptional 50mm size that is rarely seen in the world of luxury watches. The Jumbo Chrono's rhodium-plated rotor is unique and the impressive discovery dial reflects a strong graphic design: sweep-seconds chronograph in the center, hour and minute at 12:00, date at 2:00, 30-minute counter at 3:00, seconds at 6:00, and 12-hour counter at 9:00. This model is shown in black gold, but is also available in white or pink gold.

IWC

INGENIEUR DOUBLE CHRONOGRAPH TITANIUM – REF. IW376501

Weighing a mere 130g, the Ingenieur Double Chronograph Titanium presents an immediate reminder to the wrist of its extremely lightweight and practically indestructible material. The chronograph takes center stage on the dial. While the 12-hour counter at 6:00 and 30-minute subdial at 12:00 complement the small seconds at 9:00 and optimally legible day and date display at 3:00, to form the dynamic backdrop of the watch's face, the central split seconds mark a first in the Ingenieur family. The chronograph's split-seconds hand allows the wearer to record and measure as many intermediate lap times as he or she wishes, while a simple push of the button at 10:00 returns the chronograph's hands to their synchronized state.

IWC

IWC PILOT'S WATCH CHRONO-AUTOMATIC – REF. IW371701

Complementing the virtues of IWC's Pilot collection, the three-counter chronograph function of this timepiece takes this aviation wristwatch to a new level of precision timekeeping. Powered by the self-winding 79320 caliber with 44-hour power reserve, the IWC Pilot's Watch Chrono-Automatic features an optimally legible black dial, housed within a 42mm stainless steel case with soft-iron inner case for protection against magnetic fields.

IWC

PILOT'S WATCH DOUBLE CHRONOGRAPH EDITION TOP GUN – REF. IW379901

Every ounce of this timepiece evokes a fighter jet's balance of absolute precision and roaring power. With a 46mm case in black high-tech ceramic, and a crown, pushbuttons, and caseback in matte gray titanium, this watch's message extends beyond the perfection of its mechanism. Powered by the self-winding 79230 caliber chronograph movement, the Pilot's Watch Double Chronograph Edition Top Gun features a split-seconds hand, for intermediate timing. For ideal clarity on the dial, the small seconds hand and the counterpoises of the central chronograph hands are colored in bright red against the white on black theme of the watch. As constant reminders of this timepiece's identity, the Top Gun rank insignia is displayed on the caseback cover, and the date at 3:00 is designed to evoke an aero-navigational altimeter.

IWC

PORTOFINO CHRONOGRAPH – REF. IW391001

The case of the Portofino Chronograph evokes the steering wheels of the yachts anchored in Portofino's harbor. Its striking pushbuttons are reminiscent of the dynamic elegance of a 1960s Italian sports car: exciting yet understated. While the top figures of the 30-minute counter at 12:00 and the 12-hour counter at 6:00 stand out in red, the small seconds at 9:00 is decidedly low key and offers a graceful counterbalance to the day and date display on the opposite side of the dial. This energetic automatic-winding chronograph with cumulative stopwatch displays is driven by the 79320 caliber and offers a power reserve of 44 hours.

IWC

PORTUGUESE CHRONOGRAPH – REF. IW371482

The tradition behind the Portuguese family of watches stretches all the way back to the precision nautical instruments used by seafarers to discover the world. A traditional line like this needs a chronograph with a scale calibrated to an accuracy of a quarter of a second. The elegant design and moderate height of the case have made the Portuguese Chronograph one of the most sought-after Portuguese models of them all. Everything is integrated harmoniously on the clearly organized dial: the recessed totalizers, the embossed Arabic numerals and the perfectly proportioned feuille hour and minute hands. This year, two new versions join the chronograph fleet, both in cases with the warm appeal of red gold. The slate-colored dial with its shimmering sun-pattern finish and jet-black counters is simply superb. In the second new version, the blued hands for times recorded by the stopwatch provide a colorful contrast to the silver-plated dial.

IWC

PORTUGUESE YACHT CLUB CHRONOGRAPH – REF. IW390211

The name of the new Portuguese Yacht Club Chronograph harks back to the legendary Yacht Club Automatic of the 1960s and 70s, an ocean-going watch so exclusive that it became one of IWC's most successful watches ever. The Portuguese Yacht Club Chronograph has all the precision of a nautical instrument in its genes and boasts a wealth of advanced technical features. Powered by the rugged IWC-manufactured 89360 caliber, and water resistant to 6 bar, the chronograph is geared for competition use with a flyback function, an additional flange with quarter-second calibration for recording short periods of time and an analog display for longer stop times on a subdial. The Portuguese Yacht Club Chronograph is the only Portuguese model to feature crown protection along with luminescent hands and indexes. It is available in stainless steel with a black or silver-colored dial and in red gold with a slate-colored dial and black totalizers. It is supplied with a rubber strap, making it the perfect companion for water sports of all kinds.

JAEGER-LeCOULTRE
DUOMETRE A CHRONOGRAPHE – REF. 601.24.20

The Duomètre à Chronographe is a true masterpiece of micromechanics, supplied with two independent power reserves by its "Dual-Wing" caliber. One power reserve is devoted entirely to the chronograph functions: hours, minutes, seconds, a display of units per minute and a foudroyante seconds display with zero reset. A counter at 6:00 displays the jumping seconds, divided into six units and linked to the chronograph seconds hand. The attention to aesthetic detail extends to the decoration on the Jaeger-LeCoultre 380 caliber, as bridges that relate to conventional time measurement are finished differently from those involved with the chronograph functions.

JAEGER-LECOULTRE

MASTER CHRONOGRAPH – REF. 153.84.20

The Master Chronograph is powered by the automatic-winding Jaeger-LeCoultre 751 A/I caliber, which comprises 277 components and beats at 28,800 vph. Two barrels provide 65 hours of power reserve. The stainless steel case, with a diameter of 40mm, provides a perfect complement to the silver sunray-brushed dial, and provides water resistance to 50m. Small seconds tick away in a subdial at 6:00, leaving the center hand to measure chronograph seconds. The chronograph function is completed by a 30-minute counter at 3:00 and a 12-hour counter at 9:00. The piece is also available with an 18K pink-gold case.

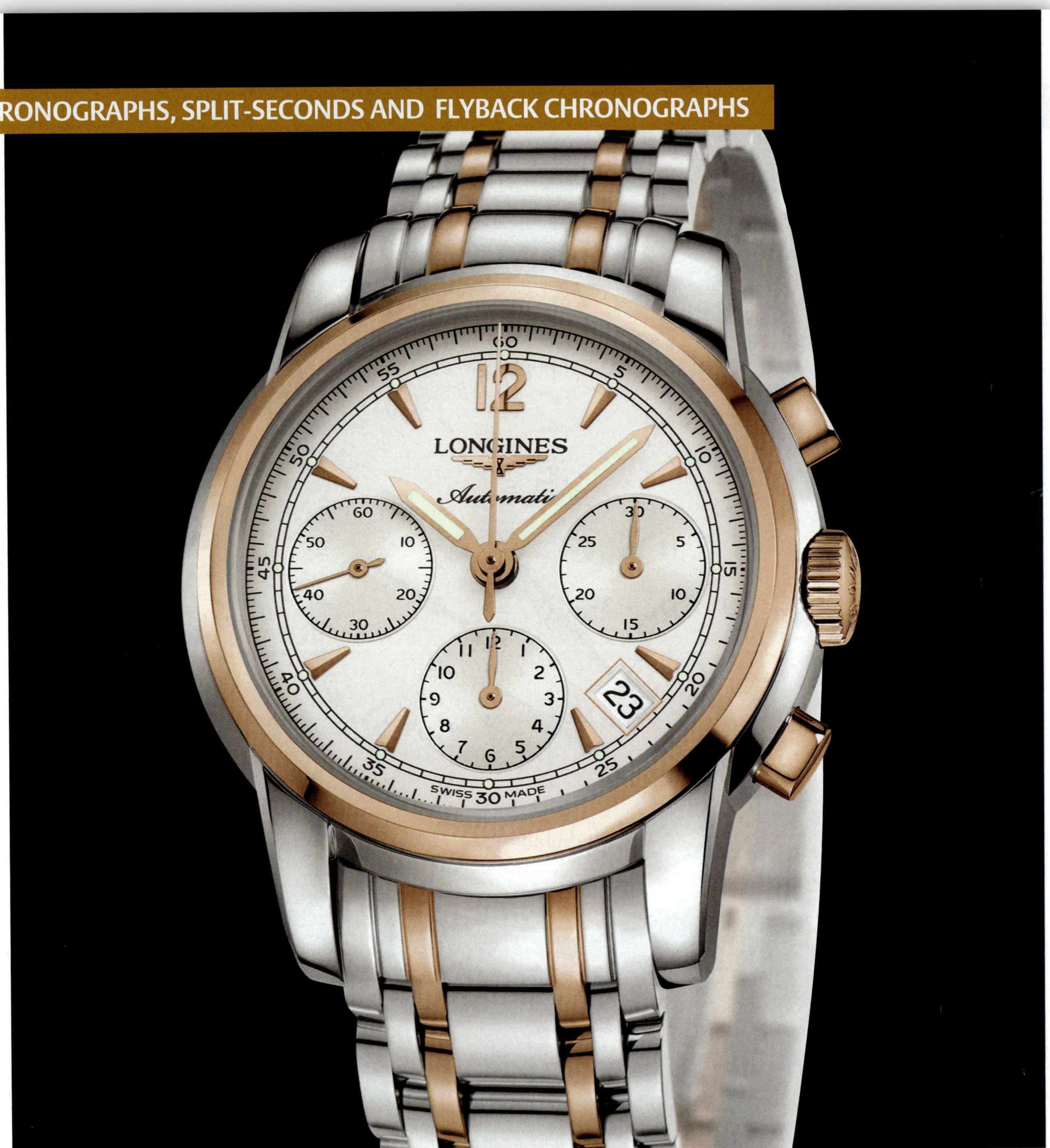

LONGINES

THE LONGINES SAINT-IMIER COLLECTION

The Longines Saint-Imier Collection has sprung from the origins of Longines's watchmaking tradition and constitutes a nice heritage combined with the latest technological advances. With a diameter of 41mm, this chronograph is fitted with the column-wheel movement L688, developed and produced exclusively for Longines. Its case in steel and rose gold displays a silvered dial and is mounted on a steel and rose-gold bracelet with a folding safety clasp.

PANERAI

LUMINOR 1950 8 DAYS CHRONO MONOPULSANTE GMT – REF. PAM00317

Innovative yet traditional, the Luminor 1950 8 Days Chrono Monopulsante GMT has an avant-garde movement fitted inside a 44mm black ceramic case that is unmistakable for its original and functional qualities. The Panerai P.2004 caliber, executed exclusively by Officine Panerai, consists of 329 components and features a second time zone with a 24-hour indicator, seconds reset and an eight-day power reserve, which is displayed via a linear indicator on the dial. Visible through the sapphire crystal caseback, the bridges are treated with a special hard black coating. This watch stands out among other sports chronographs due to reliability, water resistance to 10 bar (100m), and its single pushbutton controlling all functions.

PANERAI

LUMINOR 1950 8 DAYS RATTRAPANTE – REF. PAM00319

The Panerai P.2006/3 split-seconds chronograph caliber made of 350 components is executed entirely by Officine Panerai. This exceptional hand-wound movement is contained in a classically elegant 47mm case, which is water resistant to 10 bar (100m) and crafted of brushed 18K pink gold. With an eight-day power reserve and just two pushbuttons to control all of its functions (rather than the usual three), this rattrapante model is extremely rare in a limited edition of 300 pieces.

PANERAI

LUMINOR 1950 CHRONO MONOPULSANTE LEFT-HANDED 8 DAYS TITANIO, 44 MM

REF. PAM00345

In the history of Officine Panerai, wristwatches for the left-handed appeared for the first time in the early 1940s when the first examples were produced for the commandos of the Italian Navy. With the winding crown and bridge protecting the crown at 9:00, today these are very rare and highly sought after by collectors. Today, this historic peculiarity is the distinctive feature of the new Luminor 1950 Chrono Monopulsante Left-handed 8 Days Titanio. This piece is fitted with the hand-wound Panerai P.2004/9 caliber, a single-button chronograph caliber completely designed and produced within the Officine Panerai manufacture in Neuchâtel. The hand-wound caliber has three spring barrels, which give a power reserve of eight days, and the seconds reset function, which zeroes the seconds hand, thus enabling the watch to be perfectly synchronized with a reference time signal. From a constructional point of view, the caliber has a column wheel and vertical clutch. Water resistant to 10 bar (100m), this timepiece is a special edition of only 150 units.

PANERAI

LUMINOR 1950 FLYBACK, 44MM – REF. PAM00361

This high-performance sportsman's watch is fitted with a Panerai OP XIX caliber, COSC-certified movement. The flyback function on the subdial at 3:00 enables a timing to be interrupted, returned to zero and restarted—all with a single touch. The Luminor 1950 shaped case is brushed steel and comes with a black rubber strap. This timepiece has a power reserve of 42 hours and is water resistant to a pressure of 10 bar (100m).

PANERAI

LUMINOR 1950 RATTRAPANTE, 44MM – REF. PAM00362

This highly competitive sportman's rattrapante is fitted with the Panerai OP XVIII caliber, which is COSC-certified. The split-seconds function enables the total time and an unlimited number of intermediate times (relating to the action of a moving object) to be taken and to measure the successive arrival times of two competitors. The Luminor 1950 shaped case is polished steel and comes with a black rubber strap. This timepiece has a power reserve of 42 hours and is water resistant to a pressure of 10 bar (100m).

PANERAI

LUMINOR CHRONO DAYLIGHT, 44MM – REF. PAM00356

The Panerai Luminor Chrono Daylight is a high-performance sports watch fitted with the Panerai OP XII caliber, a COSC-certified movement with chronograph functions on three counters. Two chronograph pushbuttons on the three-part 44mm brushed steel case are integrated into the patented device protecting the crown, which ensures that the piece is water resistant to 10 bar (100m). The "Daylight" inscription at 12:00 brings back to the limelight a name reserved by Officine Panerai for Sylvester Stallone, who starred in the successful film of the same title.

PANERAI

RADIOMIR CHRONOGRAPH – REF. PAM00288

The Radiomir Chronograph, fitted with the COSC-certified Panerai OP XII calibre, is a classic model with its own sports character. It has two chronometer pushbuttons perfectly incorporated into the design of the 45mm polished steel case (at 2:00 and 4:00). These "pump-style" pushbuttons, coupled with the screw-down winding crown, ensure the watch's perfect water resistance to a pressure of 10 bar (100m).

PATEK PHILIPPE

LADIES FIRST SPLIT-SECONDS CHRONOGRAPH – REF. 7059R

Devoted to the feminine pursuit of mechanical excellence, this ultra-thin chronograph does not forget to capture a taste of elegant seduction. Meeting the rich combination of cream-colored opaline dial and rose-gold case, two sublime diamond settings adorn not only the front, but rear bezel as well. Operating brilliantly within this irresistible frame, the manually wound CHR 27-525 PS caliber provides a single-pusher split-seconds chronograph of exceptional precision, power transmission, and reduced friction and wear. Complemented by a 60-second counter, the column-wheel split-seconds chronograph's rose-gold hands add a touch of visual complexity to the alluring ambience. Boasting a power reserve of 48 hours and a sapphire crystal caseback, the Ladies First Split-Seconds Chronograph is worn on a matte pearly-beige alligator strap with square scales.

PATEK PHILIPPE

SPLIT-SECONDS CHRONOGRAPH – REF. 5950A

Launched in 2005, the caliber CHR 27-525 PS split-seconds chronograph movement has just embarked on a new career. Measuring just 5.25mm in thickness, it is the thinnest ever made, and it is still crafted one at a time. The innovative element is its armor of steel, which Patek Philippe has elevated to the status of a precious metal. The cushion-shaped case is water resistant to 30m and the sapphire crystal exhibition caseback features the same camber as the sapphire crystal covering the dial—an appropriately finished frame for the elaborate caliber with its hand-chamfered components. The orchestration of micromechanical art is gracefully complemented on the face of the watch with delicate foliage engraving that adorns the four corners of the dial.

PIAGET

LIMELIGHT EXCEPTIONAL PIECE – REF. G0A33144

This timepiece is an exceptional creation equipped with the 880P; a mechanical chronograph movement designed, developed and produced by the manufacture de Haute Horlogerie Piaget. In addition to indicating the hours, minutes, small seconds at 6:00, date at 12:00 and a second time zone, this proprietary movement features chronograph and flyback functions with 52-hour power reserve in activated chronograph mode. This haute jewelry model is adorned with 634 brilliant- and baguette-cut diamonds (approximately 10.9 carats). It is distinguished by Piaget's characteristic haute horology signature finishes, such as the circular-grained mainplate, beveled and hand-drawn bridges, blued screws, and circular Côtes de Genève.

PIAGET

LIMELIGHT EXCEPTIONAL PIECE – REF. G0A33145

The Limelight model is an exceptional creation equipped with the 880P, the first mechanical chronograph movement designed, developed and produced by the Manufacture de Haute Horlogerie Piaget. In addition to indicating the hours, minutes, small seconds at 6:00, date at 12:00 and a second time zone, this proprietary movement features chronograph and flyback functions with a 52-hour power reserve in activated chronograph mode. This haute jewelry model adorned with more than 1,148 brilliant- and baguette-cut diamonds (approximately 47.4 carats) called for almost 600 hours of development (including nearly 385 hours for the bracelet setting alone). It is distinguished by Piaget's characteristic haute horology signature finishes such as the circular-grained mainplate, beveled and hand-drawn bridges, blued screws, and circular Côtes de Genève.

PIAGET

PIAGET POLO CHRONOGRAPH GEMSET – REF. G0A35112

This watch brilliantly embodies the best of two worlds according to Piaget: haute horology and haute jewelry. Equipped with the self-winding Calibre 881P, developed and crafted by Piaget, it displays the hours, minutes, small seconds and dual time zone, as well as the flyback chronograph function. Refinement is taken to extremes with the gem-set oscillating weight. As beautiful on the outside as it is inside, its 18K white-gold case is enhanced by 700 diamonds, including 94 baguette-cut stones of 36 different sizes, all selected and calibrated by the Piaget Master Jewelers in order to ensure they adapt perfectly to the case's shape. Fitted with a mother-of-pearl dial, this model is also adorned with a gem-set caseback.

PIAGET

PIAGET POLO CHRONOGRAPH IN PINK GOLD – REF. G0A32039

The Piaget Polo Chronograph model houses the new Calibre 880P, the first mechanical chronograph movement entirely designed, developed and produced by the Manufacture de Haute Horlogerie Piaget. In addition to the chronograph and flyback functions, this proprietary movement drives the hours, minutes and small seconds at 6:00, as well as the date display at 12:00 and a second time zone indication. Within the select circle of manufacture-made chronograph movements, Calibre 880P stands out for its 24-hour dual time zone display positioned at 9:00, the place usually reserved for the standard chronograph hour counter. Featuring two barrels and a large balance with screws, this mechanical self-winding movement provides a 52-hour power reserve in activated chronograph mode. Equipped with a column-wheel mechanism and vertical coupling-clutch, the 5.6mm-thick Calibre 880P is endowed with all the attributes of an haute horology chronograph movement.

PIAGET

PIAGET POLO FORTYFIVE – REF. G0A34002

The Piaget Polo FortyFive model is made of titanium. It reinterprets the original aesthetic in a case that is watertight to 100m, mounted on a strap made of injection-molded rubber, and expanded to a diameter of 45mm. In addition to its chronograph and flyback functions, the in-house 880P caliber displays the hours and minutes, along with small seconds at 6:00, a second 24-hour time zone at 9:00 and the date at 12:00. This 5.6mm-thick self-winding mechanical movement has two barrels and a large screw balance, and offers a 50-hour power reserve when the chronograph mode is engaged. The subtle marriage of polished and satin-finished surfaces brings out this powerful timepiece's character even more strongly. The sapphire crystal caseback shows off the decoration on the movements: the plate is circular-grained, bridges are beveled and the circular Côtes de Genève pattern and blued screws are the brand's signature aesthetic; the PVD-treated dark gray winding rotor is engraved with the Piaget emblem.

PIAGET

PIAGET POLO FORTYFIVE – REF. G0A35001

In addition to the contrasts between light-colored metal and black rubber, polished steel and satin-brushed titanium, the Piaget Polo FortyFive is endowed with a technical touch thanks to multiple openings in the openworked dial, providing a view of the mechanism, which boasts a black PVD-treated circular-grained mainplate and the date disc. The numerals, hour markers and parts are entwined in a multidimensional ensemble in which every effort has been made to maintain excellent readability. The presence of bright red accents—on the hands, transfers and hour markers—stands out particularly well against the openworked dial with its black and metallic shades. Besides the chronograph and its flyback function, the Piaget 880P movement drives the hours, minutes, small seconds, date display and a 24-hour time zone indication. Thanks to its twin barrels, its power reserve lasts a full 50 hours with the chronograph in operation.

PIAGET

PIAGET POLO FORTYFIVE – REF. G0A36002

Forming an elegant visual interpretation of an aeronautical instrument, the counters at 3:00, 6:00, and 9:00 tastefully play off the black dial with 18K pink-gold luminescent hour markers. A similar choreography of contrast happens on the 45mm titanium case, where satin-brushed surfaces and pink-gold gadroons alternate to communicate this timepiece's elegant balance of power and visual refinement. Titled on their periphery, the flyback 30-minute chronograph counter at 3:00 and 24-hour second time zone at 9:00 express the range of character of this modern timepiece's complex owner. Driven by Piaget's 880P caliber, the Polo FortyFive Two-Tone chronograph reflects the sophisticated taste of the contemporary technical connoisseur of fine mechanical watchmaking.

PIAGET

PIAGET POLO FORTYFIVE – REF. G0A36017

Paying tribute to the average length of a polo match, the 45mm titanium case of this ultra-thin self-winding chronograph sets the edge of a canvas as profound as it is functional. Three deep blue counters provide a distinguished contrast to the black dial (with luminescent hour markers) that surrounds them. Along with the flyback chronograph at 3:00 and small seconds at 6:00, this elegant take on the sporty concept features a secondary 24-hour time zone at 9:00 and digital date at 12:00, and is powered by the in-house developed and produced 880P movement.

RICHARD MILLE

RM 039 E6B AVIATOR TOURBILLON CHRONOGRAPH

Now for the first time, Richard Mille presents a new tool for pilots with the introduction of the RM 039 E6B Aviator Tourbillon Chronograph. Unlike any other pilot watch on the market, the RM 039 offers the complement of functions from the well-known E6B slide rule calculator, including fuel consumption, time en route, ground speed, density altitude and much more, complemented with the full functionality of a specially designed flyback chronograph with subdial counters, a large date and time zone function. For the first time in watchmaking, the possibilities of the E6B can be used within the time recording utility of a chronograph. By uniting these functions, the applications for the E6B are greatly enriched and made even more useful for pilots.

RICHARD MILLE

RM 050 FM TOURBILLON SPLIT SECONDS COMPETITION CHRONOGRAPH

The newly designed manual-winding tourbillon movement RMCC1 with hours, minutes, chronograph, split seconds, power reserve, torque indicator and function indicator represents a new progression and development at Richard Mille Watches of the flagship RM008 Tourbillon Split Seconds model. The new RM 050 Chrono Competition Felipe Massa represents a novel movement that was researched to lower the movement weight by 20%, making the total movement weight a mere 9.5 grams. The baseplate and bridges are created from grade-5 titanium, an alloy composed of 90% titanium, 6% aluminum and 4% vanadium often used in the aeronautic, aerospace and automobile industries. Further development of the caliber with its skeletonized baseplate and bridges as well as innovative movement designs meant the creation of more than 450 new parts for the RMCC1 movement. The case is composed of polymer composite injected with carbon nanotubes.

RICHARD MILLE

RM 056 FM SAPPHIRE TOURBILLON SPLIT SECONDS COMPETITION CHRONOGRAPH

As a special creation to celebrate the release of the new RMCC1 caliber, the RM 056 has been created in a limited edition with a case created from a block of synthetic sapphire. This is the first time that such a complex case design has been realized in this material. Synthetic sapphire is very difficult to work with. The cutting tools to work with it must be specially designed and tipped with diamond; the wear and tear on the machines during its creation is extreme. The creation of just the case takes more than 1,300 hours of machining, fraction of a millimeter by fraction of a millimeter. The end result is something unique and hitherto unknown in the watchmaking industry, with a transparent case allowing a full view of the fabulous new RMCC1 movement design.

STÜHRLING PRESTIGE ACCOLADE – REF. 362

The Accolade is a member of Stührling Original's Prestige collection, a special line of timepieces made with the finest materials by the most talented and capable hands. Housed within a beautifully constructed 42mm case, the 25-jewel ETA Valjoux 7750 Swiss Made mechanical automatic chronograph movement provides this sophisticated timepiece with 30-minute and 12-hour chronograph totalizers, as well as small seconds, day, and date indications. The case's polished design extends to the dial, where individually hand-applied Roman numerals set the milestones of the central hands' revolutions.

STÜHRLING PRESTIGE MAVERICK – REF. 322A

Developed as part of Stührling Prestige's entirely Swiss Made lineup comes the Maverick with its rugged stainless steel construction. Powered by the automatic ETA Valjoux 7750 mechanical chronograph movement, this masculine demonstration of time-keeping power features the chronograph's minute counter and twelve-hour totalizer at 12:00 and 6:00, in addition to small seconds at 9:00, and day and date indications through white apertures at 3:00. This timepiece's wild and energetic personality is enhanced by its high-rising unidirectional ratcheting bezel, which features the same gear-edge design as the pushers and screw-down crown. The deeply set dial is decorated with a hydraulically embossed starburst pattern, accented with individually hand-applied markers. The Maverick is finished with a high-grade silicon rubber strap with tire tread design.

VACHERON CONSTANTIN

OVERSEAS CHRONOGRAPH – REF. 49150/000W-9501

Beating with a frequency of 21,600 vph, the Overseas Chronograph's automatic-winding 1137 caliber provides this timepiece with a precise set of functionalities. At 3:00 and 9:00, respectively, the chronograph's 30-minute and 12-hour counters join the small seconds at 6:00 and large date at 12:00, to complete the backdrop of the frontal view. While the stainless steel case and titanium bezel give the watch a powerful metallic allure, the adornment of the caseback with the two-masted Overseas ship medallion reminds the wearer of watchmaking's rich nautical heritage.

VACHERON CONSTANTIN

PATRIMONY TRADITIONNELLE CHRONOGRAPH – REF. 47192/000G-9504

This sober manual-winding chronograph makes a claim for the beauty of functional simplicity. Within an 18K white-gold case, the watch's dial lets the measuring of time intervals reign supreme. Two beautifully snailed counters—small seconds at 9:00 and 30-minute counter at 3:00—join the outer tachometer scale, and the hour, minute, and central chronograph hands, in an unostentatious telling of time. An exhibition caseback reveals splendid craftsmanship on the timepiece's heartbeat.

VACHERON CONSTANTIN

PATRIMONY TRADITIONNELLE CHRONOGRAPH – REF. 47192/000R-9352

The pink-gold version of the Patrimony Traditionnelle Chronograph uses the sheen of its material to bring out the indicative white dial, where time is kept, and measured, with sleek purity. Two counters, each with an intricate snailed pattern, represent running seconds at 9:00 and a 30-minute counter at 3:00. Joining the pink-gold dauphine hour and minute hands, a central chronograph stem completes this display of distinguished simplicity.

ZENITH

EL PRIMERO 36,000 VPH – REF. 03.2040.400/21.C496

On the black sunray dial, three counters, surrounded by nickel zones, establish the legendary architecture of Zenith's El Primero timekeepers. Anchored by a central seconds hand, the 30-minute and 12-hour totalizers, at 3:00 and 6:00, make up the high-precision chronograph of this stainless steel symbol of timekeeping accuracy. Powered by the 326-component El Primero 400 B self-winding caliber, this timepiece, with SuperLumiNova-coated rhodium-plated hands and markers, measures time to the rate of 10 beats per second, as its name suggests. Finished with a tachometric scale on the black flange, and sapphire crystal caseback, the El Primero 36,000 VPH is worn on a black alligator leather strap.

ZENITH

EL PRIMERO STRATOS FLYBACK STRIKING 10TH – REF. 03.2060.4057/69.C714

Along with its sophisticated flyback function, allowing a single button push to simultaneously stop, reset, and restart the measure of elapsed time, this 45.5mm stainless steel column-wheel chronograph puts the exceptional frequency of its 4057 B automatic-winding caliber on exclusive display. Exhibiting the smooth speed of its 36,000 beats per hour, this timepiece's central chronograph hand performs one full revolution of the dial in precisely 10 seconds. Completing the fascinating interpretation of the complication, Zenith's famous three-color counter theme integrates a 60-second totalizer at 3:00 and 60-minute totalizer at 6:00, beneath which the date occupies the spot of a luminescent hour marker, while the third subdial is devoted to displaying small seconds.

Multiple Time Zones and GMTs

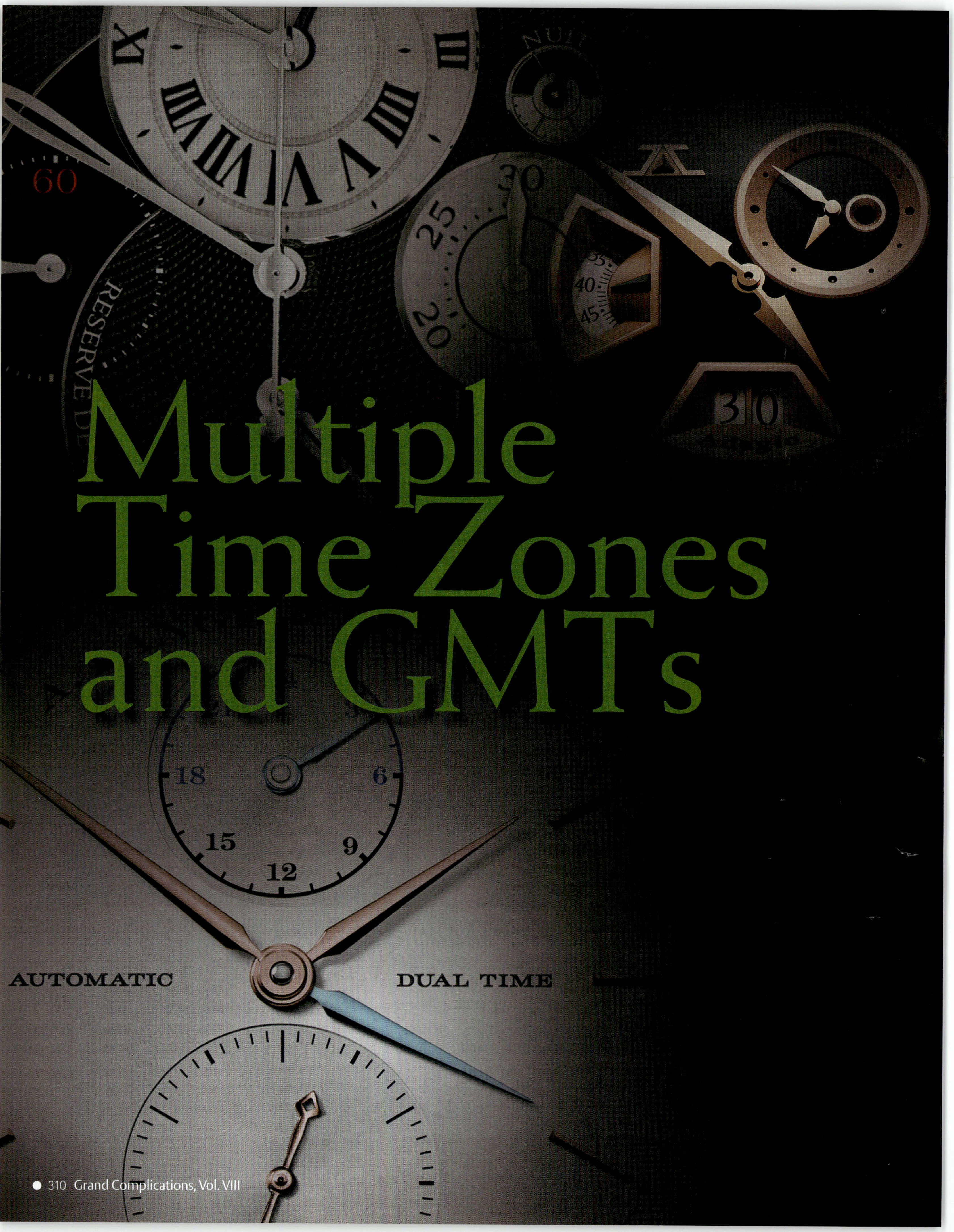

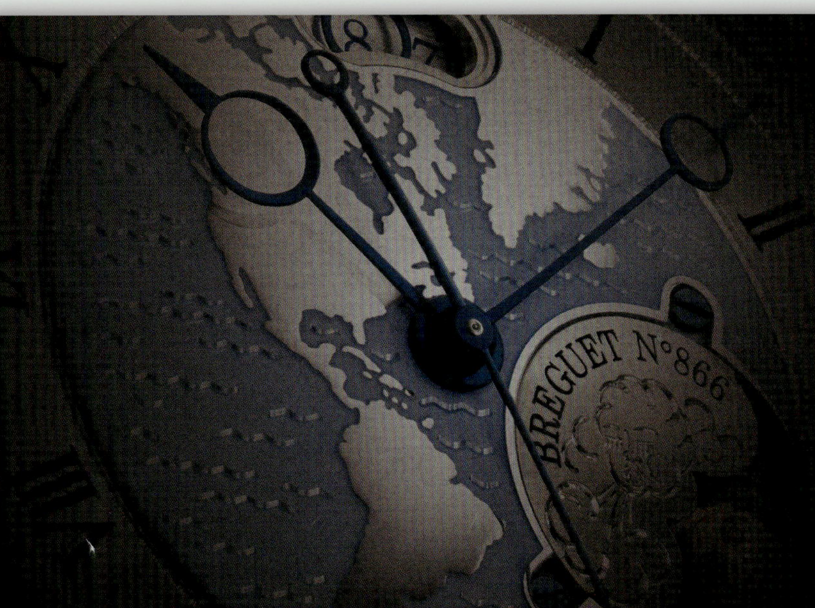

With the boom in air transport and the galloping pace of globalization, the simultaneous display of several time zones has emerged as one of the most useful functions a watch can offer. To satisfy the tastes of a clientele that travels, works and communicates across all borders, watchmakers offer a vast choice of models that present diverse technical solutions and modes of use—from double-handed systems to "world time" displays. The most sophisticated models stand out for their ease of use, legibility and the addition of functions that are most useful for travelers (24-hour displays, day/night indicators, linking the date to the local time, etc). We are also seeing a rise in watches that recognize half- or quarter-time zones—as well as timepieces that include multiple time zones and alarm mechanisms (see chapter on Alarms).

"Frédérique Constant sales grew by 25% in 2011!"

Peter Stas

President and CEO of Frédérique Constant

A leading player in the midrange arena, the Frédérique Constant brand is experiencing growing success, having sold 120,000 watches in 2011. The numbers are enough to reaffirm the initial strategic decision of its Dutch founding directors, Peter and Aletta Stas, to focus the manufacture's energy on classical luxury at an affordable price. This concept is so valuable that the couple chose to launch, or re-launch, two additional brands rather than diversify their collections. Alpina, with its sporty collections, and Ateliers deMonaco, operating in the very high end of the segment, define the present range of the Frédérique Constant group.

Peter Stas's rise to success is certainly a beautiful story. Born in Holland, the lover of Swiss watches founded his brand in 1988. By combining the given name of his wife's great-grandmother, Frédérique, with that of his own great-grandfather, Constant, he created a title that "sounded nicely Genevan," as co-founder and Chief Operating Officer Aletta Stas likes to point out. Living in Switzerland since 1997, the couple has never ceased to enhance their company. More than 20 years into the brand's history, the founding spouses maintain the status of majority shareholders with a 95% ownership of the firm they created—an independence that Aletta and Peter Stas are not nearly ready to relinquish.

You founded Frédérique Constant in 1988. What was your career path before that date?

I acquired a Masters degree in economics in Rotterdam, before moving to New York to work for a consulting firm for two years. I then joined Philips as Product Marketing Manager, first in Holland, then in the Far East, where I stayed for six years. In 1988, my wife and I founded the Frédérique Constant brand. But it was a part-time endeavor, as I hadn't left Philips at the time. We produced prototypes and received our first order in 1991, from Japan. It took us a year to honor it, between Holland, the Far East, and Switzerland.

Where did your desire to create a watchmaking brand come from?

I've always loved watches. I loved to window-shop during my family vacations in Switzerland. But above all, I love to create, to build something different. I wouldn't have wanted to work in finance, for example; I needed a product. I learned a lot with Philips in terms of investment, technology, and innovation.

TOURBILLON MANUFACTURE SILICIUM

When did you decide to relocate to Geneva?

We had a watch assembly partner in Geneva. But in 1997, we had a couple of issues with quality, which drove us to the decision to move there. We began in a small space, before expanding to 100m², then 1,000. Since 2006, finally, we've been operating in our 3,200m² facility.

How many watches did you sell in 2011?

Approximately 120,000 pieces, or a growth of 25% in relation to 2010.

Frédérique Constant was the first brand, in 1994, to incorporate an aperture in the dial, as a means of revealing a portion of the movement. How did this idea come to you?

At the time, right after the quartz crisis, nobody displayed the movement from the top, only from the caseback. We wanted to re-explain the mechanics to our clients. Today, nearly everybody has copied us...

You never patented this innovation?

No, and I regret that a little.

Revealing the inner workings of the movement is clearly close to your heart. In 2010, you launched the Junior collection, with a 38mm model for boys. In 2011, you released a feminine version. Why this line?

You're right, it has to do with helping young people discover the beauty of horology. In 2010, my son was 14 years old. Several people asked me: "Why not produce a wristwatch for him?" We gifted the first model to one of his friends. The response was such that we turned it into a complete collection.

VINTAGE RACING

How successful has it been?

In 2010, we sold 8,000 pieces for boys, and in 2011, 5,000 for girls.

At the summit of the pyramid, you also developed a tourbillon. Your positioning is however one of affordable luxury. Isn't such a timepiece, with grand feu enamel and a silicon escapement, sold for 50,000 Swiss francs, outside of that realm?

This tourbillon equips one of our two in-house made base movements, in this instance the FC-930 Heart Beat Manufacture caliber. Such a regulating organ fits nicely within our open-heart concept. But above all, we had the internal competencies to accomplish it. It's a way of showcasing our engineers' know-how.

How many have you sold?

Eighty the first year, and 60 per year since.

Is it your grandest complication?

Yes, the FC-930 caliber was launched in 2004 after three years in development. We have interpreted it since in several versions—manual-winding, automatic, moonphase with date, tourbillon and GMT. In 2009, we presented the Maxime Manufacture FC-700. It currently exists in three variations—automatic, hand-indicated date, and power reserve. More versions will be launched in the near future.

HEART BEAT MANUFACTURE GMT AUTOMATIC

Are all components manufactured in house?
No. The jewels and balance springs, for example, are outsourced.

Where do you acquire your balance springs?
From Nivarox at the moment, a Swatch Group company.

Are you very dependent on Swatch Group for the delivery of your movements?
At the moment, Swatch Group only delivers 2,000 movements per year to us. But we're in the process of developing, together with Sellita and Ronda, two movement makers that are independent of the group, a strategy designed to increase our own independence.

What portion of your production consists of mechanical watches?
We currently produce 50% mechanical watches, which adds up to 70% of our total sales.

You also founded, in 2009, the Ateliers deMonaco brand, installed in the prestigious principality. Why?
We had the opportunity to create some special movements: perpetual calendar, tourbillon, minute repeater. But such models, worth between 40,000 and 200,000 euros, did not fit the identity of the Frédérique Constant brand. We therefore sought the acquisition of an existing brand, to no avail. Creating one seemed like the only solution, but many already existed in Geneva. Monaco is one of the greatest centers of luxury in the world—a unique place. Following two years of negotiating with authorities, we were able to set up there. The production, made in Monaco, is presently very exclusive, with only 60 to 70 pieces per year.

Where do the movements come from?
A portion of the components is produced here in Geneva.

Your Geneva-based headquarters house a third brand, Alpina…
Alpina has existed since 1883; we bought it in 2002. This acquisition represents the same logic: we wanted to release sporty models, which didn't find their place within the DNA of the very classical Frédérique Constant collections. We deemed it quite important to preserve a coherent design identity across the entire brand.

MAXIME MANUFACTURE
AUTOMATIC SILICIUM

How many Alpina models did you sell in 2011?
Around 8,000, a growth of 250% for the year. But it must be said that Alpina was somewhat affected by the 2009 crisis. Our objective is to reach 25,000 annually.

You recently inaugurated a Frédérique Constant boutique in Taiyuan, the capital of the Chinese province of Shanxi. Where will the next one be opened?
We already have two in Hong Kong, one in Seoul, and one in Saudi Arabia. The next boutique will be in Europe.

In Switzerland, in Geneva?
Not yet, the rent is so expensive!

Is China an important market for you?
Very important. We have roughly 100 points of distribution in China, including seven in Taiyuan. It was self-evident for us to open our first mono-brand boutique in that city. It's a beautiful high-end 1,400ft^2 space.

What does China represent in terms of sales?
Around 15% of our revenue.

Is it your number one market?
No. That's Europe, with Germany, France, Switzerland and the Benelux (Belgium, Netherlands, Luxembourg) at the head of the pack. Together, these markets represent 38% of the sales. Next is Asia at 32%, then the United States and Russia. We have a very good overall balance.

Have you established a growth ceiling for yourselves?
No. We are presently distributed in 2,700 points of sale worldwide, and I think that we can increase that number to 3,000 or 3,500. That's a reasonable growth.

Multiple Time Zones and GMTs

Vacheron Constantin,
Patrimony Traditionnelle
World Time

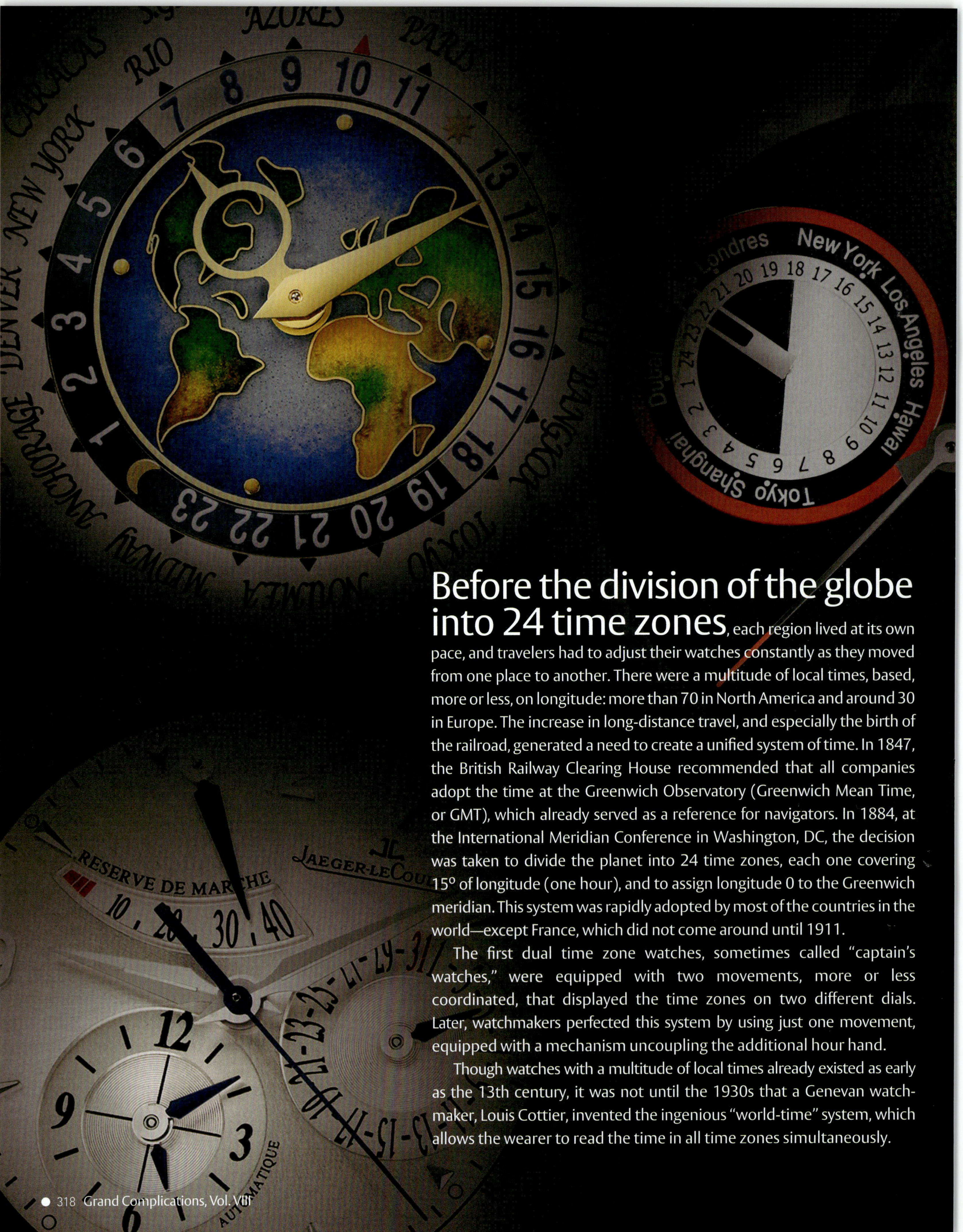

Before the division of the globe into 24 time zones

, each region lived at its own pace, and travelers had to adjust their watches constantly as they moved from one place to another. There were a multitude of local times, based, more or less, on longitude: more than 70 in North America and around 30 in Europe. The increase in long-distance travel, and especially the birth of the railroad, generated a need to create a unified system of time. In 1847, the British Railway Clearing House recommended that all companies adopt the time at the Greenwich Observatory (Greenwich Mean Time, or GMT), which already served as a reference for navigators. In 1884, at the International Meridian Conference in Washington, DC, the decision was taken to divide the planet into 24 time zones, each one covering 15° of longitude (one hour), and to assign longitude 0 to the Greenwich meridian. This system was rapidly adopted by most of the countries in the world—except France, which did not come around until 1911.

The first dual time zone watches, sometimes called "captain's watches," were equipped with two movements, more or less coordinated, that displayed the time zones on two different dials. Later, watchmakers perfected this system by using just one movement, equipped with a mechanism uncoupling the additional hour hand.

Though watches with a multitude of local times already existed as early as the 13th century, it was not until the 1930s that a Genevan watchmaker, Louis Cottier, invented the ingenious "world-time" system, which allows the wearer to read the time in all time zones simultaneously.

TECHNIQUE

HOW DOES IT WORK?

Multiple time zone watches offer such a variety of technical approaches and methods of use, that it is impossible to describe in detail all the particularities of their functioning.

Generally, they possess an additional display for the hour that is powered by the main system, but can be temporarily disengaged in order to set it to local time—without affecting the accuracy of the minutes and seconds. A pushbutton or the crown serves as a tool for setting the second time zone.

In order not to awaken a friend or a business partner who might be sound asleep, travelers often need to know if it is day or night in their home region. This is why some watches display home time on a 24-hour scale. Others use a 12-hour display, but supplement this with a day/night indication (a small aperture or subdial that changes from white to black according to the time of day), a small additional 24-hour scale or an AM/PM display.

Many watches boast another very useful function when one is traveling: automatic linkage of the date to local time.

WORLD TIME

To continuously display the time in all corners of the globe, world-time watches possess—in addition to the central hands—two mobile discs, one with 24 gradations, the other bearing the names of the reference cities. The 24-hour disc turns counterclockwise.

Double Pointer-Type Systems

The simplest system for simultaneously displaying two time zones is to add an hour hand with a distinctive design, either to the center of the dial, or—more rarely—on a small auxiliary dial. The most practical models equip their second time zone with a 24-hour scale or a day/night indicator. Luxury watchmakers also take great care to make the systems for setting the time as easy to use as possible.

Rolex, *Oyster Perpetual GMT-Master*

A classic example of the dual time zone watch, the Rolex Oyster Perpetual GMT-Master—launched in 1955—resolves the problem of daytime or nighttime with a supplementary time zone that covers all 24 hours.

Louis Moinet, *Geograph*

From Louis Moinet, the automatic chronograph Geograph possesses an additional central 24-hour hand with an indication of day (in gold) and night (in blue). The running seconds enjoy an original display via a small sun at 9 o'clock.

Breitling, *Chronomat GMT*

Equipped with a completely Breitling-made chronograph movement, the Chronomat GMT stands out for its ease of use. One needs only to turn the crown by one-hour notches to set the 12-hour hand to local time, while the red-tipped pointer maintains home time on a 24-hour scale.

Zenith, *Captain Dual Time*

The new Captain collection from Zenith presents a Dual Time model with a distinctively designed additional 24-hour hand, which the wearer can set with a pushbutton at 10 o'clock without disturbing the accuracy of the minute hand.

A. Lange & Söhne
Saxonia Dual Time

On the Saxonia Dual Time from A. Lange & Söhne, the golden central hour hand can be brought forward or back with two pushbuttons, while the blue hand maintains home time—complemented by a 24-hour subdial at 12 o'clock.

DeWitt, *Academia Double Fuseau GMT II Poetic*

The Academia Double Fuseau GMT II Poetic from DeWitt offers an original GMT complication. The wearer sets the second time zone, indicated by a red central hand, by pinpointing its position on the tiny globe at 12 o'clock.

IWC, *Portofino Dual Time*

IWC's Portofino collection, revisited in 2011, has welcomed the Dual Time model to its ranks. The crown allows the wearer to advance or bring back the central hand in units of one hour to display local time. The subdial at 12 o'clock maintains home time on a 24-hour scale.

Panerai
Luminor 1950 Tourbillon GMT

The Luminor 1950 Tourbillon GMT from Panerai is equipped with an AM/PM indicator linked to the supplementary hour hand—which allows the wearer to avoid waking anyone up with an ill-timed phone call.

Hysek, *Colosso*

On Hysek's Colosso, the second time zone display is effectuated in an innovative manner using a system of Archimedes screws and conical pinions that raise or lower two arrows pointing to the 24 hours. The three-dimensional rotating globe, which makes a complete revolution every 24 hours, can be linked to the time zone of one's choosing.

de Grisogono, *Fuso Quadrato*

On the Fuso Quadrato from de Grisogono, the hand for the additional time zone is hidden beneath a dial composed of 12 titanium shutters that opens on demand using a slide at 9 o'clock.

Louis Vuitton
Tambour Spin Time GMT

Equipped with a highly distinctive system for displaying the 24-hour scale—using small rotating cubes—the Tambour Spin Time GMT from Louis Vuitton also indicates a second time zone with a yellow central hour hand.

Piaget, *Polo FortyFive Chronograph*

The additional time zone on Piaget's Polo Forty-Five Chronograph, which uses a 24-hour scale, is displayed through an auxiliary aperture placed symmetrically opposite the chronograph's 30-minute counter.

Jaquet Droz, *Les Longitudes*

Les Longitudes from Jaquet Droz draws inspiration from regulator-style dials, with a Roman numeral subdial at 3 o'clock for the first, 12-hour time zone, a 24-hour display with Arabic numerals at 9 o'clock for the additional time zone, and a central minute hand.

F.P. Journe, *Octa UTC*

The Octa UTC from F.P. Journe uses as a reference not Greenwich Mean Time, but UTC (Coordinated Universal Time), which replaced it in 1972. The small mobile planet at 7 o'clock takes account of summer (DST) and winter times.

Superimposable Hands

On most travel watches, the additional time zone hand is always visible, even when the wearer has no use for it. Some watchmakers have improved upon this "defect" by devising hour hands that can be superposed, or placed one on top of the other, and function in a perfectly synchronized manner. This is a means of offering two watches in one.

Jaeger-LeCoultre, *Master Control*

The Master Hometime from Jaeger-LeCoultre proposes a system of dual crown-activated superimposable hour hands. The skeletonized hand on a 24-hour scale maintains home time. The date is linked to the local time.

Patek Philippe, *Aquanaut Travel Time Ref. 5164*

On the new Aquanaut Travel Time from Patek Philippe, the pushbuttons allow the wearer to bring the local hour hand forward or back in increments of one hour. When the dual time zone function is not in use, the two hour hands appear as one.

Montblanc, *Grand Chronographe Régulateur*

The Grand Chronographe Régulateur from Montblanc boasts two superimposable hour hands in a subdial at 12 o'clock, as well as a day/night indicator linked to home time.

Half- or Quarter-Time Zones

On the vast majority of travel watches, the second time zone is adjustable in increments of one hour. But there are countries in which the deviation from UTC adopts finer divisions of half an hour or even a quarter of an hour. This is notably the case with Iran (UTC + 3h30), India (UTC + 5h30) Nepal (UTC + 5h45) and the middle of Australia (UTC + 9h30). A few recent watches take these particularities into account.

Blancpain
Villeret Timezone 30 Minutes Demi-Savonnette

The Villeret Timezone 30 Minutes Demi-Savonnette from Blancpain allows the wearer to set the second time zone (which includes hours and minutes) in increments of half an hour using a crown equipped with an integrated pushbutton.

Parmigiani, *Tonda Hémisphères*

Parmigiani's Tonda Hémisphères, with a double hour/minute display and two day/night indicators, allows the wearer to set the second time zone to the nearest minute.

Franck Muller
Long Island Master Banker Lunar Moon

The Long Island Master Banker Luna Moon from Franck Muller presents, in addition to a central hour, two additional time zones adjustable to the minute, each one accompanied by a day/night indicator.

Double Hour/Minute Displays

Though the minutes generally remain the same from one time zone to the next, certain high-end watch brands prefer to include a complete display of the time in each region, with a second set of both hour and minute hands located in a small auxiliary dial. Another possibility involves indicating the two time zones on two separate dials, in watches featuring a resolutely distinctive design.

de Grisogono, *Meccanico dG*

Newly available in black titanium, de Grisogono's astonishing Meccanico dG combines an analog display for the first time zone and a digital display, driven by 23 cams, for the second time zone.

Christophe Claret, *Adagio*

The Adagio watch from Christophe Claret combines a minute repeater with cathedral chime and a patented large date with a second complete time zone with day/night indicator in a subdial at 2 o'clock.

Audemars Piguet
Jules Audemars Dual Time

The epitome of elegance and refinement, Audemars Piguet's automatic-winding Jules Audemars Dual Time displays its second time zone on a subdial at 6 o'clock, overlapping with a day/night indicator.

Epos, *3400 GMT Limited Edition*

Equipped with two mechanical movements, the Epos 3400 GMT Limited Edition displays two complete time zones on two separate dials, with day/night indication and independent date for the second time zone.

Piaget, *Altiplano Double Jeu*

Piaget's Altiplano Double Jeu possesses two superimposed cases, each containing an ultra-flat mechanical movement. The dial of the lower case displays a second time zone on a 24-hour scale.

Jaeger-LeCoultre, *Reverso Grande GMT*

The Reverso Grande GMT from Jaeger-LeCoultre makes the most of its famous reversible dial by proposing two time zones on two dials that lie back to back. The dial on the reverse side includes an indicator for the number of hours' time difference between local time and Greenwich Mean Time or another reference point.

Icelink, *Ambassador*

The brand Icelink boldly opts for an extra-extra-large size in its Ambassador line—the better to fit six quartz movements that display the time in six cities around the world.

Jacob & Co., *Grand 4*

Equipped with a quartz movement, the Grand 4 from the iconoclastic Jacob & Co. displays no fewer than five time zones—with hours and minutes—on its pentagonal case.

Systems with Discs or Rotating Bezels

Watches with multiple time zones might operate using systems based on discs or rotating bezels—either in lieu of a pointer-type system or in conjunction with it. Watchmakers generally take this opportunity to introduce complementary indications, such as the names or abbreviations for certain cities, representing precise time zones.

Cartier
Calibre de Cartier Multiple Time Zone
On the new Calibre de Cartier Multiple Time Zone, the user can select the local time using a disc that is visible on the case side—that takes summer and winter times into account. An aperture at 6 o'clock indicates the number of hours between home time and local time.

Jaquet Droz, *Les Douze Villes*
The Les Douze Villes watch from Jaquet Droz unites a disc bearing the names of twelve cities with a jumping hour display. A little pressure on the pushbutton displays the name of the desired city and its corresponding time, with minutes indicated by the large central hand.

JeanRichard, *2Timezones Zirconium*
On the 2Timezones Zirconium by JeanRichard, the first time zone is displayed traditionally, in the center, while the second appears in a window at 12 o'clock, accompanied by an AM/PM indication. An aperture at 6 o'clock reveals the 24 cities representing the world's time zones.

Breguet, *Classique 5717 Hora Mundi*

The Classique 5717 Hora Mundi from Breguet displays two preselected time zones, passing from one to the other with a simple press on a pushbutton. The system is completed by a day/night indicator and a date that is linked to the displayed time.

Richard Mille
RM 022 Aérodyne Dual Time

Built from highly futuristic materials, Richard Mille's manual-winding RM 022 Aérodyne Dual Time tourbillon displays an additional time zone in an aperture at 3 o'clock using a disc than can be set via a pushbutton at 9 o'clock.

Vogard, *Datezoner*

The new Datezoner from Vogard stands out for its patented system that allows the wearer to change the time zone and the date simultaneously, via the bezel. One needs only to pull the security lever and rotate the bezel to select the desired city.

Concord, *C1 Worldtimer*

The dial of the Concord C1 Worldtimer reveals two discs, one with cities and one with times. Pressing on the pushbutton allows the wearer to select the desired city, and the corresponding time is instantly displayed opposite.

A. Lange & Söhne
Lange 1 Time Zone Luminous

A. Lange & Söhne's Lange 1 Time Zone Luminous possesses two auxiliary hour/minute dials with day/night indicators. The wearer adjusts the second time zone with a pushbutton that turns the rotating city ring.

Glashütte Original, *Senator Navigator WorldView*

The Senator Navigator WorldView from Glashütte Original is equipped with a rotating bezel with names of cities, allowing the user to choose his time zone. It also sports the panoramic large date typical of the brand.

World Times

Queen of travel watches, the world-time complication allows the wearer to see what time it is in all 24 time zones. To this end, they are usually equipped with a mobile ring that bears the names of 24 reference cities. A few watchmakers have chosen to reinterpret this classic model by varying the configuration of the dials, taking partial time zones into account for specific time slots, such as the opening of the stock markets. The difference also finds scope for expression in the adjusting systems, whose practicality varies with the model.

Patek Philippe, *World Time Ref. 5131*

Heir to a long tradition, the World Time from Patek Philippe is distinguished by its dial in cloisonné enamel. To change the main time zone, the wearer uses the sole pushbutton, at 10 o'clock—the mechanism then simultaneously adjusts the city disc, the 24-hour disc and the hour hand.

Audemars Piguet
Jules Audemars Metropolis

The Jules Audemars Metropolis by Audemars Piguet combines a world-time mechanism with a perpetual calendar. The two rotating discs of the world-time display occupy a subdial at 6 o'clock.

Girard-Perregaux
ww.tc Financial

Dedicated to financial whizzes and nervous stock dabblers, the ww.tc Financial from Girard-Perregaux displays—in addition to the 24 time zones—the opening and closing times of the four main stock markets: Wall Street, London, Tokyo and Hong Kong.

Jaeger-LeCoultre
Master World Geographic

On its Master World Geographic, Jaeger-LeCoultre combines the indication of a second time zone with a world-time display. The crown, placed at 2 o'clock, allows the selection of a "favorite" time zone, on a subdial at 7 o'clock.

Vacheron Constantin
Patrimony Traditionnelle World Time

The Patrimony Traditionnelle World Time by Vacheron Constantin simultaneously displays no fewer than 37 time zones—including those that differ from their neighbors by a half-hour or a quarter-hour. This exclusive piece is patented.

Girard-Perregaux, *ww.tc Lady 24 Hour Shopping*

Designed for women's wrists, the ww.tc Lady 24 Hour Shopping from Girard-Perregaux does away with cities, replacing them with the most chic streets, neighborhoods and regions on the planet, such as Dubai, Ginza or Rodeo Drive.

Dior, *Chiffre Rouge T01*

Equipped with an exclusive caliber from Orny and Girardin, the Chiffre Rouge T01 from Dior simultaneously displays the local time and the time in eight other time zones, using a small satellite dial that makes a trip around the dial in 12 hours and completes a revolution on its own axis in 24 hours.

Andersen Genève, *Rodinia*

Named after Earth's long-disappeared supercontinent Rodinia, Andersen Genève's new model depicts the land mass in the center of its dial, and links the 24 continuously visible time zones to 30 of the most important cities of our time.

Antoine Preziuso, *Transworld*

Transworld, from Antoine Preziuso, offers a very attractive reinterpretation of world time, with a mobile world map in the center of the dial, depicting the Earth as seen from the South Pole and making a complete rotation over 24 hours. The display is as original as it is poetic.

Jean-Mairet & Gillman, *Sport*

In designing the Sport model, Jean-Mairet & Gillman placed the world-time display on a subdial at 9 o'clock, completed by a date window at 3 o'clock—all controlled by a multifunction crown.

A. LANGE & SÖHNE

LANGE 1 TIME ZONE LUMINOUS – REF. 116.039

Operating on the solid silver dial of the 18K white-gold Lange 1 Time Zone, the watch's luminous rhodiumed-gold hands and appliqués guide their owner even in the darkness of night. Conveniently adjusted via a pushbutton, the peripherally rotating cities ring offers a cosmopolitan and clear view of the applicable time zone's chosen reference location. Furthermore, this manual-winding timepiece is armed with a 72-hour power reserve, and boasts an ingenious synchronization mechanism that permits the seamless swapping of the indicated time between the two subdials, both of which possess an independent day/night indicator.

A. LANGE & SÖHNE

SAXONIA DUAL TIME – REF. 385.026

Powered by a completely redesigned self-winding caliber L086.2 with a 72-hour power reserve, the Saxonia Dual Time clearly indicates two time zones on the dial. The solid gold hour hand that indicates local time can be moved forward or backward in one-hour increments by two pushbuttons located at 8:00 and 10:00. A supplementary hour hand in blued steel permanently keeps time at the place of origin. The pink- or white-gold 40mm case is fitted with an antireflective sapphire crystal on the front and back. The timepiece is presented on a hand-stitched crocodile strap with a solid gold buckle.

AUDEMARS PIGUET

JULES AUDEMARS DUAL TIME – REF. 26380BC.OO.D002CR.01

The Jules Audemars Dual Time watch in 18K white gold opts for an extremely slim bezel, which ensures maximum opening on the meticulously executed silver-toned dial with a delicately satin-brushed finish. The date and dual time zone displays are surrounded by a decorative fillet highlighting their snailed inner decoration. The dial ensures pleasing readability, with the date display in a subdial at 2:00, the power reserve on the arc of a circle in the left-hand section, and the second time zone at 6:00. The day/night indication at 7:00 provides a simultaneous display of the time in two different time zones.

AUDEMARS PIGUET

ROYAL OAK "CONCEPT GMT" TOURBILLON – REF. 26560IO.OO.D002CA.01

Clad in state-of-the-art grade-5 titanium, this timepiece leans on impressive innovation to adorn the wrist with elegant simplicity. Driven by the remarkably finished manual-winding 2913 caliber, the watch features an original function indicator at 6:00 ("H" for hours and minutes, "R" for winding, and "N" for neutral), controlled by a three-position crown. Opposing the tourbillon at 9:00, the ingenious secondary time zone at 3:00 is comprised of two overlapping discs. While the numbered disc, which indicates 1 through 12, makes two revolutions per day, the disc beneath it, visible via a transparency effect, indicates, as a white or black backdrop, the occurrence of day or night.

BREGUET

CLASSIQUE HORA MUNDI – REF. 5717BR

The Classique Hora Mundi's 77F0 self-winding movement possesses a world-first synchronized instant-jump module that allows the watch to travel with the same ease as the man who wears it. With a single push of the crown, this timepiece instantly morphs all of its visible time coordinates from one pre-selected city to another. Once the wearer has selected his "destination" from the cities aperture at 6:00, the Breguet hour and minute hands, solid gold day/night indicator, and ingenious dragging date disc, transform immediately and with vivid synchronization, upon the effortless request of the watch's owner.

BREGUET

TYPE XXII – REF. 3880ST

This piece features hours, minutes and small seconds on its black oxidized dial, as well as date and second time zone display at 6:00, and a 24-hour indicator at 3:00. As the small seconds display is on a 30-second basis, a window at 12:00 lets the wearer know whether the piece is on the first or second half of the minute. The watch also features a highly precise chronograph function with a central red chronograph seconds hand that sweeps across the dial in just 30 seconds. The 44mm stainless steel case is water resistant to 100m.

de GRISOGONO

FUSO QUADRATO N°2 OPEN

de GRISOGONO invents with the Fuso Quadrato a new way to display the dual time zone indication. Refreshing the diaphragm system that the House first used on its famous Occhio Ripetizione Minuti, the Fuso Quadrato provides a fun but useful way to use this mechanism: triggered by a lock on the case side, the titanium diaphragm, made of 12 components, opens or closes to reveal or hide the dual time zone indication. The watch proudly expresses its character through a 47x47mm case, with an open sapphire caseback, and is powered by a flawless automatic movement offering 42 hours of power reserve.

de GRISOGONO

FUSO QUADRATO N°2 CLOSED

The Fuso Quadrato gives de GRISOGONO another showcase for its innovative diaphragm design, this time in the service of a dual time zone complication. Activated by a lock on the side of the case, the diaphragm, which consists of 12 "shutters" in titanium, opens or closes to show or hide the dual time zone indication. The movement provides 42 hours of power reserve and is housed within a 47x47mm case that boasts a sapphire crystal caseback.

de GRISOGONO

MECCANICO TITANIUM

de GRISOGONO ushers in a new era with its creation of the very first mechanical digital display. A masterpiece with a movement comprising 651 elements, the Meccanico dG features two time zones: an analog display of hours and minutes in the upper part and a mechanical digital display of the second time zone in the lower part—a de GRISOGONO patent. Fawaz Gruosi has achieved what others do not dare dream: propelling haute horology into a new dimension. The exclusive manual-winding dG 042, de GRISOGONO caliber with a 35-hour power reserve, is housed in a curved rectangular case of titanium and rubber. Water resistant to 30m, the case is fitted with a crown cover and correctors made of vulcanized rubber, a transparent black dial with green dauphine hands, and mounted on a black natural rubber strap with titanium. Limited edition of 177 pieces.

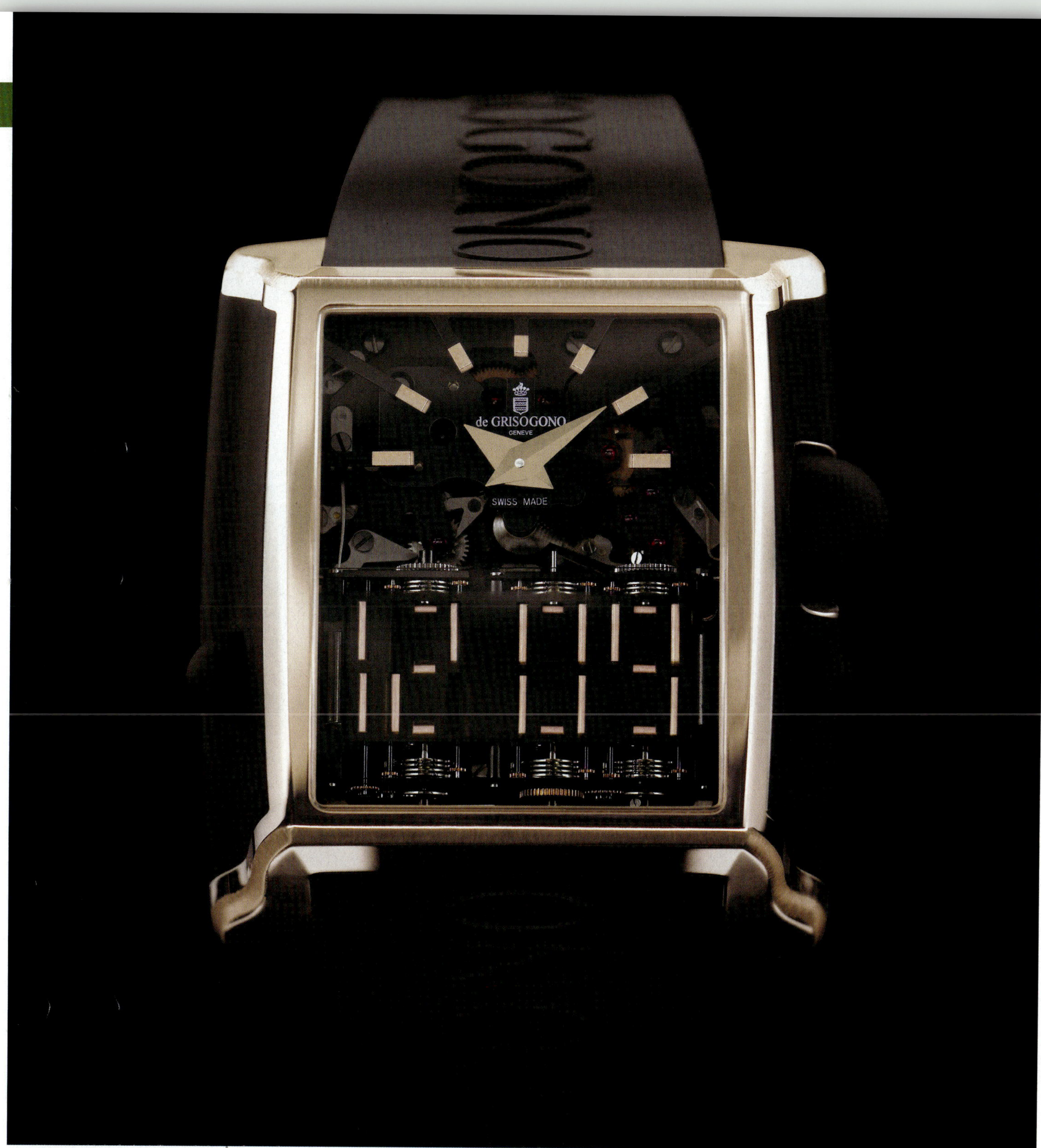

de GRISOGONO

MECCANICO ROSE GOLD

de GRISOGONO has created a world's first with the Meccanico dG's mechanical digital display. Powered by a movement comprising 651 elements, the Meccanico dG features two time zones: an analog display of hours and minutes in the upper part and a mechanical digital display of the second time zone in the lower part. The workings of this breakthrough have been patented by de GRISOGONO. A curved rectangular case of red gold and rubber houses the exclusive manual-winding dG 042, a de GRISOGONO caliber with a 35-hour power reserve. Water resistant to 30m, the case is fitted with a crown cover and correctors made of vulcanized rubber, a transparent black dial with dauphine hands, and mounted on a black natural rubber strap with a red-gold buckle. Limited edition of 177 pieces.

de GRISOGONO

DOPPIO TRE N01

The DOPPIO TRE N01 is a unique and exceptional timepiece as it features an automatic movement providing a three time zone indication on a sharp reversible case: two dials on one side, and the third time zone displayed on the other side of the case. Moreover, the back's indication is as original as it is elegant since time is indicated via two hands crossing the oscillating weight. In this version the DOPPIO TRE N01 is proposed with a steel case and a black alligator bracelet.

DIOR

DIOR CHRISTAL "8 FUSEAUX HORAIRES"

Limited edition of eight timepieces, Dior Christal "8 Fuseaux Horaires" is a tribute to Monsieur Dior and his passion for art as well as a reminder of the couturier's lucky number. This new timepiece is equipped with an exclusive automatic-winding Dior Christal "8 Fuseaux Horaires" calibre, which simultaneously displays the local time and time in eight cities worldwide, as well as the day/night indication, on a mobile satellite. This exclusive complication was developed by Les Ateliers Horlogers Dior in collaboration with watch movement designers Orny & Girardin. The playful dial was designed as a work of art in typical Art Deco materials (mother-of-pearl and gold). Mounted on a stainless steel and sapphire crystal bracelet, the Dior Christal "8 Fuseaux Horaires" is sewn with gold leaf down to the lining, revealing an haute couture oscillating weight.

FREDERIQUE CONSTANT

HEART BEAT MANUFACTURE GMT AUTOMATIC – REF. FC-938CDG4H6

The 42mm polished stainless steel case of this timepiece gently sets the tone for a silver dial of delicate intricacy. The Heart Beat aperture at 6:00 breaks the tranquility of the Clous de Paris guilloché, revealing the inner workings of the FC-938 caliber with 42-hour power reserve, 28,800 vph, KIF antishock system, Glucydur balance, and bridges decorated with Côtes de Genève and perlage. Opposing the porthole, a 12:00 subdial expresses a second time zone with day/night indicator and Arabic numerals, countering the black applied Roman numerals of the outer chapter ring. In addition to the dial-side exhibition, this wristwatch boasts a transparent caseback secured with six screws.

GUY ELLIA
JUMBO HEURE UNIVERSELLE

One of the latest creations by designer Guy Ellia is the Jumbo Heure Universelle with a movement created by Frédéric Piguet. Caliber PGE 1150 features a 72-hour power reserve, a blue sapphire disc, and Côtes de Genève-finished bridges with rhodium plating. The day/night indicator, the grand date and 24 time-zone indications define its singular functions. The Jumbo Heure Universelle bears an exceptional 50mm size that is rarely seen in the world of luxury watches. Mounted on an alligator strap with a folding buckle, this model is presented in black gold and is also available in white or pink gold.

JACOB & CO.

GLOBAL 1

Bringing to life a rarely utilized pentagonal geometry, the Global features local time with the same dimensions as the other four time zones, making a powerful statement regarding the worldwide citizenship of its wearer. Individually powered by high-precision Swiss ETA quartz movements that provide hour and minute control for each time zone, the five dedicated crowns form a synergic emblem of global modernity. While 5 powerful variations each embrace an array of materials, designs and decorative techniques, the Global adorns the four additional dials of every model with the names of cultural and economic powerhouses Tokyo, New York, Paris and Los Angeles.

JAEGER-LECOULTRE

MASTER COMPRESSOR EXTREME LAB 2 – REF. 203.25.70

Presented in a 46.8mm red-gold case, this watch's openworked dial takes the multi-function principle to the next level. Along with the conventional display of running time, the Master Compressor Extreme Lab 2 provides a discreet date aperture and second time zone with 24-hour counter. Taking full advantage of the large exhibition dial, a column-wheel chronograph, accurate to the eighth of a second, features a two-disc jumping minute counter at 12:00. On the top half of the bezel, an ingenious semicircular radial indication displays the status of the automatic 780 caliber's 60-hour power reserve. With luminescent indexes and a wealth of timekeeping measurements, this highly sophisticated instrument presents an endless supply of astounding features within a design that does not take its "Extreme" name lightly.

PANERAI

LUMINOR 1950 3 DAYS GMT AUTOMATIC – REF. PAM00329

The Panerai P.9001 caliber comes equipped with a GMT function with a 12-hour indicator, a seconds reset device (historically designed for watch synchronization) and a power reserve indicator. This 227-component movement animates the Luminor 1950 3 Days GMT Automatic. The 44mm stainless steel case is water resistant to 30 bar (300m) and its sapphire crystal caseback reveals the power reserve, which can be read from a rotating disc of the movement.

PANERAI

LUMINOR 1950 8 DAYS GMT – REF. PAM00233

In the history of Officine Panerai, 2002 was a fundamental year. Not only did it inaugurate the Manifattura Officine Panerai in Neuchatel, but it marks the year the company began development of its first in-house caliber, which celebrates the milestone with its name, the Panerai P.2002. Already in use by Panerai in the 1940s, a hand-wound eight-day power reserve has been achieved by a system of three spring barrels and linear power reserve indication, while the seconds hand is automatically returned to zero by the seconds reset device. The Luminor 1950 8 Days GMT, with its 44mm case that is water resistant to 10 bar (100m), has become an all-time favorite for those fans of Panerai's Historical Collection who live and work between multiple time zones.

PANERAI

LUMINOR 1950 10 DAYS GMT – REF. PAM00270

Unmistakably Panerai, this handsome timepiece cleanly presents a discreet linear 10-day power reserve indicator and a 24 hour GMT subdial within a 44mm steel case that is water resistant to 10 bar (100 meters). The Panerai P.2003 caliber, comprised of 296 parts, is the first automatic mechanical movement created entirely by Panerai. It has an autonomy of 10 days (240 hours). Such a prolonged power reserve is possible because of the innovative system with its unusual energy accumulator, consisting of three spring barrels: one of these is located above the second, while the third is linked through a gear train that enables the power remaining to be indicated on an appropriate graduated scale.

PIAGET

PIAGET ALTIPLANO DOUBLE JEU – REF. G0A35153

The Piaget Altiplano Double Jeu consists of two watches, featuring extremely slender cases and ultra-thin movements that enable them to be superimposed so as to form just one. The result is a decidedly avant-garde, generously sized 43mm watch equipped with two calibers driving different time displays on each dial, a particularly useful function for travelers. In developing the new Calibre 832P based on the ultra-thin Calibre 830P, the Manufacture de Haute Horlogerie wished to further enhance the sophistication of the Double Jeu concept by providing travelers with a dual time zone displayed on a 24-hour scale rather than just 12 hours. The caliber is finished with meticulous care, including beveled bridges adorned with circular Côtes de Genève, a circular-grained mainplate and traditional blued screws.

PIAGET

PIAGET EMPERADOR COUSSIN – REF. G0A32017

The Emperador Coussin watch is intended for modern-day nomads, whether businessmen or jetsetters, driven by a love of fine watchmaking craftsmanship. With its sunburst guilloché dial and two large counters indicating the dual time zone and the seconds, this model is a must-have for regular travelers. Proudly bearing the unmistakable Piaget signature, its pink-gold case features a subtle interpretation of the handsomely rounded cushion shape. As a creation truly worthy of Piaget, the Emperador Coussin watch reveals a specially tailored 850P movement adorned with superlative finishing including a circular-grained mainplate, beveled and hand-drawn bridges, blued screws and circular Côtes de Genève.

PIAGET

PIAGET EMPERADOR COUSSIN PERPETUAL CALENDAR IN WHITE GOLD – REF. G0A33018

Measuring 5.6mm thick, the Manufacture Piaget Calibre 855P self-winding movement displays the hours, minutes, small seconds at 4:00 and month and leap years at 12:00, along with retrograde day of the week and date displays at 9:00 and 3:00 respectively. In addition to the latter retrograde indications, this Calibre 855P stands out from most ordinary perpetual calendars by the addition of a double-hand dual time zone display appearing in a subdial at 8:00. The subtle architecture of the 46mm case enables to adapt to all wrists and imparts a particularly elegant profile. Subtly alternating polished and satin-brushed surfaces on the case middle, bezel and inner bezel ring, the latter is fitted with a sapphire crystal back providing admirable views of the movement finishings.

PIAGET

PIAGET POLO CHRONOGRAPH – REF. G0A33038

The Piaget Polo Chronograph model houses the Calibre 800P, a mechanical chronograph movement entirely designed, developed and produced by the Manufacture de Haute Horlogerie Piaget. In addition to the chronograph and flyback functions, this proprietary movement drives the hour, minute and small seconds at 6:00, as well as the date display at 12:00 and a second time zone indication. The 5.6mm-thick Calibre 800P is endowed with all the attributes of an haute horology chronograph movement. The generously sized 43mm-diameter case is set with 622 brilliant-cut diamonds (approximately 4.6 carats) and the dial set with 262 brilliant-cut diamonds (0.8 carats).

RICHARD MILLE

RM 022 TOURBILLON AERODYNE SECOND TIME ZONE

The RM 022 Tourbillon Aerodyne Second Time Zone is a visual and mechanical evolution of the first Richard Mille timepiece. Within its newly sculpted case design is the manual-winding caliber RM021, built on a baseplate of honeycombed orthorhombic titanium and carbon nanofiber. It provides hours, minutes, indicators for power reserve (circa 70 hours), torque indicator and function indicator for winding, neutral, and hand-setting operations. The finely finished pushbutton, located at 9:00, advances the second time zone in one-hour increments, utilizing a numbered, rotating disc of sapphire visible at 3:00.

ROGER DUBUIS

EXCALIBUR WORLD TIME – REF. EX45-1448-50-00/09R01/B

Thanks to an ingenious maximization of the surface area, the Excalibur World Time displays three time zones without making a single compromise in the field of legibility. Upon the black satin sunburst dial with transferred pink-gold and white Roman numerals, two large apertures indicate the chosen location from a total of 24 reference cities. The subdials that accompany them, at 3:00 with red transfers and 9:00 with black transfers, incorporate the added function of two day/night indicators. Despite its expressive design, and the display of three time zones, the dial remains uncluttered within its 45mm pink-gold case. The RD1448 that powers this timepiece boasts a 28,800 vph frequency and a 48-hour power reserve.

VACHERON CONSTANTIN

OVERSEAS DUAL TIME – REF. 47450/000W-9511

Within the powerful appeal of an anti-magnetic steel case with bezel and pushbutton guard made of titanium, the Overseas Dual Time employs a creative aesthetic structure to display time in two parts of the world. Seemingly overlapping, the secondary time zone and its moon-adorned day/night indicator are both concise and perfectly readable. Standing out from the satin-brushed slate-gray dial, a white luminescent strip indicates the remaining power of the self-winding 1222 SC caliber, while an intricately snailed counter at 2:00 indicates the day's date. Surrounding the functions, 12 applied 18K gold hour markers use their variable sizes to further the watch's metallic dynamism.

VACHERON CONSTANTIN
OVERSEAS DUAL TIME – REF. 47450/B01R-9404

Dressed in a case and bracelet made of radiant 18K pink gold, the 1222 SC automatic movement beats in style at a rate of 28,800 vph. A pink-gold stripe at 3:00 ruptures the dial's fine finishing to indicate the remainder of the watch's 40-hour power reserve. Enhanced with luminous materials on the hours and minutes, the three-hand time display is joined by a date subdial at 2:00, and legible secondary time zone with black and white day/night indicator. On the watch's solid caseback, a stamped medallion of the Overseas sailboat tells the story of the collection's heritage.

VACHERON CONSTANTIN

PATRIMONY TRADITIONNELLE WORLD TIME – REF. 86060/000R-9640

Combining Vacheron Constantin's rich multiple time zones heritage with a driven spirit of innovation, the self-winding 2460 WT caliber takes into account the modern reality of the world's 37 time zones. By aligning the reference city with a black triangle at 6:00, the owner has immediate access to time in all of the globe's regions, including those with partial time zones, be they half or even quarter hours. Brilliantly accomplished within a 42.5mm 18K pink-gold case, this masterpiece ingeniously uses three dials to obtain such a supreme degree of complexity with optimal legibility. In addition to driving the central hours, minutes, and seconds, with a frequency of 28,800 vph, the movement precisely rotates a sapphire dial with 24-hour chapter ring and map-overlaying day/night indicator. Simplifying the use of the watch, all indication adjustments are made via a single crown. As if the front of the watch weren't spectacular enough, the Patrimony Traditionnelle World Time features a sapphire crystal openworked caseback.

Calendars

From a simple date window to the highly complex perpetual calendar, along with large date displays, day/date subdials and complete calendars, these watches offer a vast range of different expressions and varying degrees of complication. We have even witnessed in recent years the growing popularity of a new type, known as the "annual calendar." Mechanisms are consistently fine-tuned to offer ever-increasing security, reliability and user-friendliness. In design, variety is the order of the day, with a broad palette of display modes (apertures, hands, rollers, retrograde systems, etc...); transparency-based approaches that are often very original; and appearances matching all tastes ranging from the most classic to the most daring.

The very first medieval monumental clocks

(particularly the 14th- and 15th-century cathedral clocks) already displayed a number of astronomical indications, some of which were related to the calendar. Calendar displays appeared at a relatively early stage on pocket watches—well before the minutes and seconds hands. From the late 16th century onwards, certain astronomical watches showed the time, the date, the day of the week, the month (with its length). Calendar watches subsequently proved a great success, but they were nonetheless merely "simple calendars" requiring manual adjustment after each month with less than 31 days, meaning five times a year. It was not until the late 18th century that the so-called "perpetual calendars" were developed, taking account of the variable lengths of the months and of the leap-year cycle. The 1920s saw the emergence of the first perpetual calendar wristwatches representing authentic feats of miniaturization. In 1945, Rolex claimed the launch of the first wristwatch with date window, the Datejust, which a few years later was fitted with a magnifying glass to facilitate reading of the date. The date window subsequently became a classic feature of "simple" watches. In the 1980s, with the rebirth of mechanical watchmaking, the perpetual calendar made a spectacular comeback as a symbol of technical mastery and expertise, and all the major brands were keen to perfect this already highly sophisticated mechanism. The start of the new millennium has witnessed the breakthrough of a complication that was curiously rare until then, the annual calendar, which is more practical than the simple calendar, but less complex and less expensive than the famous perpetual calendars.

TECHNIQUE

HOW DOES IT WORK?

The Gregorian calendar poses several challenges to watchmakers, particularly the varying lengths of the months and the periodical return of February 29. There are several different kinds of mechanisms, with distinct degrees of complexity.

SIMPLE CALENDAR

This is the name given to a calendar systematically indicating 31 days per month. A simple calendar must be manually adjusted on the first day of months following a month with fewer than 31 days, meaning five times a year (March 1st, May 1st, July 1st, October 1st and December 1st).

The simple calendar mechanism operates by means of a reducing gear train activated via the hour wheel. It moves one notch forward with every two turns of the hour wheel (24 hours). The display appears either on a disc bearing the date, or via a hand fixed to the 31-day star.

COMPLETE CALENDAR

A complete calendar looks very much like a perpetual calendar, in that it displays the date, the day, the month and generally the moonphase. But it does not take account of the varying lengths of the months and must therefore be corrected five times a year.

ANNUAL CALENDAR

The annual calendar automatically recognizes all months of 30 and 31 days, but does not take account of the duration of the month of February. It must therefore be corrected once a year, on March 1st. Annual calendars generally operate with the help of a wheel and pinion system of the same basic type as that driving the simple calendar, but considerably more complex.

PERPETUAL CALENDAR

The perpetual calendar is a highly sophisticated mechanism that not only recognizes months of 30 and 31 days, but also the 28 days of February and the quadrennial return of February 29th. It therefore possesses a mechanical “memory” of 1,461 days and theoretically requires no manual intervention. It does not however take account of the Gregorian correction relating to secular or century years and must be corrected for every secular year of which the first two figures are not divisible by 4—as will for instance be the case in 2100.

The perpetual calendar is distinguished from other types of calendar by the presence of a highly sophisticated toggle (or multiple-lever) system that pivots on its axis to drive the various displays. The indications may be displayed by discs or hands.

SECULAR OR CENTURY CALENDAR

The secular or century calendar takes account of the Gregorian correction made to years ending with 00. This extremely complex and rare calendar appears only on a handful of ultra-complicated watches (see the chapter on Multi-Complications).

Simple Calendars

From watches with a date window to those featuring calendars complete with day, date and month indications, there is a wide spectrum of simple calendar watches, which require correction at the end of each month lasting fewer than 31 days (i.e. five times a year). From a classic style to contemporary reinterpretation, watchmakers are giving free rein to their creativity, with an appealing selection of innovative designs, handed displays and retrograde indications—enough to satisfy any desire.

Rolex, *Oyster Perpetual Datejust II*

A modern version of the archetypal date window watch, the Oyster Perpetual Datejust II by Rolex is distinguished by its instant date change and by its famous "Cyclops" magnifying lens that enlarges the numeral two and a half times.

Rolex, *Oyster Perpetual Day-Date II*

A worthy heir to the first wristwatch to spell out the entire name of the day (launched in 1956), the Rolex Oyster Perpetual Day-Date II offers a choice of 26 languages for this indication.

Longines
Master Collection Retrograde

A festival of retrograde displays enlivens the Master Collection Retrograde by Longines, showing the date between 1 and 5 o'clock and the date at 12 o'clock, complemented by equally retrograde dual time zone and small seconds indications.

Jaeger-LeCoultre
Master Tourbillon

On the Master Tourbillon from Jaeger-LeCoultre, the patented date mechanism, adjustable in either direction, jumps between 15 and 16 so as not to hide the titanium tourbillon carriage.

Movado, *Red Label Museum Calendomatic*

Inspired by a model launched in 1946, the Red Label Museum Calendomatic by Movado combines the famous understated black Museum dial with an original date display by means of a rotating disc bearing red Roman or Arabic numerals.

Girard-Perregaux
1966 Complete Calendar

Sublimated by the gleaming metal of its palladium case, the pure dial of the Girard-Perregaux 1966 Complete Calendar features twin in-line day and month apertures, along with a pointer-type date display and a moonphase at 6 o'clock.

Hermès
Arceau Le Temps Suspendu

Arceau Le Temps Suspendu, from Hermès, is pure magic. With a simple press on the pushbutton, the hour and minute hands stand still next to 12 o'clock, while the date display disappears. Another press and all three hands return to their proper places.

a.b.art, *Serie OA*

On the Serie OA by a.b.art—a brand with German origins, now made in Switzerland—the date is indicated by a colored dot running around the dial.

Jaquet Droz, *Grande Seconde Quantième*

On the Grande Seconde Quantième from Jaquet Droz, the date display is effected with a hand on the oversized seconds subdial at 6 o'clock, while hours and minutes share the off-centered subdial at 12 o'clock.

Zenith, *El Primero Tourbillon*

On Zenith's El Primero Tourbillon, powered by a high-frequency automatic chronograph movement, the date is displayed inventively using a disc that revolves around the tourbillon carriage at 11 o'clock.

IWC, *Portuguese Tourbillon Mystère Rétrograde*

The Portuguese Tourbillon Mystère Rétrograde from IWC is equipped with a retrograde display for the date across an arc from 9 to 6 o'clock. The small seconds display is linked to the tourbillon, which seems to float, as if by magic, upon the black dial.

Alpina, *Club Regulator Manufacture*

The Alpina Club Regulator Manufacture combines a regulator-type display (central minutes, hours at 10 o'clock) with a pointer-type date display occupying the entire lower part of the dial.

Perpetual Calendars: Classic Designs

Representing the ultimate form of calendar watch, the famous perpetual calendars are characterized by their multiple displays (date, day, month, leap-year cycle), generally enriched by moonphases. In their most classic version, they generally feature three or even four subdials arranged symmetrically in relation to the dial center. But this restrained elegance sometimes conceals technical developments that considerably enhance the user-friendliness and the security of these ultra-sophisticated mechanisms.

Patek Philippe, *Perpetual Calendar Ref. 5139*
The Patek Philippe Perpetual Calendar, one of the most famous timepieces from the Geneva-based manufacturer, is distinguished by its ultra-thin self-winding movement and its understated yet readable dial, as well as its bezel with Clous de Paris decoration.

Audemars Piguet
Jules Audemars Perpetual Calendar
Equipped with an ultra-thin self-winding caliber, the Jules Audemars Perpetual Calendar model by Audemars Piguet is a perfect example of a classic and yet timeless design. The leap-year cycle appears in the center of the month subdial.

Blancpain,
Perpetual Calendar with Under-Lug Correctors
On its Perpetual Calendar with Under-Lug Correctors, Blancpain has developed an original system serving to integrate the correctors within the four bracelet lugs, on the wrist side. A press of the finger is enough to correct the date, day, month, leap-year cycle or moonphase display.

Vacheron Constantin
Patrimony Contemporaine
Perpetual Calendar
The Patrimony Contemporaine Perpetual Calendar from Vacheron Constantin presents four subdials (month, date, day and moonphase) in a perfect symmetry that is highlighted by the refined design.

Jaeger-LeCoultre
Master Grande Tradition Tourbillon à Quantième Perpétuel
Jaeger-LeCoultre has combined two major complications in its Master Grande Tradition Tourbillon à Quantième Perpétuel, featuring three subdials with date/day/month subdials, as well as the four-digit year number appearing in the center of the month window.

Perpetual Calendars: New Configurations

The design of perpetual calendars enables brands to play with various aesthetic arrangements in order to make their models stand out from traditional dials. The trend is towards a number of apertures placed either in a straight line or around the arc of a circle. Watchmakers also enjoy combining pointer- and window-type displays in sometimes highly original compositions, a sophisticated aesthetic approach that is associated with a number of technical accomplishments.

Antoine Martin
Quantième Perpétuel QP01
Equipped with a silicon escapement that needs no lubrication, the Quantième Perpétuel QP01 from Antoine Martin stands out for its original aesthetic, with vertical displays for the day and month, large date and "new-style" guillochage.

Breguet, *Classique 7717BA*
On this self-winding Classique watch by Breguet, the pointer- or window-type displays are lined up along the same vertical axis, against the brand's characteristic guilloché dial.

H. Moser & Cie., *Perpetual 1*
H. Moser & Cie. offers an unusual and extremely restrained take on the perpetual calendar. The month is displayed by a small central hand pointing to one of the 12 hour markers—such as 5 standing for May. The calendar may be adjusted forwards or backwards at any time.

Ulysse Nardin, *El Toro*
The El Toro model by Ulysse Nardin stands out not only for its exceptional outward appearance, but also for its correction system serving to adjust either forward or backward all the various calendar indications.

F. P. Journe, *Octa Perpétuelle*
The extremely original dial of the Octa Perpétuelle by F.P. Journe, with its offset hours, minutes and seconds, gives a starring role to the central retrograde hand, along with two day and month windows.

Roger Dubuis,
La Monégasque Perpetual Calendar
Launched in 2011, the new La Monégasque collection from Roger Dubuis notably offers a perpetual calendar with a double day/month window at 12 o'clock, with a hand for the date at 4:30 and moonphase at 7:30.

IWC
Da Vinci Perpetual Calendar Digital Date-Month
On its Da Vinci Perpetual Calendar Digital Date-Month, IWC has replaced the traditional subdials by two twin apertures indicating the double-digit month and date.

Perpetual Calendars: Retrograding and Roller Systems

How can one enliven a perpetual calendar model? By choosing a retrograde-type mechanism for one or several of the calendar indications, with a hand moving across the arc of a circle before jumping back to its point of departure (see the chapter on Retrograde Displays and Jumping Hours). Another, much rarer, option is that of roller-type indications. This quest for originality paves the way for all manner of fanciful visual touches calling for a superlative degree of technical mastery.

Piaget, *FortyFive Perpetual Calendar*

On its FortyFive Perpetual Calendar, Piaget presents a dynamic configuration, with retrograde date at 3 o'clock, retrograde day at 9 o'clock and subdial displaying the month and leap-year cycle at 12 o'clock.

Jaquet Droz, *Quantième Perpétuel*

Jaquet Droz, known for its consistently original designs, offers a Perpetual Calendar model with double retrograde display occupying the entire upper part of the dial, with days on the left and the date on the right.

Jean Dunand, *Shabaka*

The ultra-sophisticated Shabaka watch by Jean Dunand is equipped with a minute repeater striking on a cathedral chime, and is also distinguished by its roller-type display of the perpetual calendar indications, all of which jump instantly at midnight.

Parmigiani Fleurier
Toric Corrector

Equipped with a minute repeater and a pusher enabling instant correction of all the calendar and moonphase functions, the Toric Corrector by Parmigiani Fleurier displays the retrograde date on the arc of a circle running from 8 to 4 o'clock.

Maîtres du Temps, *Chapter Two*

The Chapter Two watch, created by Daniel Roth, Roger Dubuis and Peter Speake-Marin for the Maîtres du Temps brand, displays the months and days spelled out on two rollers—complete with two correctors housed on the caseback.

Perpetual Calendars: The Transparent Approach

Visible mechanisms are all the rage in the watch industry at the moment. After introducing sapphire crystal casebacks on virtually all their complicated models, brands are vying with each other to find ingenious means of revealing all or part of the movement through the dial side. Perpetual calendars are no exception, and there is a vast range of models with openworked dials, skeletonized movements or transparent dials that now hide almost nothing of their inner mysteries, at least in visual terms. These spectacular stagings are often matched by some exceptional technical feats accomplished behind the scenes.

Vacheron Constantin
Malte Retrograde Perpetual Calendar Openface

Vacheron Constantin has equipped its Malte Retrograde Perpetual Calendar Openface watch in platinum with a double sapphire crystal. Transparent subdials with white rotating "pallets" serve to indicate the day, month and leap-year cycle painted in black on one of the sapphire crystals.

Jaeger-LeCoultre
Master Eight Days Perpetual SQ

The Master Eight Days Perpetual from Jaeger-LeCoultre, endowed with an eight-day power reserve, is shown here in a dazzling skeletonized version featuring daringly curved bridges echoing the lines of longitude and latitude.

Parmigiani Fleurier
Tonda 42 Retrograde Perpetual Calendar

On the Tonda 42 Retrograde Perpetual Calendar by Parmigiani Fleurier, the abbreviations of the day and month appear on two discs featuring original shapes and visible through the transparent dial.

Patek Philippe
Grand Complication Ref. 5104

On the Grand Complication Ref. 5104 model by Patek Philippe, the days, months and the leap-year cycle number are printed directly on the sapphire crystal dial and dark "pallets" highlight the appropriate white transfer by contrast.

Cartier, *Tortue Perpetual Calendar*

Equipped with an in-house movement, the Tortue Perpetual Calendar by Cartier combines various types of display—including a central pointer-type date indication and a retrograde day running from 8 to 4 o'clock—appearing on an openworked dial.

Large Dates

Highly prized for their readability as well as their original touch, “large date” displays are becoming increasingly sought-after in recent years, whether appearing alone on the dial or associated with other complications. Several well-known brands have taken an interest in this ingenious mechanism, improving both its running and its reliability.

A. Lange & Söhne
Grande Lange 1 Luminous

Large date displays are closely associated with A. Lange & Söhne. A specialist in this type of display, the German brand uses its patented system on several models, including the Grande Lange 1 Luminous with an offset hours/minutes dial.

Audemars Piguet
Edward Piguet Large Date Tourbillon

Combining two superimposed discs and an ingenious system of partial gears, the display created by Audemars Piguet is intended to be the largest on the market. Witness this ultra-sophisticated Edward Piguet Large Date Tourbillon model.

Cecil Purnell
La Grande Date

La Grande Date from Cecil Purnell uses transparent effects, revealing the two discs of the oversized date display, as well as part of the movement and the tourbillon carriage.

Eterna
Madison Eight Days Spherodrive

Featuring an elegant tonneau-shaped case, an eight-day power reserve and the patented Spherodrive system, the Madison Eight Days by Eterna displays its large date at 2 o’clock, with a fast correction pusher that may be used 24 hours a day.

Carl F. Bucherer
Patravi EvoTec BigDate

Designed for feminine wrists, the Patravi EvoTec BigDate from Carl F. Bucherer displays its large date in a double aperture situated in the upper left corner of the dial. The small seconds subdial at 6 o’clock echoes the cushion shape of the case.

H. Moser & Cie, *Monard Date*

Based on two superimposed discs, the large date display on the Monard Date by H. Moser & Cie is also distinguished by its patented Double Pull Crown system, which avoids the user accidentally changing the time when simply seeking to adjust the date.

A. Favre & Fils
Phoenix 10.1 Quantième à Grand Affichage Rotatif

On the Phoenix 10.1 Quantième à Grand Affichage Rotatif by A. Favre & Fils, the units numerals remain immobile, while a red arrow (for the dates from 1 to 9) or the 1, 2 or 3 o’clock numeral move to indicate the date.

Annual Calendars

The annual calendar continues its spectacular breakthrough. Less complex than a perpetual calendar, it enables brands to create watches that are more affordable and simpler to operate, while providing a degree of user-friendliness far superior to simple calendars in that they require just one correction per year. The last few years have brought a flourishing spate of annual calendar models featuring a great variety of displays and designs, as well as occasionally associating this complication with other useful functions.

Urwerk, *UR-1001 Zeit Device*

On the new UR-1001 Zeit Device, Urwerk uses its famous satellite system, developed for hours and minutes, in the month/date calendar display. This mechanism automatically takes into account months that have 30 or 31 days.

Hysek, *Kilada Annual Calendar*

Combining rose gold and black rubber in a highly contemporary design, the Kilada Annual Calendar possesses an annual calendar with a month counter at 8 o'clock and a large date at 12 o'clock.

Blancpain

Villeret Annual Calendar GMT

The new Villeret Annual Calendar GMT from Blancpain displays the date, day and month in three highly readable apertures. The date is linked to the central hands of local time, while the subdial keeps home time on a 24-hour scale.

A. Lange & Söhne

Saxonia Annual Calendar

The first A. Lange & Söhne watch to be equipped with an annual calendar, the Saxonia Annual Calendar combines the German brand's celebrated and patented large date display with three classic windows for the day, month and moonphase.

Omega

De Ville Hour Vision Annual Calendar

Equipped with a self-winding movement, a co-axial escapement and an annual calendar with instant date jump, the Omega De Ville Hour Vision Annual Calendar displays the month and date in a double window at 3 o'clock.

Vacheron Constantin

Quai de l'Ile Retrograde Annual Calendar

On the new Quai de l'Ile Retrograde Annual Calendar from Vacheron Constantin, the month is displayed on a subdial at six o'clock and the date on an arc at 3 o'clock. The aperture at 9 o'clock also indicates the moon's age (see chapter on Moonphases).

Patek Philippe

Nautilus Annual Calendar
Ref. 5726

Launched in 1996, the patented Annual Calendar from Patek Philippe has become a bestseller for the brand. It has been interpreted in several different models, including the Nautilus Annual Calendar, Ref. 5726, with a double day/month aperture.

Pierre DeRoche

GrandCliff QA Power Reserve

The GrandCliff QA Power Reserve model by Pierre DeRoche, equipped with a Dubois Dépraz movement, combines the annual calendar with a chronograph featuring retrograding 60-minute and 6-hour counters, a flyback function and a large date.

Hermès

Dressage Annual Calendar

The Dressage Annual Calendar watch by Hermès, with its exclusive Vaucher Manufacture Fleurier movement, is distinguished by its pointer-type 270° retrograde date display and its two visible day and month discs.

Girard-Perregaux

Cat's Eye Annual and Zodiac Calendars

Designed for women, the Cat's Eye Annual and Zodiac Calendars watch combines a snail-shaped date display with a large comet's tail-shaped aperture revealing the ever-circling dance of the Zodiac signs.

A. LANGE & SÖHNE

DATOGRAPH PERPETUAL – REF. 410.032

This model is driven by the manually wound Lange L951.1 movement. It is a flyback chronograph with a precise jumping minute counter as well as perpetual calendar with a large date, moonphase display, day of the week, month, leap-year display, small seconds hand with stop seconds, and day/night indicator. The plates and bridges are made of silver and the balance cock is engraved by hand. The three-piece rose-gold case features an untreated German antireflective sapphire crystal and caseback, as well as a main pushbutton for simultaneously advancing all calendar displays, recessed pushbuttons for separately advancing the calendar displays and two chronograph pushbuttons. The hand-stitched crocodile strap is secured with a solid gold buckle.

A. LANGE & SÖHNE

GRANDE LANGE 1 – REF. 117.021

Precisely adjusted in five positions, the new manually wound L095.1 caliber provides a large diameter, upon which A. Lange & Söhne incorporates an optimal number of parts on one level. The Grand Lange 1's yellow-gold case encloses a solid silver champagne dial that uninhibitedly displays hours and minutes, small seconds, large date, and a prominent 72-hour power reserve indicator. A sapphire crystal exhibition caseback complements the slim, yet expressive, aesthetic of the watch by revealing its twice-assembled and delicately hand-decorated mechanical movement.

A. LANGE & SÖHNE

LANGEMATIK PERPETUAL – REF. 310.025

Powered by the self-winding Caliber L922.1 SAX-0-MAT, the Langematik Perpetual is the world's first self-winding wristwatch with a large date and a perpetual calendar featuring separate pushbuttons for individual corrections of the calendar indications (date, day of the week, month, leap year, and moonphase displays), as well as a main pushbutton for advancing all displays. Caliber L922.1 SAX-O-MAT has a 46-hour power reserve, stop seconds with a patented zero-reset mechanism, plates and bridges made of untreated German silver, and a hand-engraved balance cock. The Langematik Perpetual's three-piece platinum case is fitted with antireflective sapphire crystal on the front and back, and a crown for winding the watch and setting the time. The solid silver and argenté dial is topped with luminous platinum hands. The watch's crocodile strap is secured via a solid gold buckle.

AUDEMARS PIGUET

JULES AUDEMARS PERPETUAL CALENDAR – REF. 26390OR.OO.D088CR.01

The ultra-thin profile of this watch is truly fascinating and it is even more surprising when one considers that such a slim case houses the automatic-winding 2120/2802 movement, which indicates the day, date, month, moonphase and leap-year cycle, all thanks to a mechanism barely 4mm thick! The movement possesses an engraved rotor with a 21K gold segment revealed through the sapphire crystal caseback. The case is in 18K pink gold.

BLANCPAIN

L-EVOLUTION SEMAINIER GRANDE DATE 8 JOURS – REF. 8837-1134-53B

Blancpain's L-Evolution Semainer Grande Date 8 Jours is distinguished by its eight-day power reserve. The calendar displays the day, week, and large date. The 37R8G caliber is housed in the steel 43.5mm case, which is water resistant to 100atm. The L-Evolution Semainer Grande Date 8 Jours is also available in an 18K red- or white-gold case.

BLANCPAIN

VILLERET 8 DAY COMPLETE CALENDAR – REF. 6639-3437-55B

Presented in platinum with a black enamel dial, the Villeret 8 Day Complete Calendar displays a moonphase with small seconds at 6:00, date via a central hand against an outermost date ring, and day and month through nicely contrasting apertures at 12 o'clock. Powered by the 6639 self-winding caliber with eight-day power reserve, this watch features an exhibition caseback and is worn on a black alligator leather strap that complements the deep tone of the dial.

BLANCPAIN

VILLERET 8 DAY COMPLETE CALENDAR – REF. 6639-3631-55B

Blancpain's Complete Calendar 8 Jours boasts an eight-day power reserve and an automatic-winding 6639 caliber, which is housed in the rose-gold 42mm case. The complete calendar displays hours, minutes, small seconds, and moonphase. Complemented by a light brown Louisiana alligator leather strap, the Complete Calendar 8 Jours is available in a limited edition of 275 pieces.

DEWITT

ACADEMIA QUANTIEME PERPETUEL SPORT – REF. AC.7888.030A.M095

Blending the power and speed of a modern design with the finest technical pedigree that tradition has to offer, this titanium wristwatch is a perpetual calendar within a racing machine. Along with a dashboard-like month and leap-year indicator at 12:00, and celestial moonphase at 6:00, the speed-inspired black and red dial features two retrograde counters on either side of center. Both positioned on black radiator "grilles," the indicators display the numerical date, in addition to days of the week. Self-winding, with a frequency of 28,800 vph and an escapement with a 51° angle of lift, the DW 7004 caliber provides this modern perpetual calendar with a power reserve of 42 hours.

GLASHÜTTE ORIGINAL

SENATOR PERPETUAL CALENDAR BLACK CERAMIC – REF. 100.07.06.06.05

The matte black ceramic case of the Senator Perpetual Calendar lends the traditionally complicated art of watchmaking a modern appearance. The day, month, and panorama date are presented with white numerals against a black background, and a silver disk decorated with stars displays the moonphase. A display with jumping indicator located at 12:00 indicates a leap year when its red indicator points to the 4. The 42mm case houses automatic manufacture Caliber 100-07, which commands a power reserve of more than 55 hours and sports a reset mechanism that allows easy synchronization of the second hand with a time standard.

GLASHÜTTE ORIGINAL

SENATOR PERPETUAL CALENDAR RED GOLD – REF. 100-02-25-05-05

Spread spaciously across the matte black dial, the perpetual calendar indications present an elegantly modern take on the revered complication. Through four perfectly integrated apertures at 2:00, 4:00, 8:00 and 10:00, this red-gold timepiece's automatic GO 100-02 caliber displays the month, date, moonphase and date, as though they were barely there at all. As for the leap-year indicator, aesthetic discretion called for its most extreme miniaturization. Driven by a multi-colored rotating disc, a small dot just above the dial's center expresses the status of the four-year cycle, with a red spot indicating a current leap year. Through the sapphire crystal caseback, the owner can experience a view of the dazzling movement, which beats at a rate of 28,800 vph. This supremely understated perpetual calendar secures its elegance to the wrist with a Louisiana alligator leather strap that matches the color of the impeccable watch face.

GUY ELLIA

TIME SPACE QUANTIEME PERPETUEL

The Time Space, original ambassador of Guy Ellia, is transformed into a perpetual calendar for this version. A mechanical hand-winding Frédéric Piguet caliber harbored in a 46.8mm black-gold case allows the owner to read the hour, minute, day, month, date and moonphases, while taking leap years into account. With a brushed bottom plate of 7.75mm, this watch symbolizes elegance, complexity and thinness. A specific automatic winder is integrated to the watch box. This model is also available in white or pink gold.

GUY ELLIA

TIME SPACE QUANTIEME PERPETUEL – FULL SET

The case and dial of this extraordinary piece are covered in pavé-set diamonds. A mechanical hand-wound Frédéric Piguet caliber harbored in a 46.8mm white-gold case allows the owner to read the hour, minute, day, month, date and moonphase, while taking leap years into account. With a brushed bottom plate of 7.75mm, this clear allusion to the Couteaux watches symbolizes elegance, complexity and thinness. A specific automatic winder is integrated into the watch box and this model is also available in pink gold.

IWC

PORTUGUESE GRAND COMPLICATION – REF. IW377402

Limited to 50 watches per year, the Portuguese Grand Complication combines a multiplicity of extraordinary horological feats within an 18K red-gold case. The warmth of the case and dark brown alligator leather strap, stitched with 18K red-gold threads, draws the eye to a cartographic silver-plated dial design that pays tribute to Vasco de Gama's navigational exploits. Along with a full perpetual calendar, programmed until the year 2499, and a small seconds subdial, this flagship masterpiece features a chronograph with central seconds hand, as well as 12-hour and 30-minute counters, a perpetual moonphase display, and a minute repeater. On the outside of the case, the crown, chronograph pushers and the repeater's sliding activator echo the brilliance of the dial's numerous red-gold appliqués. The theme of navigational exploration extends to the caseback, on which a sextant is engraved.

IWC

PORTUGUESE TOURBILLON MYSTERE RETROGRADE – REF. IW504402

With an appearance as magical as it is distinctive, the Portuguese Tourbillon Mystère Rétrograde is guaranteed to attract inquisitive glances. Watch lovers will be particularly fascinated by the unusual arrangement of the flying tourbillon, consisting of 81 parts, against a deep black background, creating the illusion that the filigree cage containing the balance is rotating in mid-air. Set in a mirror-finished ring, it resembles an animated "12" and forms the optical centerpiece of the entire dial. The retrograde date display is not only an original complication but also makes a good deal of sense, because a conventional date disc would conceal the tourbillon. After the 31st of the month, it automatically jumps back to the 1st; in shorter months, the hand can be rapidly advanced until it reverts to the 1st. On the right-hand side of the dial, the seven-day power reserve display indicates how much energy remains in the IWC-manufactured 51900 caliber. As befitting a timepiece of this quality, the Portuguese Tourbillon Mystère Rétrograde premieres in a glamorous red-gold case with a silver-colored dial and in platinum with a dial in ruthenium black.

IWC

DA VINCI PERPETUAL CALENDAR DIGITAL DATE-MONTH – REF. IW376107

In 1884, IWC secured the rights to the Pallweber system developed by Joseph Pallweber and started producing the first "digital" watches in IWC's history. Rather than an analog display with hands, digits were presented in separate windows; only the seconds were shown via a hand. Now, WC presents the Da Vinci Perpetual Calendar Digital Date-Month with large-figure digital displays for the date and the month. The power required to switch both month and date discs at the end of the month is accumulated over the course of the entire month in a quick-action switch specially developed for this purpose. At the end of the month, the energy is released and displays are advanced, even the digital leap year if necessary. The chronograph can run continuously without having any noticeable effect on the watch's rate and, thanks to the flyback function, can be reset to zero without being stopped. The new IWC-manufactured 89800 caliber consists of 474 individual parts and builds up a power reserve of 68 hours. The movement is a massive watchmaking achievement.

IWC

PORTUGUESE PERPETUAL CALENDAR – REF. IW502307

The moonphase display on the Portuguese Perpetual Calendar, Reference 5023, is grand-scale theater on a tiny stage. Attended by a cluster of embossed stars, the moon rises behind the hemispherical cut-out on the left and waxes to full moon in the center, before disappearing on the right-hand side. IWC's design engineers have calculated that the moonphase display deviates from the duration of the moon's actual course by just 1 day in 577.5 years. No one, so far, has noticed the difference. In other respects, this elegant, up-to-the-minute timepiece leaves virtually no wish unfulfilled: perpetual calendar, four-digit year display, and a seven-day automatic movement with Pellaton winding and power reserve display. Reference 5023 is available in two versions: in a red-gold case with silver-colored dial and red-gold-plated moon against a midnight blue background; or slightly more restrained, in white gold with rhodium-plated appliqués on a slate-colored dial with a sun-pattern finish. As in the sister models (Reference 5021), the cases now measure 44.2mm in diameter.

IWC

PORTUGUESE PERPETUAL CALENDAR – REF. IW503203

The moon is useful to sailors on the open sea not only for navigational purposes. Its influence on coastal tides has always been of greater importance, because the timing of their ebb and flow is reliably dictated by the moon: at new and full moons, high tides are exceptionally high and low tides exceptionally low. In the English Channel the difference can be up to 11.5m and in the Gulf of Maine as much as 21m, which illustrates the enormous importance of the moon for shipping. Aside from the date, day, month and year in four digits, the Portuguese Perpetual Calendar also indicates the number of days remaining until the next full moon. The display showing its course and featuring mirror images of the moon in the Northern and Southern Hemispheres deviates from the moon's actual progress by just 12 seconds in one lunar period. The striking color combination found in the new version in white gold will increase its attraction to watch lovers and stargazers: the rhodium-plated moonphase indicator discs wax and wane thanks to a midnight-blue cut-out display in a dial also finished in midnight blue.

JAEGER-LeCOULTRE

GRANDE REVERSO DUO – REF. 374.24.21

As the manually wound Jaeger-LeCoultre 986 caliber drives both sides of this remarkable timepiece, the Grande Reverso Duo marks an innovative celebration of the second time zone concept. Framed by an 18K pink-gold case, two contrasting dials, with vertical and horizontal guilloché, respectively, and Clous de Paris motif, work together to offer the traveling connoisseur twice the pleasure and twice the clarity. On the white dial, local time is demonstrated through a multi-leveled architecture of central hour and minute hands, rectangular small seconds, and panoramic date aperture. On the watch's black counterpart, a 24-hour subdial that incorporates a distinctive day/night indicator complements the large 12-hour home time zone.

PATEK PHILIPPE

ANNUAL CALENDAR CHRONOGRAPH – REF. 5960R

Developed and manufactured in-house, the self-winding CH 28-520 IRM QA 24H chronograph caliber stands out with numerous features. It has a flyback column-wheel chronograph, a power reserve indicator, an annual calendar with day, date, and month, as well as a day/night indicator. The patented Patek Philippe Annual Calendar is a full-function calendar that automatically recognizes months with 30 and 31 days. On the dial's three concentric scales, it indicates elapsed minutes and hours while the chronograph is running. The day, date, and month apertures are arranged along an arc at the upper periphery of the dial. The new rose-gold case, with a diameter of 40.5mm, adds an attractive and contemporary touch of nostalgia to this impressive instrument.

PATEK PHILIPPE

PERPETUAL CALENDAR CHRONOGRAPH – REF. 5270G

The creator, in 1925, of the first-ever perpetual calendar wristwatch, Patek Philippe chooses innovation as the language that best honors its brilliant heritage. Powered by the extremely efficient, durable, and reliable CH 29-535 PS Q manually wound caliber, this 41mm white-gold timepiece lets the chronograph's precise measurement of elapsed time adorn the cleverly arranged perpetual calendar that makes its domain on an elegant opaline dial. On the right of the moonphase and date section at 6:00, a discreet aperture reveals the indication of February's variable status. On the left of the dual-function subdial, a small window demonstrates day or night via a white and blue disc that fills the opening.

PATEK PHILIPPE

SPLIT-SECONDS CHRONOGRAPH WITH PERPETUAL CALENDAR – REF. 5951P

With this masterpiece, Patek Philippe impressively demonstrates the multiple talents of the CHR 27-525 PS split-seconds chronograph movement. In the Ref. 5951P, it not only drives the rattrapante chronograph but also controls a perpetual calendar. The unequaled slenderness of the base movement inspired the developers of the calendar module to strive for compactness as well. The result is a stunning movement with an overall height of only 7.3mm. To salute this extraordinary accomplishment, it is housed in a cushion-shaped case made of 950 platinum with a sapphire crystal exhibition caseback.

PIAGET

PIAGET EMPERADOR COUSSIN PERPETUAL CALENDAR – REF. G0A35020

The Piaget Emperador Coussin Perpetual Calendar houses Calibre 856P, a mechanical self-winding movement beating at a cadence of 21,600 vph and boasting a 72-hour power reserve. Its mainplate and bridges are circular-grained and beveled, their flanks are hand-drawn, and the decoration is enhanced with blued screws and circular Côtes de Genève. Its distinctive cushion shape and the decision to combine full-cut and baguette-cut diamonds totaling 9.9 carats clearly added to the daunting complexity of the watch. Witness the extraordinary jeweling of the bezel: the succession of 60 baguette-cut diamonds—one for each minute—seems to literally give life and movement to this case offering a display of virtuoso gem-setting dexterity. The dial is also a major accomplishment, featuring a surface housing no less than 263 diamonds, 12 hour markers and five subdials.

PIAGET

PIAGET EMPERADOR COUSSIN PERPETUAL CALENDAR IN PINK GOLD – REF. G0A33019

The Piaget Emperador Coussin represents a subtle architecture of the 46mm case that enables it to adapt to all wrists and imparts a particularly elegant profile. Measuring 5.6mm thick, the Manufacture Piaget Calibre 855P self-winding movement of this watch was designed, developed and produced entirely in-house. It displays the hours, minutes, small seconds at 4:00, month and leap years at 12:00, along with retrograde day of the week and date displays at 9:00 and 3:00 respectively. In addition, this Calibre 855P stands out from most ordinary perpetual calendars by the addition of a double-hand dual time zone display appearing in a subdial at 8:00. The self-winding Piaget Calibre 855P beats at a cadence of 21,600 vph and is endowed with an approximately 72-hour power reserve.

PIAGET

PIAGET POLO FORTYFIVE PERPETUAL CALENDAR TWO-TONE – REF. G0A36001

Combining the imposing character of titanium with the warmth of 18K pink gold, this dynamic timepiece embodies the extraordinary horological achievement of a perpetual calendar. Demonstrating Piaget's mastery of design geometry, the Polo FortyFive Perpetual Calendar Two-Tone displays a dial of powerful aesthetic complexity, yet remarkable legibility. At 3:00, the retrograde date complements the retrograde day of the week indicator at 9:00, while gracefully traversing the small seconds counter that operates beneath it at 4:00. The second time zone at 8:00 completes the house's emblematic figure eight design on the lower half of the watch face. Capable of normalizing calendar irregularities until the year 2100, this 855P caliber timepiece completes the black and gold contrast of its dial with a dual month and leap year indicator at 12:00.

ROGER DUBUIS

EXCALIBUR PERPETUAL CALENDAR, MINUTE REPEATER TOURBILLON IN PLATINUM

REF. EX45-082-98-00-00-RR00/B

Limited to just eight pieces, the Excalibur Perpetual Calendar, Minute Repeater Tourbillon is lavished with features: a minute repeater with centrifugal dissipator, instantaneous perpetual calendar with oversized date, a flying tourbillon at 5:30, dual time zone display, automatic winding by double micro-rotor in platinum, 50-hour power reserve, and fine adjustment to six positions. Hours, quarter-hours, and minutes chime on demand, and display windows indicate the day of the week, date, leap year, day/night, high-precision moonphase and a dual time zone indication. The RD 0829 caliber pulses within the 45mm platinum case. The hand-stitched genuine alligator strap is complemented by its platinum folding buckle.

ROGER DUBUIS

LA MONEGASQUE PERPETUAL CALENDAR – REF. MG44-821J-59-00/0RR01/B

This miniature mechanization of time is presented in a 44mm pink-gold case with a titanium bezel coated in black DLC. With its 4Hz frequency of oscillation (28,800 vph), the 364-component RD821J caliber, with a 48-hour power reserve, is adjusted in five positions as it delivers the comprehensive indications of this perpetual calendar. Upon the rhodium-plated satin sunburst dial, this timepiece contains a lower half composed of a snailed date counter and seamlessly integrated moonphase. On the upper half, two gold windows set the frame for the French day of the week, as well as the month. Completing the nature of the calendar, a leap year indicator appears discreetly at 3:00. Finished with pink-gold applied Arabic numerals, this watch features a sapphire crystal caseback.

URWERK

UR 1001 ZEIT DEVICE ÜBER COMPLICATION

Super-resistant thanks to its coating in Aluminum Titanium Nitride, this calendar decisively proclaims that the future has arrived. Complete with small day/night, 3 x 20 seconds, and power reserve indicators, the sophisticated dial displays the date and month via a centrally rotating module, whose three arms additionally revolve vertically to prepare the correct month to enter the scale. Indicating the time, three orbiting satellites take their turn to traverse the 60-minute scale, at which point the retrograde pointer is launched back to zero, where it begins a new time-telling passage. On the watch's caseback, Urwerk complements the inner workings of its hour-satellite complication with an expression of the house's colossal vision. As the "oil change" display reaches a full revolution, the 100-year indicator above it takes a five-year leap, acting as an odometer to the movement. When the latter dial reaches the century mark, the left-side 1000-year scale marks a monumental step toward the timepiece's next millennium.

VACHERON CONSTANTIN

PATRIMONY TRADITIONNELLE OPENWORKED PERPETUAL CALENDAR

REF. 43172/000R-9241

With the clever use of vibrant colors in the 48-month and moonphase indicators, this revealing timepiece achieves legibility through contrast with the superbly revealed mechanism. Powered by the 1120 QP SQ automatic caliber, and encased in 18K pink gold, this timepiece presents its perpetual calendar on three white rings at 9:00, 12:00, and 3:00, as well as a moonphase indicator at 6:00. The 4-year display at the top of the dial cleverly highlights the leap-year quadrant in red, while the three other January indications are colored in blue, providing clear annual segments for easy reference. As the pink-gold dauphine hands display the hours and minutes, the day of the week and date are read on the rings at 9:00 and 3:00. Through a sapphire crystal, the dazzling details of the movement's finish can be further admired on the caseback.

Retrograde Mechanisms and Jumping Hours

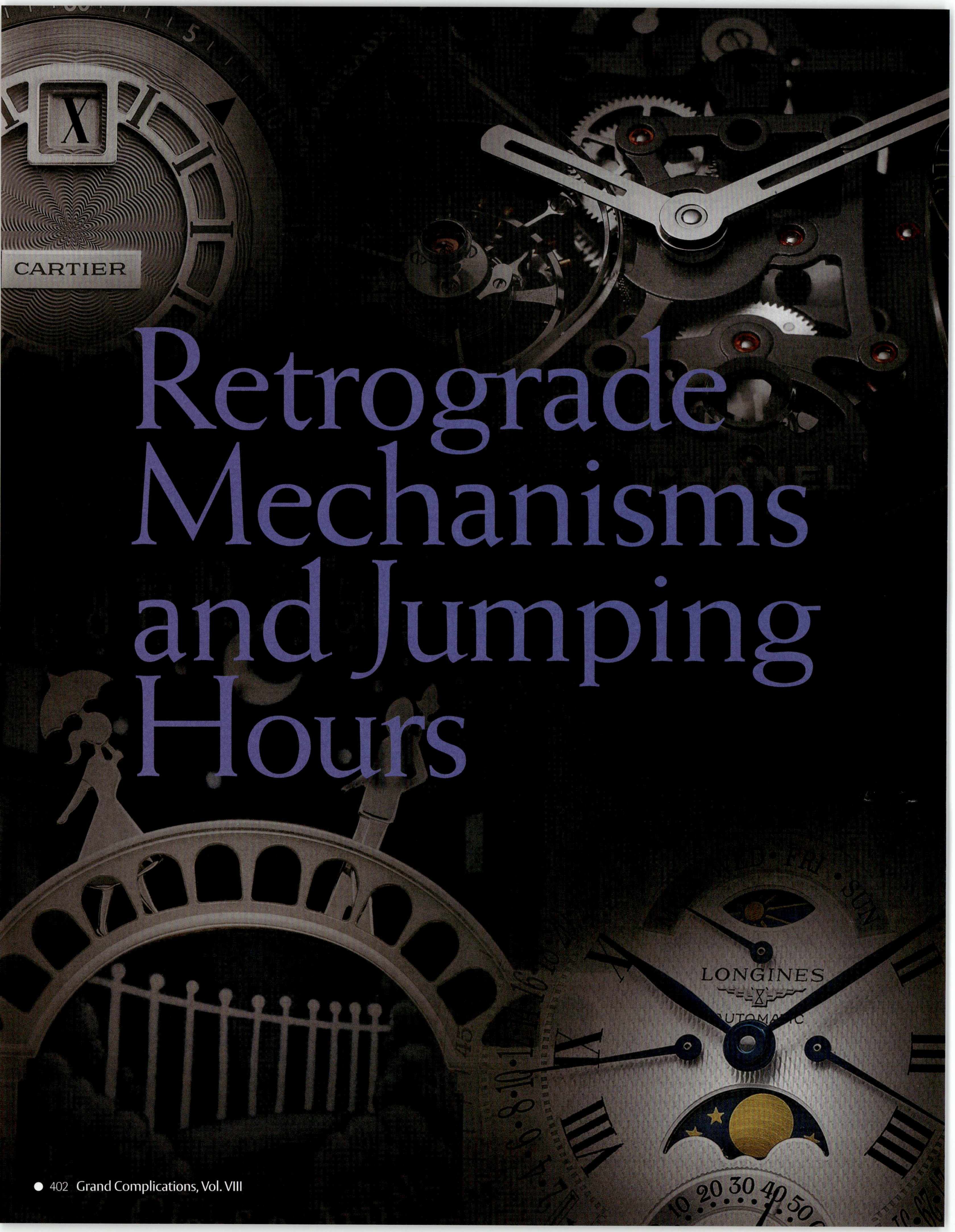

The usual system of hands turning endlessly in the same direction around the dial—just as the shadow makes its way around the sundial—has trained us in a circular conception of time. However, there have always been other modes of display, which operate according to different principles, whether retrograde indications (with a hand that traverses an arc before swinging back to its starting place) or jumping displays (which use a disc that moves forward in an aperture). Today, these alternative modes of displaying time, which had long been reserved for a few specialty models, are enjoying unprecedented popularity. Watchmakers appreciate the touch of originality and liveliness they bring to the dial, and we are now seeing a varied spectrum of new display methods and revolutionary ways of telling time (three-dimensional displays, rotating or satellite-based systems, etc.), which evince astonishing technical mastery and unbridled creativity. More than ever, time is its own spectacle.

VACHERON CONSTANTIN
GENÈVE
MONDAY
TUESDAY
WEDNESDAY
THU
FRIDAY
SATURDAY

Watchmakers have long sought to develop display methods that differ from the usual setup of hands turning… clockwise. This is why they invented the "retrograde" system (in which a hand moves across an arc, then instantaneously returns to its starting point to begin again) and the "jumping" displays (in which a disc moves behind an aperture). In the 18th century, Abraham-Louis Breguet enjoyed bringing life to his dials by using retrograde hands for certain indications, notably the date. At the end of the 20th century, the mechanical renaissance brought with it a return to prominence of these alternative display methods, allowing watchmakers to vary the looks and styles of their creations.

TECHNIQUE

HOW DOES IT WORK?

RETROGRADE DISPLAYS

On a retrograde display, the hand traces an arc before returning in the blink of an eye at its original position to begin its path again. The construction of the base movement is the same as for an ordinary watch, and the difference lies in the display mechanism placed just below the dial. A complex system of springs, racks and pawls transforms the circular movement of the hand into a back-and-forth movement with ultra-fast return and immediate restart. The more retrograde displays are featured on a watch, the more precision and expertise are required to build it.

JUMPING DISPLAYS

On jumping mechanisms, the hand is replaced with a disc that "jumps" instantly with each change of unit. The base movement has the same construction as that of an ordinary watch, but a system of drawback and jumper springs serves to temporarily halt the indicator, accumulating energy until it is time to release it all at once to advance to the next increment. The jumping display is generally used for units lasting a significant amount of time, such as the hour or the date. It requires excellent control over energy, especially when several mechanisms of this type must spring into action at the same time.

Retrograde Displays

Retrograde displays are very fashionable at the moment, and their use is no longer limited to the minute and the date, instead spreading to indications such as the hour, seconds, day, chronograph counter, second time zone and other functions. The balletic movement of a hand springing back to its initial position often lends retrograde timepieces a highly spectacular appearance—especially when the dial combines two, three or even four of these indications, or when the watchmakers have a little fun by complicating the display even further. Another popular trend opens up the heart of the mechanism, allowing the wearer to peek "backstage."

Van Cleef & Arpels
Le Pont des Amoureux

Van Cleef & Arpels poetically reinvents the retrograde display on its model Le Pont des Amoureux, with a young woman's parasol marking the hours to the left, and her suitor's rose ticking off the minutes at right. The young lovers kiss twice a day during this continuous waltz.

A. Lange & Söhne, *Lange 1 Daymatic*

Equipped with a large date and an off-center hours/minutes subdial—two specialties of the German brand A. Lange & Söhne—the Lange 1 Daymatic displays the day using a retrograde hand that swings from 9 to 11 o'clock.

Pierre Kunz, *Seconde Virevoltante Rétrograde*

On its Seconde Virevoltante Rétrograde, Pierre Kunz offers an amazing show of aerial acrobatics with a hand dipping and swooping around a 470° loop before returning to its initial position in 5/100ths of a second and starting all over again.

Pierre Kunz, *Vertigo*

On the Vertigo from Pierre Kunz, the retrograde hour hand rises vertically, like the mercury in a thermometer, before swiftly plunging back down once it reaches 12 o'clock.

Longines
The Master Collection Retrograde Moon Phases

Equipped with an exclusive new movement, The Master Collection Retrograde Moon Phases from Longines reveals no fewer than four retrograde displays—seconds, day, date, 24-hour second time zone—on a barleycorn guilloché dial.

Cuervo y Sobrinos, *Historiador Retrogrado*

On its Historiador Retrogrado model, the Cuban-Swiss brand Cuervo y Sobrinos offers an elegant Clous de Paris guilloché dial, with retrograde day at 9 o'clock and retrograde date at 3 o'clock.

Milus, *Tirion Triretrograde Minute Repeater*

The Tirion Triretrograde Minute Repeater by Milus features a retrograde seconds display based on three 20-second segments. The first hand moves across its arc of a circle before moving instantly back to its starting point, while the second hand takes over, and then passes the baton on to the third.

Atlantic, *Seaport Day Retrograde*

The new Seaport Day Retrograde from Atlantic displays the day with a hand that traverses an arc between 8 and 12 o'clock—completed by a double aperture for the large date at 1 o'clock and an oversized seconds subdial at 6 o'clock.

Jean d'Eve, *Sectora II Automatic*

The Sectora II Automatic from Jean d'Eve displays the hour and minute across a 120° arc, housed in an asymmetrical case with a highly original shape.

Thomas Prescher, *Tempus Vivendi*

Interpreted in several versions (eagles, dragons, samurais, etc.), the Tempus Vivendi from Thomas Prescher sends the hour and minute hands across two fan-shaped counters on either side of the dial.

Pierre DeRoche
GrandCliff Double Retrograde Skyscrapers

Inspired by ever more daring, ever more vertiginous skyscrapers, Pierre DeRoche created the GrandCliff Double Retrograde Skyscrapers, with two vertical retrograde displays for the hours and the minutes.

Pierre DeRoche
GrandCliff Milady Royal Retro

On the GrandCliff Milady Royal Retro from Pierre DeRoche, equipped with an exclusive Dubois Dépraz mechanism, the seconds are indicated via a succession of six retrograde displays activated via a system of gears and springs that is visible on the dial.

Vacheron Constantin
Patrimony Contemporaine day-date bi-retrograde

The highly original Patrimony Contemporaine day-date bi-retrograde from Vacheron Constantin indicates the date on an arc from 9 to 3 o'clock, which is echoed by a second segment for the day from 7 to 5 o'clock.

Maurice Lacroix
Masterpiece Double Retrograde Limited Edition

The Masterpiece Double Retrograde Limited Edition from Maurice Lacroix offers retrograde displays for the date and the 24-hour second time zone. It is powered by an in-house automatic-winding movement.

Retrograde/Jumping Combinations

The jumping hour is often partnered with a retrograde minute, or other similar indications. This offers a fascinating spectacle on the hour and at midnight, when the numerals jump in their apertures and the hands leap to their starting position.

Hautlence, *HL2.0*

The new automatic HL2.0 models from Hautlence associate a retrograde minute with a semi-dragging jumping hour that consists of a 12-link chain and a crank-connecting rod system. Each hour, the movement of the chain leads to a 60° rotation of the baguette movement, which compensates for the effects of gravity on the regulating organ.

Bulgari

Octo Chronograph Quadri-Retro

A true animated ballet, the Octo Chronograph Quadri-Retro, from Bulgari, associates a jumping hour aperture with four retrograde indications: central minute, date at 6 o'clock and chronograph hour and minute counters at 3 and 9 o'clock, respectively.

MB&F, *Horological Machine N° 2*

The Horological Machine N° 2 by MB&F stands out for its resolutely original two-dial look. The right-hand dial displays jumping hours and concentric retrograde minutes, while the left-hand provides retrograde date as well as twin-hemisphere moonphase displays.

Jumping Displays

In jumping displays, the indication is provided by a disc on which are written numerals that "jump" by one increment at each change—as the date does on instantaneous calendars. This system is most often used for the hour display. However, horologers are increasingly intrigued by "digital" jumping indications, which they also use for other units (minutes or seconds), often revealing the discs upon the dials.

Cartier, *Rotonde de Cartier Jumping Hours*

A watch without hands, the Rotonde de Cartier Jumping Hours associates an aperture with jumping hours at 12 o'clock with a dragging minutes system equipped with a rotating disc. The hours are displayed in Roman or Arabic numerals.

Hysek, *IO Jumping Hour*

Outfitted with an exclusive movement and an atypical look, the IO Jumping Hour from Hysek presents a multi-level dial with jumping hours and dragging minutes displayed on a disc and day/night indicator.

De Bethune, *Digitale*

The Digitale from De Bethune presents an entirely disc-based display, with an upper aperture for day, date and month, one in the center for the minutes and an aperture in the lower half of the dial for the hours.

A. Lange & Söhne, *Lange Zeitwerk Luminous*

The Lange Zeitwerk Luminous from A. Lange & Söhne associates traditional and digital displays, with a jumping hour on a double disc at 9 o'clock, jumping minutes at 3 o'clock and two counters with conventional hands for the small seconds and power reserve.

RSW, *Outland*

On Outland from the brand RSW, the traditional hands make way for three concentric discs (hours, minutes and seconds) that move around a fixed point.

Vincent Calabrese, *Baladin*

Vincent Calabrese, on his Baladin, proposes an unusual way of reading the time by displaying the jumping hour in a small round window that marks off the minutes by rotating around the dial.

Harry Winston, *Opus 3*

For the Opus 3 by Harry Winston, Vianney Halter created an all-digital display with jumping hours, minutes, seconds and date appearing in six separate "portholes," and ten independently rotating discs driven by two mechanisms totaling 250 parts.

Audemars Piguet
Jules Audemars Jumping Hour Minute Repeater

On the Jules Audemars Minute Repeater with Jumping Hours from Audemars Piguet, the hour appears in a bisected aperture at 12 o'clock, while the minute holds court by itself at the center of the dial.

F.P. Journe, *Vagabondage II*

On the Vagabondage II from F. P. Journe, the only indication with a hand is the small seconds counter at 6 o'clock. Three discs appearing through a mostly openworked dial indicate the hours (at 12 o'clock) and the minutes (in the center) in two bisected apertures.

New Displays

Over the last few years, we have seen an explosion in the number of watches that revolutionize the indication of time, as well as its read-off. Whether three-dimensional, linear, pivoting, retractable or satellite systems, these alternative displays have become a favored field of exploration for young, creative watchmakers—who occasionally work behind the scenes with the biggest names in the industry. Though they do not always promise ease of reading, they are proof of a stunning ingenuity, served by unparalleled technical mastery.

Louis Vuitton, *Tambour Spin Time GMT*

The Tambour Spin Time GMT by Louis Vuitton marks the hours using 12 rotating rods arranged in a star shape, each tipped with a small cube. Every time the minutes move from 59 to 00, one of the cubes pivots to reveal the following hour, while the cube displaying the previous hour also makes a quarter-turn to reveal its neutral face.

de Grisogono, *Meccanico dG*

The Meccanico dG dual time zone watch by de Grisogono combines an analog display of the first time zone with a digital display of the second, with both driven by a completely mechanical movement comprising 651 parts. The digital second time zone indication, which is reminiscent of old airport display panels, is composed of mobile micro-segments driven by a set of 23 cams.

MCT, *Sequential One All Black*

The Sequential One by MCT puts on a fantastic show. The hour appears in turn in one of the four display zones on the dial by means of an original system of triangular prisms closely resembling animated advertising panels. The minutes appear over a 270° arc, and at each change of hour, the mobile minute ring makes a one-quarter turn to the left to reveal the following hour.

Pierre Kunz, *Infinity Looping*

On its Infinity Looping model, the Genevan watchmaker Pierre Kunz invented a spectacular new way of reading the time. Thanks to the gravitation of a satellite pinion that moves around a fixed rack, the hours and minutes whirl around the dial, tracing a rosette shape.

Harry Winston, *Opus 7*

For Harry Winston, in the Opus 7, the watchmaker Andreas Strehler created an "alternating display." A first press on the crown guard turns the disc to bring the correct figure opposite the marker at 10 o'clock, a second press displays the minutes, and a third the power reserve.

Harry Winston, *Opus 8*

For the Opus 8 by Harry Winston, Frédéric Garinaud devised a system of digital hours and minutes display inspired by pin art games. Activating a bolt on the side of the case causes the digits corresponding to the time to "rise up" from the dial, while the minutes are marked off on a vertical scale.

Harry Winston, *Opus 9*

The Opus 9 by Harry Winston, developed by design engineer Eric Giroud and watchmaker Jean-Marc Wiederrecht, features a linear display of the hours and minutes by means of two small brass chains set with emerald-cut diamonds, along with vivid mandarin garnets serving as hour markers.

Harry Winston, *Opus 11*

Harry Winston's Opus 11, created by Dennis Giguet, has no hands at all. Every 60 minutes, the large central numeral for the hour explodes into chaos before being reconstituted in a fraction of a second, using 24 mobile "pallets."

Bulgari, *Papillon Chronographe*

On the Bulgari Papillon Chronograph the minutes are displayed by an ingenious central device that completes a 360° rotation in two hours and boasts two independent pivoting hands that take turns traversing a 180° segment that marks 0 to 60 seconds.

Cyrus, *Klepcys*

Created by the watchmaker Jean-François Mojon, the movement of the Klepcys—the inaugural timepiece of the new company Cyrus—displays the hour using a retrograde hand mounted upon two rotating cubes that indicate the day and night. The minutes and seconds are read off on two central discs, and the date is indicated by a retrograde hand with a three-dimensional rotating tens column.

Urwerk, *UR-201*

On the highly futuristic UR-201 from Urwerk, the time is read off on three satellites spinning around a central carrousel. Each satellite rotates once every 12 hours, successively revealing its four sides ((1-4-7-10 / 2-5-8-11 / 3-6-9-12). The three satellites carry tiny telescopic hands that extend or retract to follow the minutes scale appearing along the bottom of the dial.

Urwerk, *UR-103T Mexican Fireleg*

Urwerk—star of planetary devices—continues to innovate with its UR-103T Mexican Fireleg, an entirely black watch equipped with four satellites that replace the classic hour hand while also marking the minutes.

Urwerk, *UR-CC1 Black Cobra*

Inspired by the speedometers on certain 1950s cars, the UR-CC1 Black Cobra from Urwerk presents the linear display of the hours and minutes via two cylinders. Upon reaching the far end of its trajectory, the minute cylinder returns to its initial position in one tenth of a second, and this retrograde movement pushes the hour cylinder one unit forward.

Urwerk, *UR-110 Torpedo*

The new Urwerk UR-110 Torpedo stands out for its satellite display system, with three hour modules that act as minute hands and remain horizontal throughout their revolution.

Chanel, *J12 Rétrograde Mystérieuse*

The central minutes hand of Chanel's J12 Rétrograde Mystérieuse runs in a traditional manner for the first ten minutes, before bumping up against the retractable crown appearing on the dial at 3 o'clock. This sets off a retrograde motion that takes another ten minutes to bring the hand to the other side of the crown, on the 20th minute.

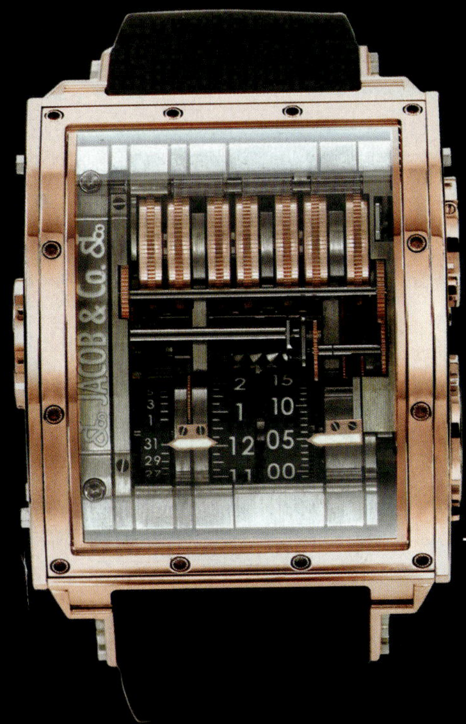

Jacob & Co., *Quenttin*

The imposing Quentiin from Jacob & Co. possesses no fewer than seven barrels—visible through the crystal—that ensure a power reserve of one month. The hour, minute and power reserve can be read off on vertical discs assembled on the same axis.

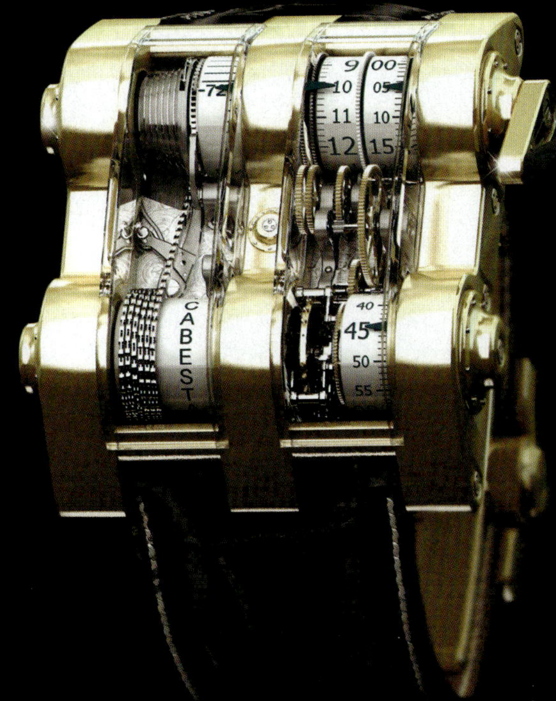

Vianney Halter and DMC
Cabestan

The Cabestan from Vianney Halter and DMC is wound using a movable crank. The displays for hour, minute and power reserve are shown using engraved rotating drums.

Christophe Claret, *DualTow*

On his DualTow watch (with tourbillon and single-pusher chronograph) Christophe Claret presents an hour and minute display by notched rubber belts inspired by caterpillar-track vehicles.

Jean Dunand, *Palace*

For Jean Dunand's Palace model, Christophe Claret designed a flying tourbillon caliber with a second time zone and power reserve indication, situated in two vertical cartridges traversed by two ovals with arrows on them.

A. LANGE & SÖHNE

LANGE ZEITWERK – REF. 140.025

The Lange Zeitwerk is powered by the manual-winding Lange proprietary L043.1 caliber, which contains 388 components and 68 jewels. Decorated and assembled by hand, the movement beats at 18,000 vph and possesses a precision beat-adjustment system with lateral setscrew and whiplash spring. The dark tinted sapphire crystal glass has a special UV-transparent PVD coating that permits light to enter and charge the numerals with enough photonic energy to reliably emit the time for several hours during the night. The case is platinum and the series is limited to 100 pieces.

AUDEMARS PIGUET

JULES AUDEMARS SKELETON MINUTE REPEATER WITH JUMPING HOUR AND SMALL SECONDS

REF. 26356PT.OO.D028CR.01

Housed in a 950 platinum case fitted with a sapphire caseback and an opaline openworked dial with black printed numerals and a skeleton jumping hour disc, this Jules Audemars model marries two great horological specialties: the minute repeater and the jumping hour. This marvel of precision and harmony extends Audemars Piguet's savoir-faire in the realm of complicated watches. With its classically reinvented case and dial, the watch is a fresh addition to the Jules Audemars collection.

BVLGARI

GEFICA BI-RETRO – REF. BGF47BBLDBR

The Gefica Bi-Retro features retrograde minutes and date displays, as well as a jumping hour positioned at 12:00. The 46mm case is crafted in sand-blasted bronze and satin-finished titanium, providing a sturdy and chic home for the automatic-winding Calibre GG 1004 within, which beats at 28,800 vph and provides a 45-hour power reserve. Its black dial matches the black alligator strap, which bears a three-blade titanium folding buckle.

BVLGARI

OCTO BI-RETRO – REF. BGO43BSCVDBR

This decidedly sporty model houses a sophisticated movement powering a jumping date window, as well as retrograde minute and date indications via superimposed hands. The Octo Bi-Retro is driven by in-house made Calibre GG 7722, an automatic-winding movement that beats at 28,800 vph. The jumping hour, visible through a wide aperture at 12:00, is a perfect match for the retrograde minute indication provided by a hand running over a 210° arc featuring a graduated scale divided into 10-minute zones. The date can be read off a 180° segment at the bottom of the dial. The Octo Bi-Retro is housed in a 43mm steel case with a black ceramic bezel and sapphire crystal caseback.

BVLGARI

OCTO CHRONOGRAPHE QUADRI-RETRO – REF. BGOP45BGLDCHQR

The Calibre GG 7800 driving the Octo Chronographe Quadri-Retro features four retrograde functions—minutes, date, chronograph hour and seconds counters—along with jumping hours through a window at 12:00 and a large chronograph seconds hand appearing at 6:00. This choice ensures that the hour indication is never hidden from sight. The traditionally built column-wheel movement is treated to impeccable finishing and is housed within an imposing 45mm case. The two chronograph pushers at 2:00 and 4:00, respectively controlling the stop/start functions and reset function, are perfectly integrated within the case middle. The well-structured visual composition of the dial combines a jet black lacquered surface, silvered segments and white arcs with a minute track at 12:00 and date at 6:00, as well as chronograph and minute counters at 9:00 and 12:00.

CHANEL

J12 RETROGRADE MYSTERIEUSE – WHITE CERAMIC

When technical prowess compliments the aesthetics
CHANEL RMT-10 Calibre

- R for Retrograde
- M for Mysterious
- T for Tourbillon

After introducing the first tourbillon featuring a highly innovative high-tech ceramic bottom-plate, CHANEL confirmed its status as a pioneer of contemporary watchmaking by creating the J12 Rétrograde Mystérieuse. The Rétrograde Mystérieuse is a concentrated dose of innovation, bringing together complications and world première:

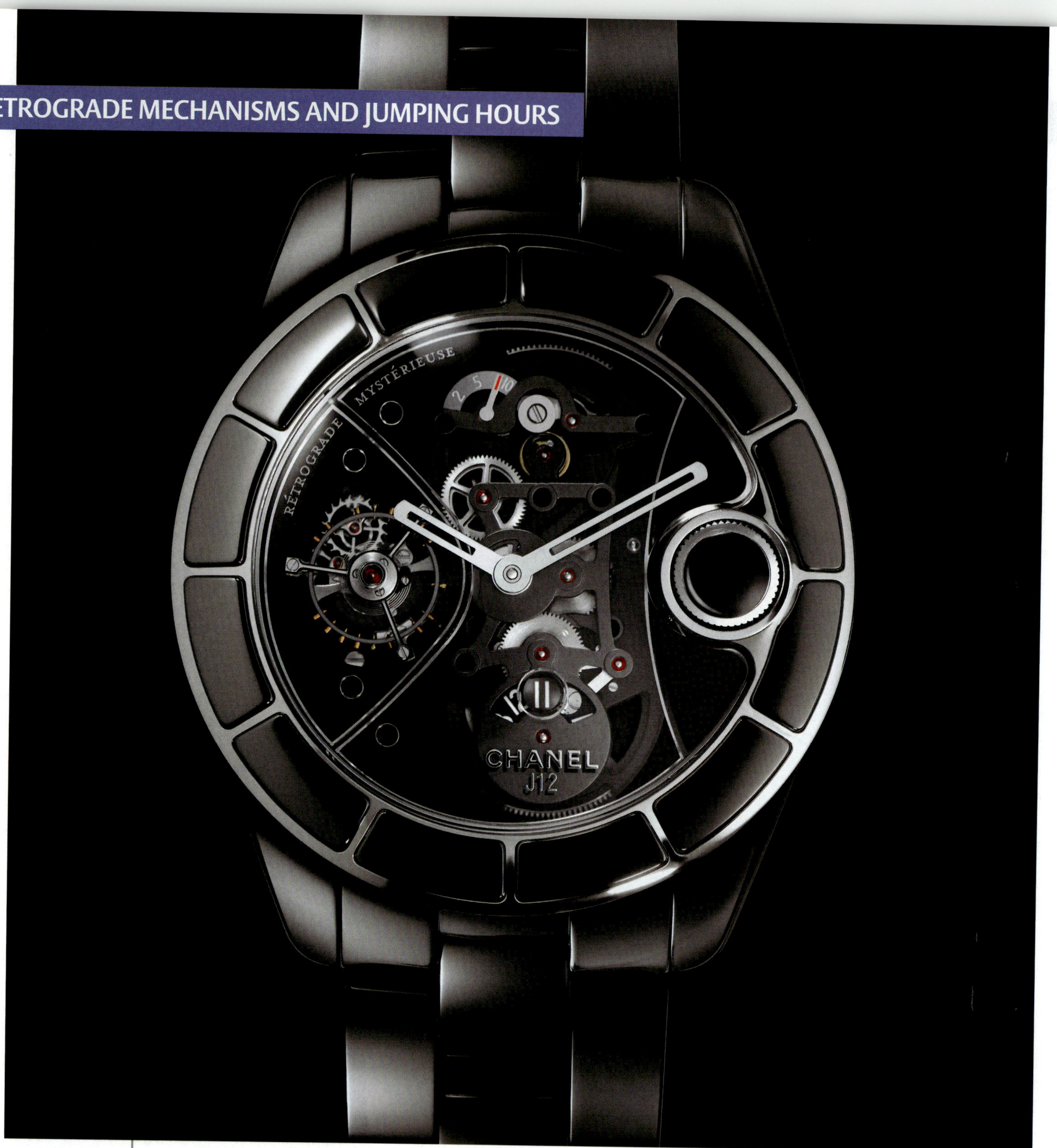

CHANEL

J12 RETROGRADE MYSTERIEUSE – BLACK CERAMIC

1. A tourbillon
2. A digital minutes display
3. A retrograde minutes hand
4. A 10-day power reserve
5. A retractable vertical crown

This perfectly round watch with a 47mm diameter has been designed without a side crown to ensure optimum comfort on the wrist. The work on this complication was entrusted to one of the most "state-of-the-art" watchmaking design/construction workshops: the Giulio Papi team (APRP SA).

Limited and numbered edition of ten pieces in black high-tech ceramic and 18K white gold or ten pieces in black high-tech ceramic and 18K pink gold. The white high-tech ceramic edition is a unique piece.

HUBLOT

KEY OF TIME – REF. 902.ND.1140.RX

With this extremely imaginative timepiece, Hublot surrenders the notion of time to the owner's governance. A tri-positional crown permits a variable rate of motion, whereby each chosen setting offers a unique interpretation of the pace at which time passes. Position 1 presents time slowed by four, thus representing one hour as a quarter thereof on the watch's display. Position 2 offers a conventional perception, or "real time," while in position 3, an accelerated hand transforms 15 minutes into the visual illusion of a full hour. While the complex mechanism can be kept indefinitely in the altered modes, a simple return to the second position lets the wearer admire the hands readjust to a conventional time display. The demonstration of seconds via a vertical flying tourbillon cage adds a veritable third dimension to this time traveler of haute horology.

PIAGET

PIAGET EMPERADOR – REF. G0A33072

The large size of this Piaget Emperador model particularly accentuates the design of the rectangular case with its subtle blend of straight lines and curves. The warm shade of the 18K white gold further enhances its aura of harmony and strength. The silver-colored dial provides a highly contemporary reinterpretation of classicism by combining a sunburst guilloché motif with slender baton-shaped applied hour markers and the historical Piaget coat-of-arms in white gold. Beneath this supremely distinguished face lies a self-winding Manufacture-made Calibre 560P with large date display at 6:00 and retrograde seconds at 12:00—the flagship movement within the new Piaget collection of ultra-thin mechanisms.

PIAGET

PIAGET EMPERADOR COUSSIN PERPETUAL CALENDAR IN WHITE GOLD – REF. G0A33018

This watch is equipped with a Piaget Calibre 855P self-winding movement, designed, developed and produced entirely in-house. It displays the hours, minutes, small seconds at 4:00 and months and leap years at 12:00, along with retrograde day of the week and date displays at 9:00 and 3:00 respectively. The case middle actually carries a mention of the function of each of the four correctors for the month, date, day of the week and second time zone. Subtly alternating polished and satin-brushed surfaces on the case middle, bezel and inner bezel ring, the case of the Piaget Emperador Coussin Perpetual Calendar is fitted with a sapphire crystal caseback that provides admirable views of the movement finishings.

PIAGET

PIAGET EMPERADOR COUSSIN REGULATOR – REF. G0A34024

This Piaget Emperador Coussin Regulator is driven by the Calibre 835P, an ultra-thin mechanical handwound movement measuring 3.92mm thick. This caliber is equipped with a large balance with screws and a large barrel providing a power reserve of around 60 hours. Like all movements by the Manufacture, the Calibre 835P is graced with extremely meticulous finishes. The mainplate is circular-grained and bridges are beveled, while the decorative elements such as circular Côtes de Genève and blued screws are in line with the brand's aesthetic codes. Its case measures 42.5mm in diameter and is fitted with a sapphire crystal caseback. A finely satin-brushed charcoal gray dial is guilloché-worked at 12:00 for the retrograde seconds.

PIAGET

PIAGET RECTANGLE A L'ANCIENNE – REF. G0A33061

This powerful and extremely masculine watch, with its oversized white-gold case housing a 561P movement driving the retrograde seconds and power reserve displays, is intended for men with a taste for distinctive design and fine watchmaking. This model is equipped with an ultra-thin mechanical hand-wound movement endowed with superlative finishing including circular Côtes de Genève, a circular-grained mainplate, beveled and hand-drawn bridges, as well as blued screws. Piaget thereby confirms its longstanding tradition and undeniable know-how in the field of exceptional haute horology.

ROGER DUBUIS

EXCALIBUR BI-RETROGRADE JUMPING DATE – REF. EX45-14B-20-00/01R00/B

This bi-retrograde timepiece offers automatic winding and a 48-hour power reserve. Finely adjusted to five positions, this Excalibur is powered by the RD 14B movement and housed in a 45mm white-gold case. The bi-retrograde jumping date is situated at the center, and the date corrector is at 2:00. The fully adjustable, hand-stitched alligator strap is outfitted with a white-gold adjustable buckle. The Excalibur Bi-Retrograde Jumping Date is part of a limited edition of 88 pieces.

VACHERON CONSTANTIN

PATRIMONY CONTEMPORAINE RETROGRADE DAY AND DATE – REF. 86020/000R-9239

Powered by the mechanical automatic-winding Vacheron Constantin Caliber 2460 R31 R7, this Patrimony Bi-Retrograde is hallmarked with the Geneva Seal. Beating at 28,800 vph and offering 43 hours of power reserve, the 27-jeweled movement is equipped with a guilloché rotor. Retrograde day is provided at 6:00 and retrograde date is shown at 12:00. The three-piece case is polished and water resistant to 3atm. The sapphire caseback reveals the exquisite movement.

VACHERON CONSTANTIN

PATRIMONY CONTEMPORAINE RETROGRADE DAY AND DATE – REF. 86020/000R-9239

In this 18K pink-gold timepiece, the noble hue of the case, indexes, and hour and minute hands plays a clever game with the resolute modernity of the bi-retrograde design. Via two semicircles, the automatic 2460 R31 R7 caliber, beating at 28,800 vph, dictates the date and day of the week in a borderless manner that seems to float freely on the dial. The Patrimony Contemporaine Retrograde Day and Date displays the oscillating weight and inner workings of its Geneva Seal-certified movement through an open caseback.

VACHERON CONSTANTIN

QUAI DE L'ILE RETROGRADE ANNUAL CALENDAR – REF. 86040/000G-M936R

Due to its sophisticated annual calendar movement, this 18K white-gold timepiece requires only one correction per year, addressing the irregular length of the infamous second month. Upon the satin-brushed vertical finishing dial, the retrograde date makes its presence known as it assertively ruptures the opaline chapter ring just below 2:00. Completing the calendar, the 2460 QRA self-winding caliber, endowed with an oscillation frequency of 28,800 vph and 40-hour power reserve, additionally drives a month indicator at 6:30 and comprehensive moonphase with small seconds at 9:00.

Equations of Time

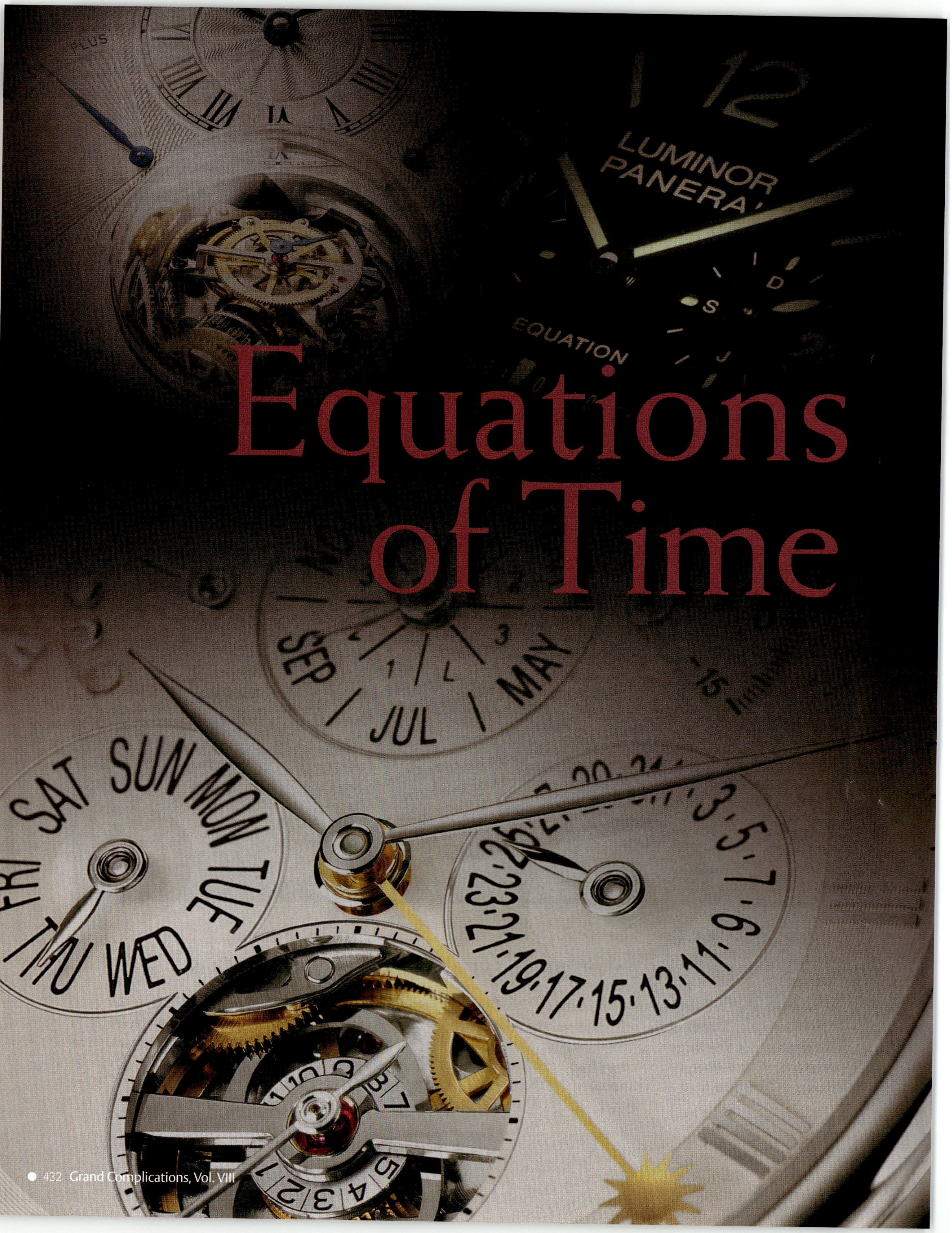

The 2004 appearance of the first wristwatches with "running" equation of time, i.e. watches that simultaneously display true solar time and mean solar time, let us believe for a moment in the triumphant return of the equation of time. However, we must admit that, aside from a few models that can be counted on both hands, this astronomical function is still reserved for ultra-complicated timepieces. It is certainly true that the display of the difference between conventional time (what we see on our watches) and astronomic time (what we would see on a sundial) is not the most useful one in our day-to-day life. But it does bring a note of poetry to the dial, reminding us that our first clock was the sun, and thereby renewing our immemorial bond with Mother Nature...

Jean-Frédéric Dufour

President and CEO of Zenith

"The new Christophe Colomb will be even more precise!"

The 2010 launch of the Academy Christophe Colomb model was a sensation in the watch world. Equipped with a gyroscopic mechanism that maintains the regulating organ in a horizontal position, the timepiece is based on the principles of marine chronometers. The now completed 75-piece series made way in 2011 for the Christophe Colomb Equation of Time model. The 2012 model concentrates even more intensely on precision by featuring constant torque.

Now in his mid-forties—he was born on December 3, 1967—Jean-Frédéric Dufour certainly enjoys being active on multiple fronts. He has just finished redeveloping the brand's collections and is now taking on the complete renovation of Zenith's factories and workshops. This dynamism reflects that of his career as a whole, which began in 1992 at Chopard, where he set up the L.U.C movement manufacturing facility in Fleurier in 1997. A year later, by then director of the site, he left Chopard for Ulysse Nardin. A new change came in 2000 when he joined the Swatch Group, where, under the supervision of a certain Jean-Claude Biver (then CEO of Blancpain), he was put in charge of founding the brand Léon Hatot. However, he was soon called upon to act as Biver's second-in-command at Blancpain, before returning to Chopard's team as director of product development, where he served until 2009 when he was recruited to be the president and CEO of Zenith.

You have held this position since June of 2009. How would you sum up these almost three years at Zenith? What is left to do?

The collections have reached maturity in 2012, with 130 models that represent about 15 lines. We are leaders in the field of ultra-precise high-frequency chronographs, and we plan to keep it that way. This has led to double-digit growth for us, and we are moving in the right direction. Meanwhile, with 146 years of existence behind us, we have undertaken an important renovation program in our factories, in order to move on to the next stage.

What is that next stage?

Today, our ateliers are spread out over 19 different buildings—a real labyrinth. We've decided to renovate the historic buildings at the Zenith site in Le Locle, those built between 1898 and 1905, and to demolish more recent ones that hold no architectural interest. You must understand that Zenith is one of the last watch manufacturers still in its original location. It is extremely important for the continuity of the Swiss horological heritage.

ACADEMY CHRISTOPHE COLOMB
EQUATION OF TIME

Are you also investing in new machines?
Yes, of course—in Swiss machines. The total investment is 20 million Swiss francs.

When will all this be ready?
We are planning to move in the summer of 2012.

Is the goal to produce more watches than the 30,000 Zenith currently makes?
No, we only make as many as we need, even though we have enjoyed swift success—indeed much faster than we had anticipated! Our goal is to be better organized to optimize our work.

You say you are the leader in high-frequency chronographs. To prove your point, at BaselWorld 2011, you presented an impressive prototype beating at 50Hz (360,000 vibrations per hour), whereas most mechanical movements beat at 3 or 4 Hz. Where are you currently with this prototype?
Research is ongoing, but it's like high-wire acrobatics. We're using silicon and the project is extremely complex, but represents an excellent exercise for making progress within our teams.

Will this watch come out as a series?
This watch is highly specialized. You wouldn't take a Formula 1 racecar to go buy bread... If we do have a series, it will be limited to 100 pieces. Think about it: the fully wound mainspring boasts a massive 4.8 kg torque, compared with just 800g in our star El Primero movement. That gives you a good idea of the challenges involved.

How do you see the future of watchmaking?
In the mid-1980s, a huge change swept over horology: the watch went from being an object of necessity to an object that fulfilled an emotional need. The watch companies that were able to successfully negotiate this paradigm shift are still around; the others are gone. Today, the mechanical watch is halfway between a work of art and an industrial object. It's not a painting, but it's not a car, either. If you can create an emotion, if you can transform a watch into a vector for dreaming, the future belongs to you.

How does that translate at the product level?
That depends on fashion and trends. Over the last few years, we have returned to a neo-classicalism, to tried and true values... But anyone who can predict the future is very clever indeed.

Several brands have made substantial investments in R&D, with silicon, for example, but also in the field of magnetism in relation with the escapement. Does the future belong to sweeping innovations?
Magnets spark our dreams, and they effectively showcase the capabilities of the brands that work with them. But it's not what I would call a real breakthrough, because the problems are so numerous.

What would you call a real breakthrough?

Silicon is one. But I have the feeling that the future is in playing around with the functions. Our new Captain Windsor, for example, features an ingenious annual calendar that needs adjustment just once per year. That is a real asset for horology!

In 2010, you presented the superb Academy Christophe Colomb. The series was limited to just 75 models—25 in rose gold, 25 in white gold and 25 in yellow gold—and each watch cost 210,000 Swiss francs (about $210,000). Were they all sold?

Yes, that series is over. We have a new model—the Academy Christophe Colomb Equation of Time—and another Christophe Colomb with constant torque that will feature another technical innovation.

Zenith's collections include another tourbillon, the El Primero Tourbillon model. Will you be releasing another version soon?

We have some new dials, but no new variations as such.

What does the El Primero Tourbillon represent for a brand such as yours?

Quite simply, it is the only chronograph with tourbillon and date on the market! No other brand has introduced this combination, so it remains exclusive to Zenith. Throw in the fact that it beats at 36,000 vibrations per hour, and you have a unique model.

What new products does Zenith intend to roll out for the coming year?

We will be focusing our efforts on aviation watches. The "Pilot" brand belongs to us; it is one of the three oldest in aeronautical history. We have discovered that the pioneering aviator Louis Blériot owned a Zenith altimeter and a Zenith watch. We have been present throughout the development of aviation, through to equipping Italian fighter pilots in the 1970s and French fighter pilots in 1997. We are therefore preparing a small Zenith Pilot collection.

After Moscow, Dubai, Shanghai, Wuhan and Beijing, you recently opened a new boutique in Hong Kong. Where will the next one be?

In Geneva, on Rue du Rhône. Then Sao Paulo. We plan to open three or four boutiques per year.

Is this the end of multi-brand retail stores?

No, we need them. But we also need passionate devotees, people who will fight for us, people who are selling art. Not just merchants who won't lift a finger except to wrap up the product and open the cash register.

How are the various markets evolving?

Asia is very much the driving force, but you already knew that...

In Asia, what could be the next big thing after China? We're hearing more and more about Vietnam...

Myanmar also has a lot of potential. There are still lots of virgin territories. But one thing is certain: it is the commodity-producing countries that will experience the strongest growth in the next few years.

Such as?

Russia, the Middle East and South America.

EL PRIMERO TOURBILLON

Equations of Time

Blancpain,
Villeret Running Equation

There are actually two times:

true solar time and mean solar time. True solar time, which you might see on a sundial, corresponds to natural rhythms. The Earth describes an ellipse in turning around the sun, and its axis is inclined in relation to its orbit. This means that the lapse of time between two passages of the sun through its highest point in the sky (noon) is not the same length year-round. It actually lasts 24 hours only four times a year: on April 15th, June 14th, September 1st and December 24th. Otherwise, it is sometimes longer and sometimes shorter, following an immutable curve. This difference ranges from 16 minutes and 23 seconds, on November 4th, to 12 minutes and 22 seconds, on February 11th and is called the "equation of time." As for mean solar time (also called civil time), it is a convention based on the average of all days in a year. The greatest watchmakers have rivaled each other in ingenuity to develop systems that reproduce the variations in the equation of time. This function has become an indispensable feature of all ultra-complicated watches—particularly the astronomical ones—but it is much more rare to find it flying solo. In 2004, the "running" equation of time (see "How does it work?"), long reserved for pocket watches, made its wristwatch debut.

TECHNIQUE

HOW DOES IT WORK?

Since the variable lengths of true solar days are identically repeated on the same days, they can be "programmed" by means of a so-called "equation" cam that performs one full rotation per year. Its profile resembles that of an "analemma," representing the figure eight traced in the sky by the sun's various positions as recorded each day at the same time and from the same place throughout the calendar year. The extreme precision of this shape determines the accuracy of the equation of time.

DISPLAY METHODS

The equation of time display may be presented in various ways. Most watches are equipped with a subdial or auxiliary segment swept over by a hand running from -16 to + 14 minutes (sometimes from -15 to +15); to know true time, the user must then do a mental addition or subtraction of this difference in relation to mean time.

RUNNING EQUATIONS

Distinctly more user-friendly yet far more complex in terms of their construction, "running" equation of time watches have two hands fitted coaxially with the minute hand, respectively indicating mean time and true time. They are equipped with a sensor system that searches out the information from the cam, as well as a differential that corrects the running of the supplementary minute hand. They require no mental arithmetic, since true time is continuously displayed directly on the dial.

A Very Rare Complication

Extremely rare as a solo complication, the equation of time is most often joined by a perpetual calendar, even an annual calendar, or with astronomical indications. It is usually displayed on a small fan-shaped segment covered by a hand, but certain watchmakers prefer to innovate by spotlighting the complication with a central hand or opting for a linear indication.

Zenith,
Academy Christophe Colomb Equation of Time
Equipped with an escapement that maintains a horizontal position, whatever the position of the watch—as with the gimbals used in maritime navigation—the new Academy Christophe Colomb Equation of Time from Zenith displays the equation of time across a fan-shaped segment at 9 o'clock.

Breguet,
Classique Complications

On its finely guilloché dial, this grand complication watch from Breguet's Classique collection combines a perpetual calendar, power reserve display and an equation of time indication in a fan shape at 1:30.

Girard-Perregaux
1945 Vintage Perpetual Calendar and Equation of Time

Housed in a rectangular Art Deco-inspired case, the 1945 Vintage Perpetual Calendar and Equation of Time from Girard-Perregaux has been released in a version with a perpetual calendar and an equation of time segment-type display appears in the upper left corner of the dial.

Girard-Perregaux
1966 Annual Calendar and Equation of Time

The 1966 Annual Calendar and Equation of Time by Girard-Perregaux is distinguished by its dial, on which an extremely original configuration features the date in a small subdial at 1:30, the small seconds at 9 o'clock, the month in a panoramic window at 7 o'clock and the equation of time on the arc of a circle at 4:30.

Panerai,
Luminor 1950 Equation of time Tourbillon Titanio 50 mm L'Astronomo

The most sophisticated ever developed by Panerai, the Luminor 1950 Equation of time Tourbillon Titanio 50 mm L'Astronomo provides an innovative linear display of the equation of time at 6 o'clock. It also indicates the times of sunrise and sunset for a reference city chosen by the client, and its caseback bears a depiction of the night sky as seen from that same city.

Chopard, *L.U.C 150 All-in-One*

Chopard uses the back of its anniversary model L.U.C 150 All-in-One as a second dial: it features a power reserve display, 24-hour night and day indication, sunrise and sunset times, an orbital moonphase and an equation of time—all set to correspond to what may be observed in Geneva.

Vacheron Constantin

Patrimony Traditionnelle Calibre 2253 Collection Excellence Platine

The Vacheron Constantin Patrimony Traditionnelle Calibre 2253 Collection Excellence Platine is endowed with a tourbillon movement powering indications of the perpetual calendar and times of sunrise and sunset, as well as the equation of time on the arc of a circle at 10:30.

Taking Longitude into Account

By convention, all the places situated in one time zone have the same time. But "true" solar noon varies by longitude, and it is distinctly earlier in Warsaw than in Madrid. Executing a correction of -16 to +14 minutes over an average applicable to the entire time zone (60 minutes) is therefore not of any great scientific interest, but innovative watchmakers are remedying this flaw with models that take into account the exact degree of longitude.

Audemars Piguet, *Royal Oak Equation of Time*

The first brand to have developed an equation of time indication system adjusted to the exact degree of longitude, Audemars Piguet equipped its Royal Oak Equation of Time with a large central hand for the complication's display. The inner bezel ring bears the name of the reference city chosen by the client, as well as the time of true noon in that city. When the hour hand corresponds to the hour indicated on the inner bezel ring, and the equation of time and minute hands line up exactly, the owner of the watch knows that the sun is exactly at its zenith. This is also one of the rare wristwatches to display sunrise and sunset times while taking into account three parameters: date, longitude and latitude.

Arnold & Son, *True North Perpetual*

The True North Perpetual watch from Arnold & Son takes account of longitude, thanks to a dial featuring two mobile rings. The model features another unprecedented characteristic: when the 24-hour solar hand indicates the true solar noon, the wearer need only point it towards the sun for the mobile outer dial to indicate true geographical North—hence its name.

Running Equations of Time

Distinctly more user-friendly yet far more complex in terms of their construction, "running" equation of time watches have two hands fitted coaxially with the minute hand, respectively indicating mean time and true time. They require no mental arithmetic, since true time is continuously displayed directly on the dial. This system, which had long been regarded as the exclusive preserve of pocket watches, first appeared on wristwatches in 2004 and represents a genuine feat in terms of miniaturization.

Jaeger-LeCoultre
Gyrotourbillon 1

The Gyrotourbillon 1 by Jaeger-LeCoultre, equipped with a spherical tourbillon (see chapter on Tourbillons), also features an offset hour/minute subdial bearing a running equation of time displayed by an additional minute hand adorned with a tiny golden sun.

Blancpain
Villeret Equation Marchante Pure

Blancpain has associated a running equation of time display and a perpetual calendar in a model from the Villeret collection named Equation Marchante Pure. A circular opening at 6 o'clock allows the wearer to contemplate the cam that governs the equation, as well as the sensor in action.

Blancpain, *Le Brassus Equation Marchante*

The Le Brassus Equation Marchante by Blancpain is distinguished by its double equation of time display: the running equation of time itself appears in the center with an additional central minute hand tipped with a golden sun; and a subdial at 2 o'clock boasts a retrograde hand indicating the number of minutes of difference. This sophisticated device is combined with an ultra-thin perpetual calendar.

AUDEMARS PIGUET

JULES AUDEMARS EQUATION OF TIME – REF. 26053PT.OO.D02CR.01

Powered by the manufacture's self-winding 2120/2808 skeleton caliber, this exceptional wristwatch expresses the equation of time with stunning legibility. Roman numeral sunrise and sunset dials, at 9:00 and 3:00, are automatically synchronized with the movement's perpetual calendar. Along with month, date, and day of the week, this timepiece distinctly indicates the equation of time with a third blued-steel hand, differentiated from the hour and minutes indicator by its wavy form and golden sun tip. Displaying the discrepancy in the length of the day, caused by the tilted axis of the earth's rotation, this calculation is located on the watch's bezel for optimal legibility without obstructing the intricate view of the watch's dials and interior.

AUDEMARS PIGUET

ROYAL OAK EQUATION OF TIME – REF. 26603ST.OO.D092CR.02

The Royal Oak Equation of Time is housed in a stainless steel case and powered by an automatic-winding 2120/2808 movement, which beats at 19,800 vph and is endowed with a 42-hour power reserve. Visible through the sapphire crystal caseback, the 41-jewel movement depicts conventional time and real solar time and offers hours and minutes, sunrise and sunset times, equation of time, perpetual calendar and moonphase. The solar zenith is calibrated to the reference city chosen by the owner. The openworked oscillating weight may be personalized on request (the standard version has the "AP" logo). Mounted on a large scale hand-sewn crocodile leather with AP folding clasp in stainless steel, this model is also available in 18K pink gold.

BLANCPAIN

VILLERET EQUATION MARCHANTE PURE – REF. 6038-3442-55B

The Equation Marchante Pure, based on the Le Brassus model that was the first wristwatch capable of displaying the separate solar and civil times by two minute hands, was launched in 2005 as part of the Villeret collection, characterized by its pure lines and formal beauty. This limited edition of 50 pieces is crafted in platinum and houses the 364-part caliber 3863A, equipped with 72 hours of power reserve.

BLANCPAIN

VILLERET RUNNING EQUATION OF TIME – REF. 6638-3431-55B

Bridging the gap between watchmaking and astronomy, the Villeret Equation of Time displays its spectacular innovations with absolute clarity. Fitted with a three-subdial perpetual calendar complete with a retrograde moonphase, this red-gold masterpiece delights with an aperture at 6:00, through which the owner is treated to the precise analemma-shaped equation of time cam. This astronomical complication is in fact where this timepiece earns its admirable virtue. Achieved through a sophisticated secondary mechanism of independent satellite gears, the movement provides two sources of rotation for the solar hand alone. Translating the retrograde equation of time indication into a visible revolving manifestation, the secondary blue hand, finished with a symbolic golden sun, joins the principal minute indicator in illustrating the true discrepancy between the time that we conveniently accept, and that which is defined by the earth's imperfect orbit.

JAEGER-LECOULTRE

HYBRIS MECHANICA GYROTOURBILLON 1 – REF. 600.34.30

In Jaeger-LeCoultre's 177 caliber, which powers the Hybris Mechanica Gyrotourbillon 1, the three-dimensional rotations of the balance-wheel are at the very heart of an extraordinary horological invention. The ultra-light outer carriage makes a complete turn about its axis every sixty seconds. The inner carriage rotates far more rapidly, completing 2.5 turns per minute. Beside the remarkable three-dimensional tourbillon, this timepiece also displays hours, minutes, perpetual date and month with retrograde displays. Far from being satisfied with these accomplishments, the master watchmakers also decided to add an equation of time, one of the most challenging of complications. For an extra challenge, the display is of a "running" equation of time, displaying civil time with thicker blue hands and true solar time with a thinner, star-tipped dial.

PANERAI

LUMINOR 1950 EQUATION OF TIME TOURBILLON TITANIO, 50MM – REF. PAM00365

Officine Panerai's approach to the most complicated of all grand complications, the equation of time, has set a new industry standard. The Luminor 1950 Equation of Time Tourbillon Titanio, also called L'Astronomo, is the ultimate tribute to the genius of Galileo Galilei and showcases some of the rarest, most exclusive and fascinating specialties in watchmaking. Completely customized for the owner, L'Astronomo showcases a tourbillon with equation of time functionality, sunrise/sunset times for the city chosen by the wearer, and depiction of the star map of the night sky for that locality on the back plate. All of these functions are powered by the hand-wound, 375-component Panerai P.2005/G caliber which also features a four-day power reserve and Panerai tourbillon regulator, and housed inside a 50mm titanium case which thanks to its patented crown protecting device is water resistant to 10 bar (100m). Produced in just 30 examples, it is the most technically sophisticated timepiece ever produced by Officine Panerai.

VACHERON CONSTANTIN

PATRIMONY TRADITIONNELLE CALIBRE 2253 – REF. 88172/000P-9495

A hand-stitched dark blue alligator strap with platinum threads traces the path to a truly astonishing spectacle. Limited to 10 numbered pieces, this 44mm 950 platinum timepiece houses a remarkable manually wound caliber honored with the Geneva Seal. While the perfectly finished tourbillon with small seconds at 6:00 completes its rotation in precisely one minute, the rest of the dial looks at time on a significantly grander scale. Set to the owner's reference city of choice, the sunrise and sunset indicators surround the exposed carriage on either side. On the upper half of the watch face, the perpetual calendar, complete with day of the week, month, date, and leap-year indicator, is joined by the equation of time between 10:00 and 11:00. Merging the tourbillon's symbolism of horological history with a wealth of highly sophisticated functions, the Patrimony Traditionnelle Calibre 2253 makes a magnificent statement regarding the grandeur of time.

ZENITH

ACADEMY CHRISTOPHE COLOMB EQUATION OF TIME – REF. 18.2220.8808/01.C631

Presented as a 75-piece limited edition, this tribute to horology's rich navigational heritage is as much a feat of ingenious technical mastery as a bold exploit of design architecture. Beneath the spectacular dome at 6:00, the owner is treated to a 167-component self-regulating gyroscopic module that ensures the organ's perfect horizontal positioning. Further adorning the handmade silver rounded barleycorn guilloché dial, two retrograde counters at 3:00 and 9:00 indicate the power reserve and equation of time, respectively. Completing this 18K rose-gold 45mm masterpiece's stunning multi-dimensional geometry, two blued-steel hour and minute hands at 12:00 are steered across a black lacquered Roman numeral circumference at a spectacular oscillating rate of 36,000 vph.

Minute Repeaters and Sonneries

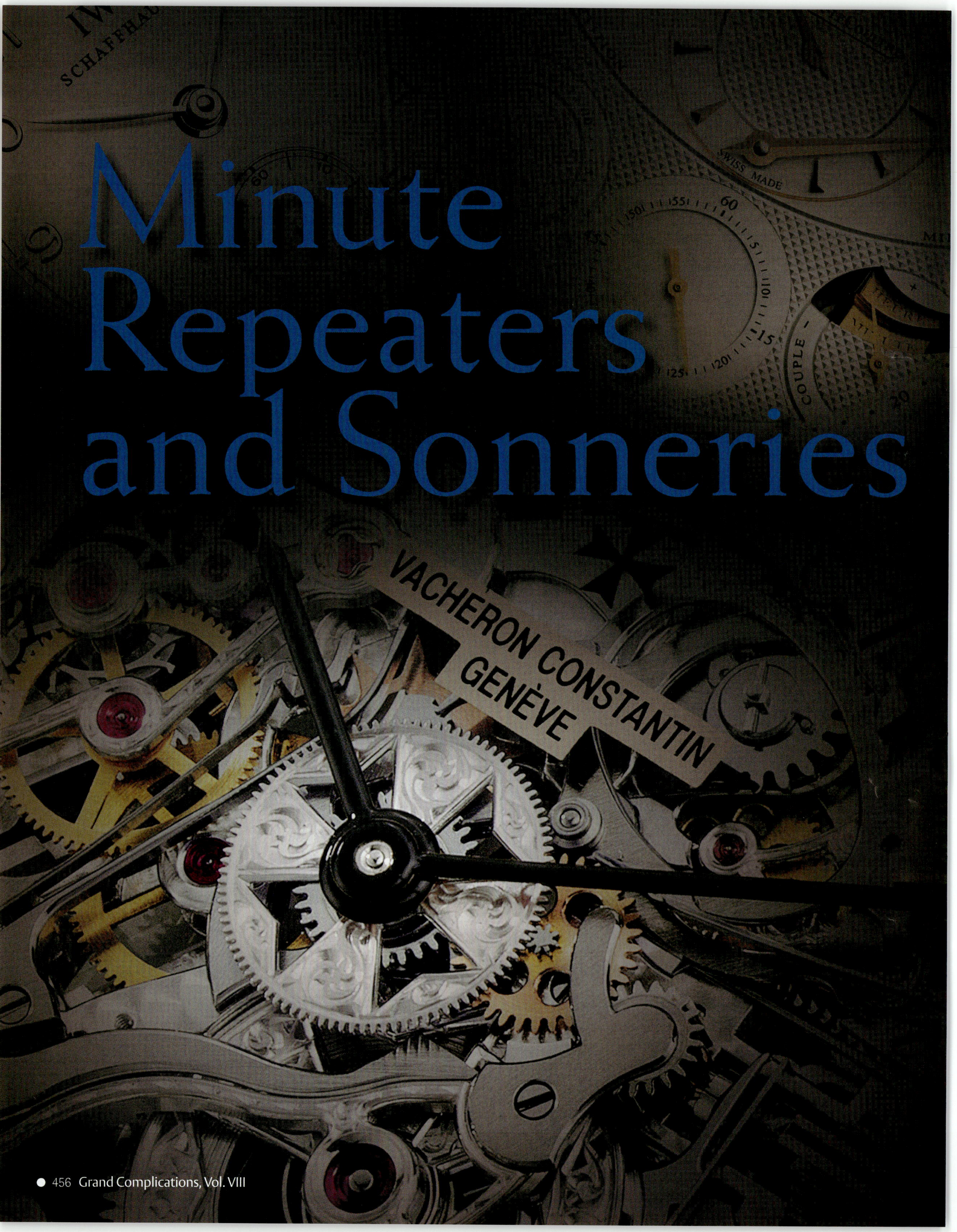

With their tiny hammers that strike chimes to make the hours, quarter-hours and minutes sing, watches with audible indications are regarded by many connoisseurs as the most sophisticated complication—the supreme consecration of the watchmaker's art. Though they are less well known than tourbillons, minute repeater watches (which sound on demand) and grand and small strike watches (which strike "in passing," or automatically) actually demand extreme technical skill coupled with a true musical ear. Today, to enhance the acoustics of the complication, watchmakers are focused on more than just exceptional artisanal savoir-faire. They are also inventing new striking systems and exploring all the potential of high-tech metal alloys—sometimes using the most up-to-date software to handle the sound components. But lovers of rare and exclusive pieces should rest easy: given their extreme complexity, these visual and audible treasures will long remain the prerogative of a few manufactures, master watchmakers and preternaturally gifted artisans.

Striking watches appeared in pocket watches at a very early stage. By the late 15th century, there are already records of watches striking the hours in passing, like church bells. By the late 18th century, the quarter repeater mechanism had been created and could strike the hours and quarter-hours on demand—an extremely practical system of keeping track of time at night. Watches at the time were equipped with hammers striking a small bell. The development of the minute repeater is generally attributed to the English chronometer-maker Thomas Mudge, in about 1750. By the end of that same century, the famous Abraham-Louis Breguet had the idea of replacing bells with gongs, meaning hardened steel blades wrapped around the case, thereby serving to reduce the thickness of the watch, as well as achieving a purer sound. In the 20th century, in the miniaturized form of wristwatches, watches providing audible indications of the time established themselves as one of the most eloquent demonstrations of watchmaking expertise.

TECHNIQUE

HOW DOES IT WORK?

There are two main types of audible indication: striking in passing, or automatically (grand and small strike) and striking on demand (repeater mechanisms). The striking system includes minuscule metal hammers that hit chimes (also called gongs), i.e. steel or specialized alloy blades that are firmly fixed at one end and wrap around the movement. The chimes produce a higher or lower note corresponding to their length.

REPEATER WATCHES

Repeater watches sound the hour on demand when the wearer activates a slide or pushbutton. "Quarter repeaters" indicate the number of hours followed by the quarter-hours elapsed. "Five-minute repeaters" sound the hours, quarter-hours and increments of five minutes that have elapsed.

MINUTE REPEATERS

Minute repeaters sound the time down to the minute. They are generally equipped with two chimes, a low one for the hours, a high one for the minutes, and a low-high alternation for the quarter-hours. If the wearer activated the minute repeater at 11:47AM, he or she would hear 11 low tones, three dual tones and two high tones. Unparalleled skill is needed to fabricate this complex system of mechanical "memory," based on "feeler-spindles" or sensors picking up the information from the hour, quarter-hour and minute "snails," then passing it on to "gathering-pallets" that raise the hammers. It takes an extremely sensitive musical ear to adjust the gongs as one would a musical instrument.

"CATHEDRAL" CHIMES

The term "cathedral" chime generally refers to chimes that wrap around the movement more than once, offering a richer and more profound tone.

GRAND AND SMALL STRIKE

Grand and small strikes automatically sound the hour and the quarter-hours in passing, like a church bell. Grand strikes sound the hours and quarter-hours, repeating the hours every fifteen minutes. Small strikes sound the hours or the quarter-hours, without reiterating the hours. A "silent" mode, activated by a slide or a pushbutton, allows the wearer to mute the sound.

WESTMINSTER CHIMES

The systems called Westminster chimes sound each quarter hour by striking on four different chimes consecutively. Contrary to popular belief, the tone does not necessarily reproduce the one played by Big Ben, the bell in the clock in London's Palace of Westminster, whose melody was originally composed by Handel.

Minute Repeaters: Innovation at Work

In recent years, watchmakers seems determined to revive interest in minute repeater models by exploring new technical paths, with changes to construction of the chimes, alloys used for their fabrication, transmission of the sound, ways of activating the strike or the increasing water resistance of these ultra-sophisticated watches.

Breguet
Classique Grande Complication Minute Repeater 7637
Beneath its traditional appearance, the Classique Grande Complication Minute Repeater 7637 from Breguet conceals an entirely reinvented striking mechanism that uses new materials and innovative positions for the chimes, chime-holders and hammers.

IWC, *Portuguese Minute Repeater*
A sober, classical aesthetic dominates IWC's Portuguese Minute Repeater, equipped with a large case in platinum or rose gold and a manual-winding pocket watch movement.

Jaeger-LeCoultre, *Master Grande Tradition Minute Repeater*
Equipped with a silicon escapement, the Master Grande Tradition Minute Repeater from Jaeger-LeCoultre benefits from an unusual system for transmitting sound, in which square-section gongs are welded directly to the sapphire crystal—a system that was patented by the manufacture.

Manufacture Royale, *Opéra*
The first creation from the hyper-exclusive brand Manufacture Royale, the Opéra tourbillon and minute repeater model stands out for its case, which resembles a metallic accordion bellows and acts as a resonance chamber for the gongs.

Christophe Claret, *Adagio*
On the new minute repeater model from Christophe Claret, Adagio, the cathedral chimes of the striking mechanism are equipped with a patented device that prevents the chimes from hitting each other while they vibrate under the hammers.

Roger Dubuis
Excalibur Minute Repeater

A new kind of function-starting device equips Roger Dubuis's Excalibur Minute Repeater: the wearer activates the strike with a turn of the rotating bezel.

Audemars Piguet
Jules Audemars Minute Repeater Tourbillon Chronograph

On its Jules Audemars Minute Repeater Tourbillon Chronograph, Audemars Piguet resolved to develop a new striking system, with new hammers as well as two gongs crafted all of a piece for a more consistent tone.

Blancpain, *Léman Minute Repeater Aqua Lung*

Blancpain has opted to tackle one of the trickiest issues with minute repeater watches—the Achilles heel in their water resistance represented by the slide-piece—with its Léman Minute Repeater Aqua Lung, water resistant to 100m.

Jaeger-LeCoultre, *Reverso Répétition Minutes à Rideau*

Unveiled last year, Jaeger-LeCoultre's Reverso Répétition Minutes à Rideau invents a new sensation with a sliding shutter system that hides one of the faces of the case—while activating the strike mechanism.

Cvstos, *Challenge RMT-S*

The Challenge RMT-S from the Genevan brand Cvstos, with anti-shock tourbillon carriage, combines a minute repeater with water resistance to 100m—in a distinctly futuristic manner.

Minute Repeaters: Open-Hearted Mechanisims

On classical minute repeater watches, nothing signals the presence of this sophisticated complication—besides the presence of a small slide or bolt on the side of the case. Following a general trend in haute horology, many watchmakers today prefer to reveal the mechanism by openworking the dial.

Blancpain, *Le Brassus Minute Repeater Carrousel*

Le Brassus Minute Repeater Carrousel from Blancpain associates a flying carrousel (see chapter on Tourbillons) with a minute repeater whose cathedral chimes are affixed to the interior side of the case, a configuration that provides a sound of peerless volume and clarity.

Seiko, *Credor Spring Drive Minute Repeater*

Signed Seiko, the Credor Spring Drive Minute Repeater features a skeletonized movement that is visible through an openworked dial and a sapphire crystal caseback. Its hammers are shaped from a special kind of steel forged by one of the most famous Japanese steelmakers.

Harry Winston, *Midnight Minute Repeater*

On the Midnight Minute Repeater from Harry Winston, with an off-centered hours/minutes display, a large "porthole" at 10 o'clock allows the wearer to admire the striking hammers, engraved with the initials H and W.

Milus

Tirion TriRetrograde Minute Repeater

Equipped with a highly original display of the seconds over three retrograde segments, the Tirion TriRetrograde Minute Repeater from Milus reveals the hammers and gongs of its striking mechanism through its openworked dial.

Audemars Piguet

Millenary Minute Repeater

Housed in an oval titanium case, the Millenary Minute Repeater from Audemars Piguet stands out for its three-dimensional architecture that reveals the new Audemars Piguet escapement, a double balance-spring, as well as the hammers and gongs of the striking mechanism.

Vacheron Constantin,
Maîtres Cabinotiers Skeleton Minute Repeater

Vacheron Constantin aims for maximum transparency—and slenderness—with its Maîtres Cabinotiers Skeleton Minute Repeater. The 3.3mm-thick movement comprises over 330 parts, most of them openworked, decorated and chased.

Badollet
Observatoire 1872 Répétition Minutes
A wristwatch with a pocket watch look, the Observatoire 1872 Minute Repeater from Badollet provides ample views of its hammers, gongs and inertial flywheel through an opaline openworked dial.

de Grisogono, *Occhio Ripetizione Minuti*
de Grisogono plays the iconoclast with its Occhio Ripetizione Minuti. Based on the principle of reflex cameras, the watch features an aperture in place of a dial; when the minute repeater is activated, the twelve ceramic shutters open to reveal the movement and remain open while the cathedral chime is sounding.

Repeater Watches: New Rhythms

The most popular repeater watches are currently the minute repeaters, which sound on demand the hours, quarter-hours and minutes. A few horologers have opted to reinterpret this classic model by revisiting the old-fashioned "five-minute repeater," proposing variations on the frequency and type of the strike, or creating repeaters that sound the time of another time zone.

Kari Voutilainen, *Masterpiece N°7*

On his one-of-a-kind model, the Finnish-born watchmaker offers a minute repeater striking not only hours/quarter-hours/minutes, but also hours/ten minutes/minutes, a system designed to enable a more intuitive division of time.

Franc Vila

FVa35 SuperSonico 5-Minute Repeater

Limited to just 88 pieces, the new FVa35 SuperSonico 5-Minute Repeater from Franc Vila stands out for its "five-minute repeater" mechanism equipped with two chimes, one sounding the hours, the other marking increments of five minutes with a double high-low strike.

Louis Vuitton
Tambour Répétition Minutes
On the Tambour Répétition Minutes from Louis Vuitton, with a dual time zone, the minute repeater sounds the home time, not local time—a pleasant way to feel connected with close friends and family.

Edox
Classe Royale Répétition 5 Minutes
On its Classe Royale Répétition 5 Minutes, Edox offers an audible indication of the time to five minutes, using a mechanism that sounds the hours on a chime, then one strike for five minutes, two for ten minutes, and so on.

Seiko, *Credo Spring Drive Sonnerie*
The Japanese brand Seiko has revived the antique hour repeater mechanism in a high-end model named Credo Spring Drive Sonnerie. The mechanism strikes in three modes: the number of hours on each hour; three strikes every three hours (3, 6, 9 and 12 o'clock); and silent mode.

deLaCour, *Birépétition minutes*
Equipped with a Christophe Claret movement, the Birépétition minutes from deLaCour strikes the hours, quarter-hours and minutes for either the local time or a second time zone.

Grand and Small Strikes

Like a church bell on the wrist, grand and small strike systems mark the hours and quarter-hours in passing. This extremely rare function is the prerogative of ultra-complicated wristwatches (see chapter on Multi-Complications), but also of some highly sophisticated watches where it most often joins the minute repeater—sometimes in chiming the famous melody of Big Ben.

Bulgari
Octo Grande Sonnerie Tourbillon
Thanks to its four gongs, the Octo Grande Sonnerie Tourbillon can play the famous melody of the Big Ben bell, in Westminster, London. It is equipped with a grand and small strike as well as a minute repeater.

Philippe Dufour, *Grande Sonnerie*
Launched in 1992, the Grande Sonnerie from Philippe Dufour—one of the preeminent members of the Académie Horlogère des Créateurs Indépendants—was the first minute repeater watch with grand and small strike.

FP Journe

Sonnerie Souveraine

Possessing grand strike and minute repeater capabilities, the Sonnerie Souveraine is distinguished by its extreme functionality and security assured by ten patented devices. FP Journe actually designed it "so an eight-year-old child could use it without damaging it"—which required a high degree of technical sophistication in the conception and design.

A. Lange & Söhne

Zeitwerk Striking Time

The new Zeitwerk Striking Time from A. Lange & Söhne strikes each quarter-hour in passing with a high note, then the hour with a low one—thus reproducing in slow motion the famous tune from the beginning of Beethoven's Fifth Symphony.

Jaeger-LeCoultre

Hybris Mechanica à Grande Sonnerie

The Hybris Mechanica à Grande Sonnerie is part of the Hybris Mechanica trilogy of ultra-complicated watches presented by Jaeger-LeCoultre (see chapter on Multi-Complications). Its movement, comprising over 1,300 parts, incorporates a grand and small strike as well as a minute repeater, along with a Westminster chime that sounds a tune lasting much longer than normal.

Chopard, *L.U.C Strike One*

On its L.U.C Strike One, Chopard presents a mechanism striking each hour with a single note (hence its name), while an opening in the dial serves to reveal a small hammer at work.

Feminine Melodies

In a still tentative trend, we have recently seen the first watches with minute repeater or "in passing" strike mechanisms created especially for women.

Breguet
Reine de Naples 8978
To celebrate the 200th anniversary of the wristwatch created for Caroline Murat, Queen of Naples, Breguet presented the Reine de Naples 8978, with a mechanism that marks each full hour with two strikes repeated three times.

Patek Philippe
Ladies First Minute Repeater Ref. 7000
Patek Philippe recently launched its first minute repeater wristwatch created specifically for women, the Ladies First Minute Repeater, Ref. 7000, with an extra-thin automatic movement, rose-gold case and cream-colored dial.

Ellicott, *Lady Tuxedo Midnight*
Ellicott's Lady Tuxedo Midnight model is equipped with a self-winding movement striking the hours and quarter-hours on request. Its sensual case, partially or entirely set with diamonds, is crafted in rose gold, white gold or steel.

Watches with Automatons

In terms of a grand visual and acoustic spectacle, watches with automatons, which are extremely rare, unquestionably occupy an echelon all to themselves.

Ulysse Nardin, *Genghis Khan*

The Genghis Khan from Ulysse Nardin possesses a minute repeater with a Westminster chime (E-C-D-G) as well as a system of jaquemarts or jacks. It sounds the hour by a G, the minutes by an E, and indicates the quarter-hours on all four gongs by means of three different sound sequences. The black onyx dial is adorned with hand-engraved gold figurines that spring to life when the striking mechanism is activated, and are perfectly synchronized with the sound of the gongs.

Bulgari, *Il Giocatore Veneziano*

Inspired by a painting by Caravaggio, Il Giocatore Veneziano associates a minute repeater mechanism (with cathedral chime) with an automaton that throws two dice with a total of 504 possibilities. The automaton movement operates independently of the minute repeater mechanism, and may thus be activated either at the same time as the striking mechanism, or on demand.

Bovet Fleurier

Amadeo Fleurier 44 Minute Repeater Tourbillon Triple Time Zone Automaton

The Amadeo Fleurier 44 Minute Repeater Tourbillon Triple Time Zone Automaton watch by Bovet Fleurier features a dial bearing an automaton with bells reminiscent of the first *jaquemart* (jack) mechanisms.

A. LANGE & SÖHNE

LANGE ZEITWERK STRIKING TIME – REF. 145.029

The most recent addition to the Lange Zeitwerk family is endowed with a chiming mechanism that is visible on its dial. The Lange Zeitwerk Striking Time is the first Lange wristwatch with an acoustic signature. It strikes the quarter-hours with high-pitched tones and the full hours at a lower pitch. The chiming mechanism consists of two black polished steel hammers that are integrated in the dial layout on either side of the subsidiary seconds. The manually wound L043.2 caliber is crafted to the most exacting Lange quality standards and largely decorated and assembled by hand. The sonorous timepiece comes in a 44.2mm white-gold case with a black dial or in a limited edition of 100 pieces with platinum cases and rhodium-plated dials.

AUDEMARS PIGUET

JULES AUDEMARS JUMPING HOUR MINUTE REPEATER – REF. 26151OR.OO.D002CR.01

This complicated wristwatch in 18K rose gold takes full advantage of the contrast between the blue of the hands and minute markers, and the sober white of the dial. The creative use of a jumping hour window at 12:00—or rather 60 minutes—brings a decisively modern character to the seemingly classical design of this manually wound minute repeater wristwatch. The presence of a single hand at the center of the dial generates a clever visual tension that holds the eye for an extra second, dazzled by the gamesmanship of Audemars Piguet's ingenious creation.

AUDEMARS PIGUET

MILLENARY HAND-WOUND MINUTE REPEATER WITH AP ESCAPEMENT

REF. 26371TI.OO.D002CR.01

The Millenary Minute Repeater is a concentrated blend of expertise, technical sophistication and innovative materials. Its titanium oval case provides an atypical setting for a truly magnificent sight featuring offset gold subdials. The AP escapement and the double balance-spring, as well as the hammers and the striking gongs, all become key players in a truly three-dimensional creation. Conceived, developed and produced by Audemars Piguet, the new hand-wound 2910 caliber driving the Millenary Minute Repeater is also distinguished by the atypical construction of the regulating organ. The oval Millenary case in brushed titanium—a material featuring exceptional acoustic qualities—is framed by a polished titanium bezel. The various organs within are barely concealed by the anthracite gray hours and minutes subdial offset at 3:00, and by the small seconds at 7:00. Limited edition of eight pieces.

BLANCPAIN

CARROUSEL REPETITION MINUTES LE BRASSUS – REF. 0233-3634-55B

Blancpain's Carrousel Répétition Minutes Le Brassus is powered by the 1736 caliber residing in its 18K red-gold 45mm case, and features a flying one-minute carrousel. A slide lever operates the minute repeater and a cathedral gong sounds the hour. The skeletonized and openworked dial reveals the Blancpain movement. The Carrousel Répétition Minutes Le Brassus is available in a limited edition of 10 pieces.

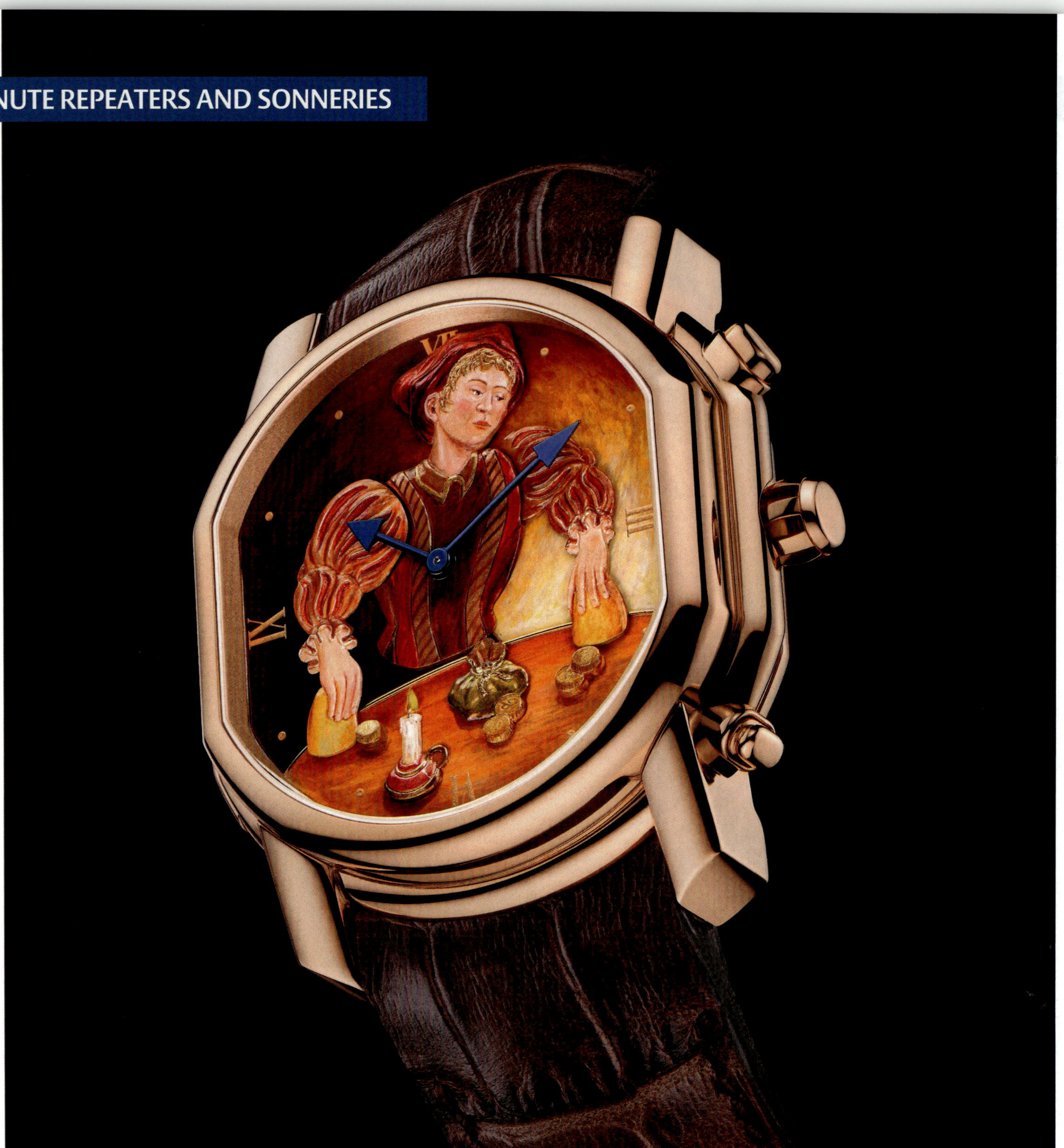

BVLGARI

IL GIOCATORE VENEZIANO – REF. BRRP46GLGV/2

An enchanting combination of art and motion, this 46mm 18K pink-gold timepiece features a hand-painted enameled gold dial with five separate animations. In addition to the visual spectacle, the finely decorated, hand-wound DR 7300 caliber provides the sonorous charm of a minute repeater. Subtitled Automaton with 504 Combinations, this Venetian player is hand-painted, offering unique subtlety to each piece. Adding to this luxurious taste of the Renaissance, the crown, pusher, and correctors, are made of 18K pink gold, and the caseback is transparent for infinite delight.

BVLGARI

OCTO REPETITION MINUTES RETRO – REF. BGOP43BGLMR

The Octo Répétition Minutes Retro is distinguished by a combination of a minute repeater mechanism with a jumping hour display and retrograde minutes indication. The piece features an exquisitely crafted dial with a guilloché and cloisonné decoration, featuring a retrograde minute hand running across a 180° arc on the right-hand side of the dial, while the jumping hour window is located in the traditional position at 9:00. The 43mm white-gold case of the Octo Répétition Minutes Retro is adorned with two beaded crowns. The one at 3:00 serves to adjust the usual time functions, and the second to activate the repeater mechanism.

CHRISTOPHE CLARET

ADAGIO – REF. MTR.SLB88.107-807

This exceptional watch is equipped with the 455-component Calibre SLB88, created entirely in-house. The Adagio features central hour and minute hands, small seconds at 9:00 in a window or subdial, along with a large date at 6:00 and a dual time zone (hours and minutes) display complete with day/night indication in a subdial at 2:00. In tribute to his manufacture's first caliber introduced over 20 years ago, Christophe Claret equipped this timepiece with a minute repeater, a particularly intricate complication that has become one of the great specialties of the manufacture. Striking the hours, quarters and minutes on demand, the "cathedral gongs" of the striking mechanism feature a patented device preventing them from knocking against each other when they vibrate under the hammers. The patented large date display boasts an unprecedented construction.

de GRISOGONO

OCCHIO RIPETIZIONE MINUTI TITANIUM

The exceptional Occhio Ripetizione Minuti boasts a mechanism very similar to the one found in a reflex camera. Comprising 12 titanium blades, the diaphragm opens to reveal the movement as the mechanism chimes. The watch's sapphire crystal caseback reveals the movement of the three hammers (to strike the hours, quarter-hours, and minutes) on the gongs, as well as the movement's signature decorative finishing. Originally released in a more sedate version, this model is now available in a spectacular diamond-set version, which features 154 baguette-cut diamonds (18 carats in total) on the bezel, case flanks and lugs.

de GRISOGONO

OCCHIO RIPETIZIONE MINUTI ROSE GOLD OPEN

The exceptional Occhio Ripetizione Minuti boasts a mechanism very similar to the one found in a reflex camera. Comprising 12 titanium blades, the dial is actually a diaphragm that opens to reveal the movement as the mechanism chimes. The wearer can either enjoy the spectacle on the front of the watch, or the one on the back, as the watch's sapphire crystal caseback reveals the movement of the three hammers on the gongs, as well as the movement's signature decorative finishing.

de GRISOGONO

OCCHIO RIPETIZIONE MINUTI ROSE GOLD CLOSED

The Occhio Ripetizione Minuti more than holds its own as a minute repeater, striking the hours, quarter-hours and minutes. At first glance, it looks like any other beautifully designed watch. However, its dial holds a secret: it is made of twelve titanium blades that open to reveal the movement underneath. As the three hammers inside strike the gongs to sound the time, the dial reveals the delightful play inside; the sapphire crystal caseback shows off the movement of the hammers and the trademark de GRISOGONO finishing on the movement.

GUY ELLIA

REPETITION MINUTE ZEPHYR

The ambassador of Guy Ellia's complicated timekeeper, the Répétition Minute Zephyr with its complications and intricate manufacturing process, is considered a particularly exceptional piece. The Caliber GEC 88 was created by Swiss manufacture Christophe Claret and features a power reserve indicator, minute repeater function and five time zones with day/night indication. The movement beats at 18,000 vph in a solid, convex, high-resonance sapphire crystal case of impressive proportions (53.6x43.7x14.8mm). Mounted on an alligator strap with a folding buckle, this model is also available in pink gold or titanium.

IWC

PORTUGUESE MINUTE REPEATER – REF. IW544906

For Portuguese explorers out on the open sea, timekeeping was of crucial importance. Using a log line together with a special sandglass—the log glass—they were able to measure the vessel's speed. The ship's bell clock was used to signal the beginning and end of sailors' watches: the bell would be struck once every half-hour and twice every full hour, with four double strikes signaling the end of a watch. The abstract concept of time was thus being converted into acoustic tones even back then. In the Portuguese Minute Repeater, depressing the slide causes a delicate strike train to sound the time out audibly in hours, quarters and minutes. In 2009, the case was increased by 1.7mm in height and 1mm in diameter, but in a move destined to appeal to fans of classic dial design, the small seconds display was shifted from 9:00 to 6:00. To achieve this, the original 95-calibre Lépine open-face movement was replaced by a 98950 caliber hunter pocket watch movement and some of the stylish elements of the early Jones calibers were adopted. A number of these, such as the elongated index, the balance with its high-precision adjustment cam and the distinctively decorated nickel-silver plate and bridge with gold-plated engravings, can be seen through the sapphire crystal caseback. Both versions are limited to 500 watches.

JAEGER-LECOULTRE

MASTER GRANDE TRADITION MINUTE REPEATER – REF. 501.T4.50

With the interaction of its retrograde two-week power reserve and barrel-torque indicators on the intricately openworked dial, this audible member of the Master Grande Tradition collection is a comprehensive reflection of the house's vast range of horological expertise. Housed within a titanium case, the hand-wound 413-piece 947 caliber lets time resonate with perfect clarity and authority. Rich with handcrafted decorations, this timepiece oscillates at 21,600 vph and opts for an exceptional revealing design, with central dauphine hands, as the visual backdrop for its revered resonant complication. It is worn on an alligator leather strap.

JAEGER-LeCOULTRE

REVERSO REPETITION MINUTES A RIDEAU – REF. 235.35.20

Poetically, this timepiece's minute repeater is activated by the owner's hand uncovering the openworked front dial by pushing aside the symbolic veil of a finely crafted spring-loaded Venetian blind. On the reverse side, the hand-wound 944 caliber continues its revelation, with an exposure of its bridges beneath the hour and minute hands. Presented as a 75-piece 18K white-gold edition, worn on an alligator strap, this orchestral composition grants its owner a wealth of creative freedom in expressing his sonorous vision of time, merging innovation with the manufacture's legendary swiveling case. Powered by a 340-part movement with two barrels, the Reverso Répétition Minutes à Rideau boasts a power reserve of 35 hours.

Moonphases

H. Moser & Cie.
Glashütte ORIGINAL
MOONPHASE
SWISS
MADE
MER JUIN
BLANCPAIN
Fifty Fathoms
Flyback
MON • WED • FRI • SUN
LONGINES

The days when the small moonphase window was content to play a secondary, almost decorative role at the bottom of the dial on a perpetual or complete calendar are over. Today, the display has come into its own as a complication in its own right, with stagings that can be spectacular as well as poetic. On a growing number of watches—for men as well as women—the moonphase occupies a place of honor, and each year brings a bumper crop of technical and aesthetic innovations. It is a beautiful way to remind us that our conception of time is inextricably linked to the movement of heavenly bodies and the grand cycles of nature.

The observation of the moon's cycle has always constituted—along with the course of the sun, the return of the seasons and the alternating of day and night—one of the primary foundations of calendar systems. This cycle famously inspired the ancient Egyptians to divide the year into twelve months, a system we inherited via the Greeks and Romans. Despite the near-universal adoption of the Gregorian calendar, essentially based on the course of the sun, the ancient lunar or luni-solar (i.e. based on both the sun and moon) calendars retain their full importance in certain cultures, and are notably used to determine the date of traditional or religious holidays, or for astrological calculations. This is the case, for example, in the Chinese and Jewish luni-solar calendars. Such is also the case for the Muslim calendar, in which the year contains twelve lunar months of 29.53059 solar days—adding up to about 11 days fewer than the Gregorian calendar.

In the West, the moonphase display was an essential component of the first great clocks of the Middle Ages. It plays a role on the clock of Saint-Etienne Cathedral in Bourges, in France (1424), and on Prague's Old Town Hall (15th century). It is featured on the dials of the first pocket watches, from the 16th century—well before watchmakers could present the minute or the second. The moonphase later became an inescapable element of watches devoted to astronomical, astrological or calendar indications—especially the famous perpetual calendars. In the 20th century, although the moon had lost much of its magnetic force over the human mind, watchmakers took it upon themselves to miniaturize the mechanism to the wristwatch format, while conserving a maximum of precision (see sidebar: "How does it work?").

TECHNIQUE

HOW DOES IT WORK?

The moonphase is generally displayed via a mobile disc on which are depicted two perfectly round moons. A specially shaped window, with two rounded cutouts representing the "dark" side of the moon, allows the display to represent the diverse aspects of the heavenly body throughout its cycle (waxing, full, waning and new moons). The indicator changes once a day, as a rule.

A VARIABLE LEVEL OF PRECISION

Though they are all based on the same principle, not all window moonphase displays offer the same level of precision. Their exactitude depends to a large extent on the number of teeth on the moonphase disc. The length of one synodic, or lunar, month (the length of time from one new moon to another) is actually 29 days, 12 hours, 44 minutes and 2.8 seconds, or 29.53 days—making it impossible to simply multiply any units from solar civil time. The more teeth the disc has, the more precise the moonphase will be.

ORDINARY MOONPHASES

On ordinary moonphases, the disc bearing the two moons is linked to a wheel with 59 teeth, corresponding to two lunar months (2 x 29.5 days). This system falls behind 44 minutes and 2.8 seconds per month, or close to nine hours per year, a discrepancy that reaches a full day after two years, seven months and around 20 days.

ASTRONOMICAL MOONPHASES

High-end watches are equipped with a more complex device, called "astronomical moon," with a 135-toothed wheel. With this system, the lag between the mechanism and the actual lunar cycle comes to just one day after 122 years and 44 days. Certain recent timepieces have surpassed even this feat with impressive displays of precision (see the "Precision Records" section).

DOUBLE MOONPHASES

Some timepieces feature a simultaneous indication of the moonphase in both hemispheres. This particular feature is generally not a technical advance in and of itself (since it requires only revealing the two moons already present on most mobile discs), but it nonetheless gives the dial a charming touch of originality.

THE MOON'S AGE

Moonphases are sometimes completed by the indication of the moon's "age," i.e. the number of days that have passed since the last new moon.

Calendars with Moonphase

The moonphase indication has long been an almost inescapable element on complete or perpetual calendars (see chapter on Calendars). On these pieces, it most often occupies a small window at 6 o'clock. However, numerous brands have now chosen to reinterpret this tradition with more creative designs, moons at 12 o'clock, oversized windows or off-center displays.

Longines
Master Collection Retrograde Moon Phases
On the Master Collection Retrograde Moon Phases from Longines, launched in 2011, the large moonphase window at 6 o'clock is complemented by four retrograde hands for the day, the date, small seconds and a 24-hour additional time zone.

Pequignet, *Rue Royale*

Equipped with a manufacture-made caliber, the Rue Royale model from the French brand Pequignet displays the moonphase in a large vertical window—complemented by a double day/date window and a power reserve indicator.

Harry Winston

Premier Perpetual Calendar

On Harry Winston's Premier Perpetual Calendar, the moonphase shines at 6 o'clock on the off-center hours/minutes subdial, while the retrograde displays of the month and date compose a perpetually moving arrangement.

Hermès

Arceau Grande Lune

In 2011, Hermès completed its Arceau collection—recognizable by its stirrup-inspired design—with the presentation of the Arceau Grande Lune, with moonphase and complete calendar (day and month via windows, date display with a hand).

Jaquet Droz, *L'Eclipse*

On the "grand feu" black enamel dial of L'Eclipse from Jaquet Droz (equipped with day, date and month displays), a moon with a smiling face inspired by 19th-century engravings plays peekaboo with a mobile black disc surrounded by stars.

Blancpain
Fifty Fathoms Flyback Chronograph Complete Calendar and Moonphase

The newest addition to Blancpain's sporty Fifty Fathoms collection, this flyback chronograph also boasts a complete calendar, as well as a rather anthropomorphic moonphase.

Chopard, *L.U.C Lunar One*

The perpetual calendar L.U.C Lunar One from Chopard offers an "orbital" moonphase: the small round window, in which the silver moon waxes and wanes, itself rotates around the small seconds axis on a disc that simulates the star-spangled night sky.

Epos, *3391 Moonphase*

On a midnight blue dial sprinkled with stars, the 3391 Moonphase from Epos displays—in an unusual configuration—a moonphase, along with windows for the day and month, and a hand for the date.

Dubey & Schaldenbrand
Grand Dôme DT

In designing the dial of the Grand Dôme DT, Dubey & Schaldenbrand arranged multiple displays—date, day, month, chronograph counters and moonphases—on a vertical axis, creating a highly original geometry.

Breguet
Classique 7337

Breguet's Classique 7337 associates an off-center hour/minute subdial with two windows for the date and day. The moonphase window at 12 o'clock also displays the "age" of the moon, i.e. the number of days since the last new moon.

Jaeger-LeCoultre
Duomètre à Quantième Lunaire

The Duomètre à Quantième Lunaire, from Jaeger-LeCoultre, with the Dual-Wing movement, features a moonphase window complemented by two hands, one for the moon's "age," the other for the moonphase in the Southern Hemisphere.

The Moon is the Star

Over the last several years, the moonphase indication has been breaking free of the perpetual or complete calendar "straitjacket", and establishing itself as a complication in its own right. On certain timepieces, it is even the main attraction—with displays that can be quite poetic.

Bulgari, *Grande Lune*

The Bulgari Grande Lune stands out for the original configuration of its two-tone dial, with an asymmetrically positioned oversize moonphase aperture and a pointer-type date display.

Hermès

Dressage Platinum Moonphase

On the Dressage Platinum Moonphase from Hermès, the retrograde pointer-type display moves across the arc of a circle between 8 and 4 o'clock, above a large moonphase aperture at 6 o'clock.

MB&F,
Horological Machine N°2-SV – Final Editions

Equipped with a rectangular case and two juxtaposed dials, the very avant-garde Horological Machine N°2-SV – Final Editions, from the watchmaking collective MB&F, uses the leftmost dial to display a double moonphase that refers to both the Northern and the Southern Hemispheres.

Louis Moinet, *Variograph*

On its Variograph model, Louis Moinet has opted to display, not the course of the moonphase, but the exact day of the full moon in the window at 6 o'clock.

Perrelet,
Grande Phase de Lune centrale

Perrelet gives pride of place to the moonphase, with an aperture that occupies the entire top half of the dial as well as an indication of the moon's "age."

Glashütte Original

PanoMatic Lunar XL

Boldly playing with asymmetrical design, the PanoMaticLunar XL from Glashütte Original displays the moonphase in a large vertical aperture at 2 o'clock that also indicates the "age" of the moon.

Zenith

Class Tourbillon Moon & Sunphase

Equipped with the automatic chronograph movement El Primero, the Class Tourbillon Moon & Sunphase from Zenith uses two superimposed discs to display not only the moonphase (at night) but also the course of the sun (during the day).

Maurice Lacroix

Pontos Décentrique Phases de Lune

In the large crescent-shaped Pontos Décentrique Phases de Lune from Maurice Lacroix, two superimposed discs reveal the moonphase and day/night indication. The design is daring and boldly asymmetrical.

Hermès

Arceau Moonphase

Retrograde Pocket Watch

Powered by a movement from Vaucher Manufacture Fleurier, this Arceau Pocket watch from Hermès displays a large moonphase between 5 and 6 o'clock, as well as a retrograde date with central pointer. It is available in rose or white gold.

Patek Philippe, *Celestial Ref. 5102*

Equipped with a mobile map of the starry night sky, the highly complex Celestial from Patek Philippe provides a perpetual view of the exact configuration of the night sky over the Northern Hemisphere, complete with the visible movement of the stars and the moonphases, as well as the moon's position in the sky.

Ulysse Nardin, *Moonstruck*

A worthy heir to Ulysse Nardin's astronomical watches, the Moonstruck continuously indicates the position of the moon and sun relative to any point on the globe; it thus allows its wearer to read the current moonphase and the state of the tides wherever one may be.

Round Apertures

Alongside traditional apertures, we are also seeing an increasing number of round apertures equipped with mobile covers that represent the dark side of the moon. This enables horologers to create majestic extra-large and even extra-extra-large displays.

Martin Braun, *Selene*

On its Selene watch ("Selene" is the word for "moon" in ancient Greek), Martin Braun has opted to meld poetry and realism; a large moon based on a photograph is alternately hidden and revealed by a mobile cover.

Piaget
Emperador Coussin Moonphase

On Piaget's Emperador Coussin Moonphase, shown here with rose-gold case and blue dial, the disc representing the moon is a plaque of white gold that is heated to create craters such as those found on the face of the moon. Its hand-crafted production renders each watch one of a kind.

Sarpaneva, *Korona K3*

On the highly original Korona K3 from the Finnish watchmaker Sarpaneva, the moonphase display operates with a large central disc bearing two moons with human faces, visible through the openworked dial.

Pierre Kunz
A014 HMRL Tahitian Moon

On the A014 HMRL Tahitian Moon from Pierre Kunz, with retrograde hour and minute displays, the moonphase is displayed in the center of a large oval decorated with metal stars and black mother-of-pearl from Tahiti.

Andersen Genève, *Kamar*

For its Kamar model ("kamar" means "moon" in Arabic), Andersen Genève has created a round aperture equipped with a mother-of-pearl disc bearing both a dark and a light moon, all on a dial of aventurine or guilloché 22-karat blue gold.

Three-Dimensional Displays

A handful of watchmakers—most often independent artisans—have chosen to supplant the classic aperture systems with innovative three-dimensional displays. In these, the moon is depicted by a small mobile sphere (or a stationary sphere equipped with a mobile cover) reproducing the different faces of the moon throughout its cycle. This leads to very evocative stagings.

Konstantin Chaykin, *Lunokhod*

On the Lunokhod from Russian watchmaker Konstantin Chaykin, the heavenly body is represented by a stationary sphere sculpted in wootz steel, an Indian metal whose granular quality recalls the lunar surface. The moonphase is displayed by means of a semi-circular cover.

Thomas Prescher

Mysterious Automatic Double Axis Tourbillon

On the Mysterious Automatic Double Axis Tourbillon from Thomas Prescher (whose movement is entirely hidden within the bezel), the two cylinders for the hours and minutes frame a spherical moonphase display.

De Bethune, *DB25 QP*

The DB25 QP from De Bethune presents an original, patented system with a mobile sphere. The two hemispheres, in steel and platinum, are flame blued; the steel oxidizes and changes color, while the platinum maintains its natural hue.

Precision Records

On ordinary moonphase watches, the complication will eventually show a one-day discrepancy after two years, seven months and around 20 days. On the moonphase complications within the luxury watches at the high end of the market, that difference has been reduced to one day over 122 year and 44 days. A few great brands have recently opted to face this technical challenge and develop moonphases that are much more precise—even resulting in no lag at all.

H. Moser & Cie.
Moser Perpetual Moon
The Perpetual Moon from H. Moser & Cie would need to run 1027.3 years to differ from the real lunar cycle by one full day—thanks to a continually revolving display linked to the hours mechanism (as opposed to most moonphases, which advance once per day). The vertical lines marking the eight quarters of the moon, fixed by international standards, allow an ultra-precise reading.

A. Lange & Söhne, *1815 Moonphase*
The German company A. Lange & Söhne has equipped its 1815 Moonphase with a gear train fitted with a particular gear-train ratio that guarantees a difference of just 6.61 seconds per lunar month, or just one day every 1,058 years!

Arnold & Son
True Moon
True Moon, from Arnold & Son, claims to provide a precise reproduction of the waxing and waning of the moon, adhering to the exact duration of synodic periods.

IWC, *Portuguese Perpetual Calendar*
Using an innovative system comprised of thee toothed wheels, the moonphase indication on IWC's Portuguese Perpetual Calendar has a discrepancy of just one day over 577 years. The double hemisphere display for the Northern and Southern Hemispheres is completed by two countdowns signaling the number of days until the next full moon.

The Feminine Side of the Moon

The moonphase display remains one of the favorite complications of ladies' watches, though it is still more widespread on masculine wrists. Catching the wave of this longstanding interest, both large brands and independent watchmakers offer a beautiful palette of quite refined ladies' models, most often adorned with diamonds and mother-of-pearl.

Bulgari, *Bulgari Bulgari Moonphase*

The Bulgari Bulgari Moonphase, from... Bulgari combines a white mother-of-pearl dial (with a diamond-pavé crescent) with a bezel adorned with the brand's famous double signature. The moonphase appears in an aperture at 9 o'clock.

Patek Philippe, *Ref. 4958*

Equipped with Patek Philippe's smallest complicated movement, Ref. 4958 sets the stage with a guilloché dial bounded by a mother-of-pearl perimeter and adorned with a small seconds subdial—all framed by a diamond-set bezel.

Saskia maaike Bouvier
8 Moons

Created by a woman for women, The 8 Moons timepiece from Saskia maaike Bouvier sports a starry night sky as a backdrop for eight spheres that show not only the current phase of the moon (at 12 o'clock), but also those for the seven following nights.

Girard-Perregaux
Cat's Eye Moon Phase

Equipped with an oval white-gold case set with 66 diamonds, as well as a mother-of-pearl dial, Girard-Perregaux's Cat's Eye Moonphase displays the moon's cycle in a large aperture at 6 o'clock that also features small seconds.

Antoine Preziuso, *Starmoon*

Glamour and excitement permeate Antoine Preziuso's Starmoon, introduced as the largest moonphase display ever made. The black ceramic dial with luminescent numerals is framed by a case that uses diamonds and sapphires as stars in the night sky.

AUDEMARS PIGUET

JULES AUDEMARS MOON-PHASE CALENDAR – REF. 26385OR.OO.A088CR.01

The Jules Audemars Moon-Phase Calendar watch reveals the full measure of this pure form. The pink-gold case and slender bezel ensure maximum dial opening and thus enhance readability. The date and moonphase displays are surrounded by a decorative fillet highlighting the snailed inner decoration. The date, day and moonphase are some of the most useful watch functions in daily life. In this model, beauty also lies beneath the dial. All the bridges are beveled, polished and adorned with Côtes de Genève, and the mainplate is circular-grained.

AUDEMARS PIGUET

MILLENARY STARLIT SKY – REF. 77316BC.ZZ.D007SU.01

The Millenary Starlit Sky's off-centered midnight blue disc initiates the artistic architecture of the multi-layered dial, joined by a diamond-pavé crescent that completes the irresistible backdrop of this automatic timepiece. Framed by a case entirely set with 392 diamonds, the central seconds, date, moonphase and power reserve perpetuate the controlled visual chaos, confirming the fascinating aesthetic of this masterful display of luxury and mechanical sophistication.

BREGUET

CLASSIQUE HORA MUNDI – REF. 5717BR

The Classique Hora Mundi's 77F0 self-winding movement possesses a world-first synchronized instant-jump module that allows the watch to travel with the same ease as the man who wears it. With a single push of the crown, this timepiece instantly morphs all of its visible time coordinates from one pre-selected city to another. Once the wearer has selected his "destination" from the cities aperture at 6:00, the Breguet hour and minute hands, solid gold day/night indicator, and ingenious dragging date disc, transform immediately and with vivid synchronization, upon the effortless request of the watch's owner.

BREGUET

CLASSIQUE MOON PHASES – REF. 7787BR

The elegance of this 18K rose-gold timepiece is accentuated by the elongated power reserve hand, which reaches the scale all the way from its axis at 3:00, reflecting the slender grace of the blued-steel hour, minute and seconds indicators. Via an aperture in the white, solid gold, finely enameled dial, the comprehensive moonphase makes its appearance at 12:00, with a shape and level of detail that make it the star of the watch's visual identity. The Classique 7787 Moon Phases is powered by the exceptionally flat, 3.02mm-thick, self-winding Breguet Calibre 591 DRL, whose double barrel permits a power reserve of 38 hours, as is expressed by the arrow-adorned indicator on the lower half of the dial.

BVLGARI

GRANDE LUNE – REF. BRRP46C14GLDMP

The astronomical moonphase of this manually wound timepiece is so artfully crafted that it appears to be a window into the night sky above. Matching the 18K pink-gold brilliance of the 46mm case, the detailed moon takes center stage of the simple yet cleverly designed dial. Playing off the circularity of the shimmering chapter ring and Arabic numeral date, the small seconds are indicated as an ingenious three-arm, three-scale semicircle. Ranging in length, the arms relay responsibility to one another every 20 seconds, distinctly pointing to the appropriate half-ring. Boasting a 40-hour power reserve, the watch's DR 2300 caliber is decorated with perlage, Côtes de Genève and chamfering finishing.

de GRISOGONO

OTTURATORE

The understated clarity of the Otturatore's Clou de Paris cobbled dial is at the heart of this watch's conceptual genius. With the press of the stylish gold pushbuttons that surround the crown on the side of the case, the patented high-performance sequential display selector rotates its aperture 90° to reveal one of the four secondary functions that loom beneath the watch face. Like a racecar instantly accelerating to its top speed and immediately braking to a full stop, this innovative sequencer mechanism completes its module transition 15 times faster than the blink of an eye. To the casual observer, this watch possesses a charming, unassuming elegance. To the connoisseur, the Otturatore is a truly spectacular feat of unprecedented innovation and de Grisogono expertise.

FREDERIQUE CONSTANT

FREDERIQUE CONSTANT MANUFACTURE TOURBILLON MOONPHASE DATE 24H

REF. FC-985ABS4H9

Powered by the sophisticated FC-985 self-winding caliber, completely developed in-house, this multi-complication timepiece presents a black Clous de Paris guilloché dial, through which the ingeniously balanced, individually numbered tourbillon rises to glory. Matching the 44mm 18K rose-gold case, the central hands are joined in their time-telling journey by two multi-function subdials that magnify the extreme precision of the watch. At 9:00, the 24-hour indicator features an internal day/night indicator for optimal coherence. Positioned at 12:00, the moonphase indicator is surrounded by a contrasting small date ring. Designed with a silicon escapement wheel and lever, the movement of this limited edition horological work of art is finely decorated with Côtes de Genève and perlage, as well as chamfered and rhodium-plated bridges.

FREDERIQUE CONSTANT

RUNABOUT MOONPHASE & DATE – REF. FC-360RM6B4

Honoring the distinguished heritage of timekeeping's adornment of the sea, the Runabout Moonphase & Date embellishes the wrist with a clean elegance reminiscent of the legendary boats whose name it proudly bears. Presented as a rose-gold-plated limited edition, this uncluttered wristwatch offers the intricate craftsmanship of a Pavé de Paris guilloché dial center. As the SuperLumiNova hands indicate the hours and minutes, a central running seconds stem circles the dial, driven by the automatic FC-360 caliber's 28,800 vph frequency. Finding their place on the silvered face, the day and date subdials frame a precisely proportioned moonphase indicator at 6:00. Worn on a dark brown crocodile calfskin strap, this timepiece is delivered in a handmade wooden case, accompanied by a Runabout boat miniature.

GLASHÜTTE ORIGINAL

PANOMATIC LUNAR XL – REF. 90-02-36-12-05

The gray Louisiana nubuck alligator leather strap is the perfect choice for this stainless steel timepiece. Playing off the shade of the ruthenium dial, the tones offer a level of refinement that highlights the gentle contrasts of the face. On the milled and galvanized principal and small seconds counters, white-gold hands with luminescent coating draw perfect clarity within the white and gray monochrome theme. The automatic winding 90-02 caliber, with three-quarter plate, swan-neck fine adjustment, and hand-engraved balance cock, additionally powers a panorama date in the lower right of the dial, and a moonphase indicator in the top right. Featuring an oscillating frequency of 28,800 vph, the 90-02 self-winding movement provides a power reserve of 42 hours.

JAEGER-LECOULTRE

DUOMETRE A QUANTIEME LUNAIRE – REF. 604.24.20

The partially openworked dial of the Duomètre à Quantième Lunaire allows a peek at its exceptional manual-winding Jaeger-LeCoultre 381 caliber, which comprises 369 components and provides 50 hours of power reserve. Hours and minutes are displayed in a subdial at 2:30, and jumping seconds complete the time indication. A subdial at 9:30 indicates the date, as well as the moonphase in the Northern and Southern Hemispheres. The 42mm pink-gold case reveals the movement through a sapphire crystal caseback and is water resistant to 50m. A chocolate brown alligator strap completes the ensemble.

LONGINES

THE LONGINES MASTER COLLECTION RETROGRADE MOON PHASES

The Longines Master Collection Retrograde Moon Phases is fitted with an exclusive self-winding caliber (L707.2) developed especially for Longines. With a diameter of 44mm, it shows the time, day, night and phases of the moon, as well as four retrograde functions. The silvered dial features eleven black Roman numerals and 6 blued steel hands. The stainless steel case has a transparent caseback and is mounted on a brown alligator strap with a folding safety clasp.

PIAGET

PIAGET EMPERADOR COUSSIN MOON PHASE – REF. G0A34022

This model is a paragon of purity and understatement, featuring a generous 46.5mm case with an original and attractive moonphase display at 6:00. With its broad opening measuring 12mm in diameter, this large moon reveals a wealth of subtle craftsmanship exercised on a heated gold plate featuring reflections symbolizing moon craters. The moonphase indication is provided by a mobile mask that gradually uncovers the white-gold moon disc, before covering it up again. This complication beats to the rhythm of the new Calibre 860P, a self-winding movement. In addition to its approximately 72-hour power reserve, it features Piaget's signature finishes such as circular Côtes de Genève motifs, a circular-grained mainplate, beveled bridges, and blued screws.

VACHERON CONSTANTIN
PATRIMONY TRADITIONNELLE CHRONOGRAPH PERPETUAL CALENDAR
REF. 47292/000P-9590

Housing the outstanding 1141 QP caliber within a 43mm 950 platinum case, the Patrimony Traditionnelle Chronograph Perpetual Calendar finds a material worthy of its exceptional performance. A clever arrangement of the perpetual calendar makes the sophisticated complication an elegantly understated companion to the central second chronograph with 30-minute counter. With every component finished to the highest standard, and a splendid caseback exhibition of the movement's precise inner workings, this timepiece makes a powerful statement in the field of graceful luxury.

VACHERON CONSTANTIN

PATRIMONY TRADITIONNELLE CHRONOGRAPH PERPETUAL CALENDAR

REF. 47292/000R-9392

This 1141 QP caliber is comprised of 324 parts, and can be admired through the 18K pink-gold watch's transparent sapphire caseback. At 6:00 on the dial side, a hand-engraved moonphase is enclosed within the circular date component of the perpetual calendar, whose day of the week, month, and leap-year indicators are neatly arranged via small apertures for an optimal use of space. Oscillating with a rate of 18,000 vph, the manually wound movement additionally drives the central chronograph hand, 30-minute counter at 3:00, and small running seconds at 9:00.

Diving

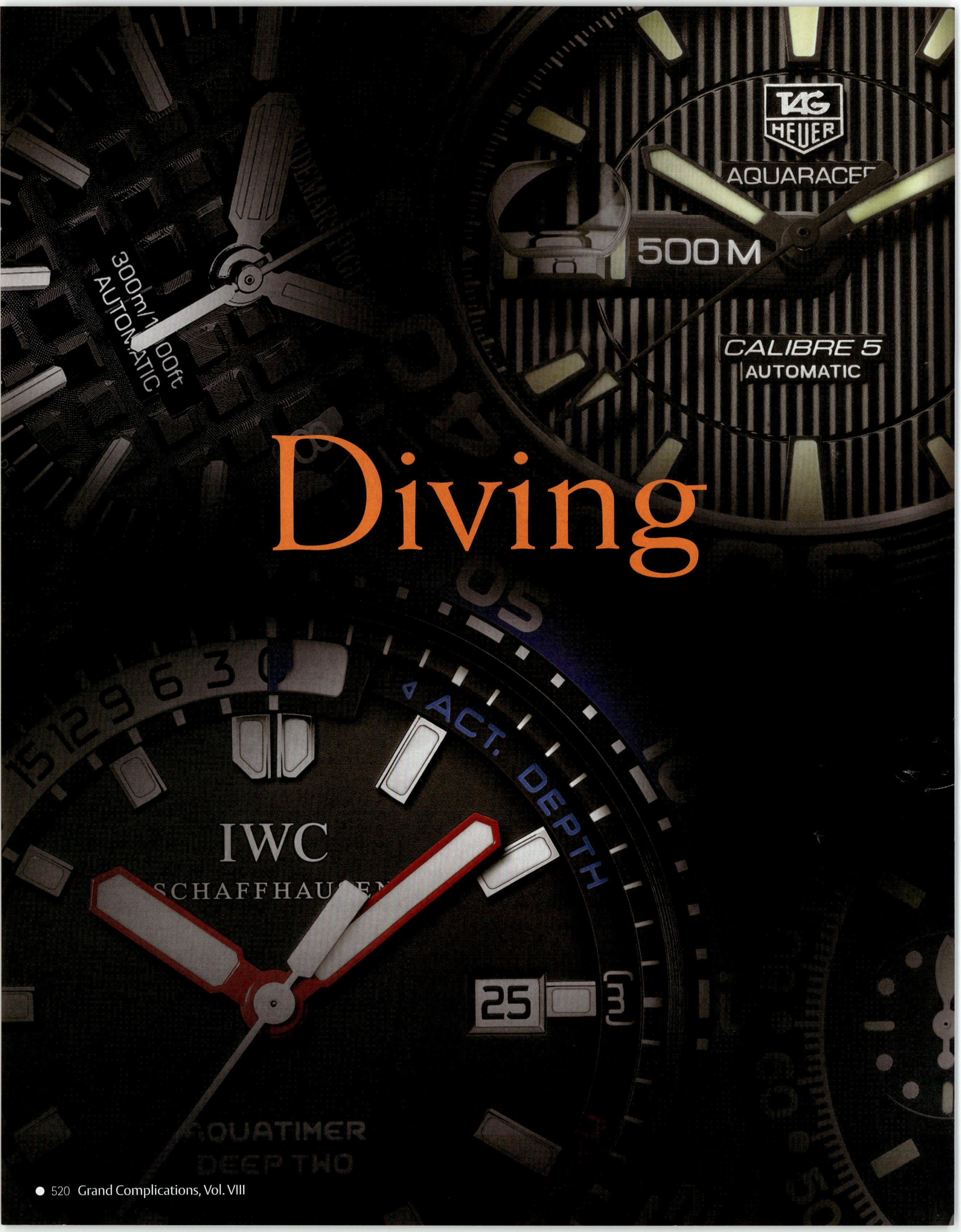
TAG HEUER
AQUARACER
500 M
CALIBRE 5
AUTOMATIC
300m/1000ft
AUTOMATIC
ACT. DEPTH
IWC
SCHAFFHAUSEN
25
AQUATIMER
DEEP TWO

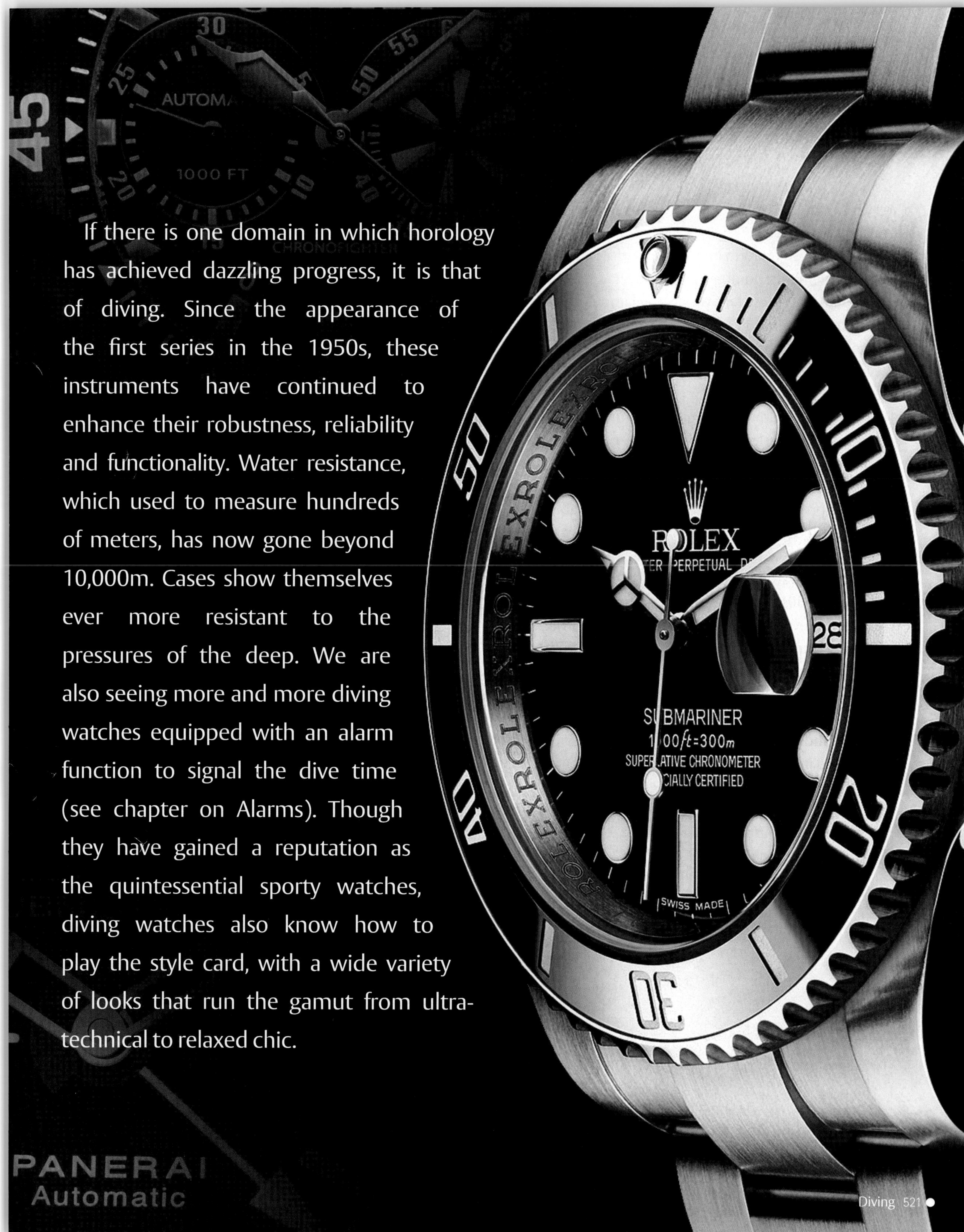

If there is one domain in which horology has achieved dazzling progress, it is that of diving. Since the appearance of the first series in the 1950s, these instruments have continued to enhance their robustness, reliability and functionality. Water resistance, which used to measure hundreds of meters, has now gone beyond 10,000m. Cases show themselves ever more resistant to the pressures of the deep. We are also seeing more and more diving watches equipped with an alarm function to signal the dive time (see chapter on Alarms). Though they have gained a reputation as the quintessential sporty watches, diving watches also know how to play the style card, with a wide variety of looks that run the gamut from ultra-technical to relaxed chic.

Water resistance, as well as lubrication, has always constituted one of horologers' main concerns. This is not to say that all horological aficionados are budding Jacques Cousteaus. However, water resistance represents a welcome protection, even on terra firma, against the two great enemies of watch movements: humidity and dust.

The first water resistant watch, the famous Oyster from Rolex, arrived on the scene in 1926, thanks to the invention of the "Screw Crown." In 1953, the brand created for Professor Auguste Piccard a watch that would accompany his bathyscaphe to 3,150m under the sea. In 1960, the Deep Sea Special would descend to over 10,916m down in the Marianna Trench in the Pacific Ocean, and ascended to the surface intact after having undergone pressure of more than a ton per square centimeter.

Besides explorers and scientists, the first diving watches often equipped the armed forces. This was notably the case with Panerai in the 1930s and 1940s, made for the Italian Navy, with the models' luminescent indications on the dial and a crown system guaranteeing water resistance to 200m.

In the 1950s, with the rise of water sports, came the first collections devoted to diving watches. Rolex set the tone in 1953 with its famous Submariner, water resistant to 100m (now 300m). That same year, Blancpain launched its Fifty Fathoms, created in collaboration with two "frogmen" from the French Army. This watch, initially resistant to 50 fathoms of depths—hence its name—stands out for its black dial, bezel and strap. It would later be released in countless other versions.

Ever since, diving watches have become the quintessential sporting watch, and horologers have continued to increase their resistance and robustness.

TECHNIQUE

HOW DOES IT WORK?

The definition of an authentic "diving watch" conforms to an official Swiss industry standard, or "norme de l'industrie horlogère suisse" (NIHS 92-11).

To earn the title of diving watch, a timepiece must not just possess a water resistance superior to the average watch (minimum 100m), usually ensured by a screw-down crown and caseback. It must also offer all the functions that are indispensable to amateur or professional divers, notably a system that allows one to preset and check the time of the dive, with a device preventing any accidental manipulation. This is usually done by a turning bezel whose unidirectional rotation prevents the diver from inadvertently extending the remaining dive time.

The dial usually features large numerals and highly visible hands, generously covered in luminescent coating. The metal strap or rubber bracelet is often equipped with an extension system that stretches over the diving suit. The highest-performance models possess a valve that eliminates any helium within the watch. This highly volatile gas, used to facilitate breathing in pressurized chambers, gets inside the watch case very easily, but the case must be totally evacuated of helium when re-ascending to avoid the build-up of excessive pressure.

A SMALL REMINDER ABOUT WATER RESISTANCE

Contrary to what is all too often believed, the indication of water resistance in meters is a technical standard that does not correspond to an absolute value. The phrase "water resistant to 30m" does not imply that the watch can be worn to that depth under any conditions whatsoever. The movements of the wearer (diving, jumping, swimming, etc.) can increase the pressure considerably. For all aquatic activities, it is therefore best to stick to watches that possess a water resistance of at least 100m.

DIVING CHRONOGRAPHS

The inherently sporty nature of the two functions means that horologers often add chronographs to diving watches. However, it bears noting that most of these instruments, though perfectly "water resistant," cannot be activated in chronograph mode during the dive, or else water will seep into the case via the pushbuttons.

Re-Releasing Flagship Models

Several well-known brands are re-releasing or re-interpreting their emblematic diving watches, especially the pioneering models of the 1950s. Though their look might be similar to the original, their performances usually benefit from the enormous progress made in the intervening years.

Rolex
Oyster Perpetual Submariner
Heir to the legendary 1953 model, the Rolex Oyster Perpetual Submariner is water resistant to 300m thanks to a patented Triplock screw-down crown system. The unidirectional rotating bezel is in ultra-resistant scratchproof ceramics.

Omega, *Seamaster PloProf 1200M*
Omega re-interpreted its 1970 Seamaster 600M model, also called PloProf (for “plongeurs professionnels,” or professional divers), in a modernized version that is water resistant to 1,200m, with a co-axial escapement and a security pushbutton that locks and unlocks the rotating bezel.

Blancpain
Fifty Fathoms Flyback Chronograph
Blancpain revisited its historic 1953 model Fifty Fathoms by creating a whole new collection, notably including a flyback chronograph and water resistant pushbuttons that are functional to 300m.

Super Luminous

Diving watches must offer optimal readability in the extreme darkness prevailing at great depths. For this purpose, they are generally equipped with oversized numerals, indexes and hands that are treated with luminescent coating. Some brands have developed "lighting" systems offering even higher performance.

Ball Watch
Engineer Hydrocarbon Spacemaster
The indexes on the Engineer Hydrocarbon Spacemaster from Ball Watch are equipped with micro-tubes containing a gaseous form of tritium. This Swiss technology guarantees, for the next 20 years, a luminosity one hundred times more intense than other processes.

Luminox, *Deep Dive*
The Luminox Light Technology System, in operation on the Deep Dive by Luminox, guarantees visibility in any conditions, thanks to its micro-tubes reflecting a blue light—the last color perceivable by the human eye after a certain depth.

Champions of Style

From sporty chic models destined mainly for poolside cocktails to professional instruments equipped for confronting the watery depths, from ultra-technical looks to timepieces focused on class and elegance, diving watches exist in a vast array of choices. Steel occasionally gives way to unusual materials—ceramics, titanium, bronze—and the quest for high performance is increasingly paired with close attention to style. These are watches that shine underwater, but also on dry land.

Omega
Seamaster Planet Ocean 45.50 mm Titanium Liquidmetal

The new Omega Seamaster Planet Ocean 45.50 mm Titanium Liquidmetal pairs a titanium case, water resistant to 600m, with a case in black ceramics and Liquidmetal®—two materials that are ultra-hard and ultra-resistant to scratches and corrosion.

Corum
Admiral's Cup 46 Chrono Dive

Corum's sport collection has welcomed a new diving model called Admiral's Cup 46 Chrono Dive, with a titanium case that is water resistant to 300m. The dial is adorned with 12 nautical pennant symbols, as well as the brand's logo.

Perrelet, *Seacraft Chronograph*

Introduced in 2011, Perrelet's Seacraft Chronograph is water resistant to 777m, the brand's lucky number. It possesses a unidirectional turning bezel, a helium valve and a thick sapphire crystal with antireflective treatment on both sides.

Panerai
Luminor Submersible 1950 3 Days Automatic Bronzo

Water resistant to 300m, the new Luminor Submersible 1950 3 Days Automatic Bronzo from Panerai stands out for its large case in bronze—a material often used on the old sailboats that the Italian-Swiss brand so admires.

JeanRichard, *Diverscope JR1000*

The Diverscope JR1000 from JeanRichard boasts an inner turning bezel operated using one of the two crowns. The steel case is coated with injected vulcanized rubber that offers great resistance to shocks, scratches, abrasion and UV rays.

Audemars Piguet
Royal Oak Offshore Diver Automatic

Recognizable by its octagonal bezel decorated with eight screws, the Royal Oak Offshore Diver Automatic from Audemars Piguet features an antimagnetic steel case that is water resistant to 300m, as well as an interior rotating bezel that is governed by a crown at 10 o'clock.

Richard Mille, *RM 032*

The new diving chronograph RM 032 from Richard Mille, with a 60-minute countdown and annual calendar, is water resistant to 300m and possesses a patented system that prevents any accidental manipulation of the crown or the pushbuttons.

Graham
Chronofighter Oversize Diver Deep Black

The British-Swiss brand Graham has updated its Chronofighter, originally created for fighter pilots in the Second World War, to fit modern tastes with its diving model Chronofighter Oversize Diver Deep Black, water resistant to 300m.

Chanel, *J12 Marine*

Equipped with a ceramic case and rubber strap, the J12 Marine from Chanel—water resistant to 300m—marries elegance and performance in versions for men and women in black, white or blue.

TAG Heuer, *Aquaracer 500M Calibre 5*

TAG Heuer plunges into the depths with the Aquaracer 500M Calibre 5. The case is equipped with six sprockets that facilitate use with diving gloves, and the elegant, readable dial is underscored with vertical streaks.

Super Divers

Certain companies have chosen to compete by developing exceptional instruments capable of descending to 1,000m, 3,000m, 6,000m or even 11,000m underwater! These super divers possess ultra-robust and innovative architectures, reinforced water resistance systems and even—for the highest performers—cases filled with liquid that is immune to pressure.

Breitling
Avenger Seawolf Chrono Blacksteel
With its patented system of magnetic pushbuttons, the Avenger Seawolf Chrono from Breitling is presented as the only chronograph that is water resistant and functional to 1,000m. It is equipped with a SuperQuartz™ movement ten times more precise than ordinary quartz movements.

Oris

Regulateur Der Meistertaucher

The Oris model Regulateur Der Meistertaucher in titanium, water resistant to 1,000m, utilizes a regulator-style dial to spotlight the central position of the diving watch's most important indication: the minutes.

Blancpain, *500 Fathoms*

In 2009, Blancpain presented the "big sister" of Fifty Fathoms, the 500 Fathoms model, which is water resistant to 1,000m and possesses a titanium case, decompression valve and transparent sapphire crystal caseback—a rare feat for a timepiece with such extreme water resistance.

Doxa,

Doxa SUB 4000T Professional

Created for the tenth anniversary of the Doxa SUB collection, the new Doxa SUB 4000T Professional is distinguished by its water resistance to 1,220m (4,000ft), its helium valve at 9 o'clock and its rotating bezel that displays the stages of decompression.

Porsche Design, *P'6780 Diver*

On the P'6780 Diver from Porsche Design, water resistant to 1,000m, the automatic movement is lodged inside a pivoting chamber. When the chamber is locked, the rotating bezel and crown are immobilized. The user must unlock it to set the dive time.

Girard-Perregaux, *Seahawk II Pro*

On its Seahawk II Pro, water resistant to 3,000m, Girard-Perregaux has shifted the crown to 4 o'clock to prevent it from getting in the way of the movements of the wrist, and equipped it with a large crown-guard that is both ergonomic and highly original.

Hublot, *Oceanographic 4000 Titanium*

Water resistant to 4,000m, the Oceanographic 4000 from Hublot possesses a 6.5mm-thick sapphire crystal, an interior turning bezel for calculating the dive time and a valve to eliminate helium.

Rolex, *Sea-Dweller Deepsea*

Rolex has reaffirmed its sovereignty over the deep seas with its launch of the Sea-Dweller Deepsea, water resistant to 3,900m. To resist such colossal pressures, this extraordinary instrument benefits from a patented new case architecture called Ringlock.

Watches with Depth Gauges

Over the last few years, we have witnessed the return of a function that is not strictly horological, but very useful for divers: the depth gauge, or bathometer. It is a tempting alternative—or complement—to the electronic wristworn computers that are currently flooding the market.

IWC, *Aquatimer Deep Two*

The Aquatimer Deep Two from IWC is equipped with a mechanical depth gauge with two differently colored hands, one indicating the current depth (up to 60m), and the other the maximum depth achieved during the dive. With these two references, the diver can plan for the decompression stages and pause at the required depths to finish the dive safely.

Jaeger-LeCoultre

Master Compressor Diving Pro Geographic Navy SEALs

The Master Compressor Diving Pro Geographic Navy SEALs from Jaeger-LeCoultre, water resistant to 300m, stands out for its mechanical depth gauge equipped with a membrane that dilates or contracts according to the water pressure. The movements of this membrane operate on a large arrow-shaped hand using a clever transmission system that is partially visible on the dial. The depths measured range from 0 to 80m.

Panerai, *Luminor 1950 Submersible Depth Gauge*

On its Luminor 1950 Submersible Depth Gauge, Panerai pairs an automatic caliber with an electronic depth gauge using a membrane and microchip system that activates a large yellow central hand. The levered bridge protecting the crown ensures water resistance to 120m.

AUDEMARS PIGUET

ROYAL OAK OFFSHORE DIVER – REF. 15703ST.OO.A002CA.01

For its diver's watch, Audemars Piguet has opted for a pared-down approach. The Royal Oak Offshore Diver is equipped with the Manufacture Audemars Piguet automatic 3120 movement with a 22K gold oscillating weight decorated with the Audemars and Piguet family crest. The case components—particularly the gaskets, the thickness of the back and that of the crystals—have been adapted to guarantee water resistance to depths of 300m. Its exclusive black "Mega Tapisserie" dial, which has a inner rotating ring with diving scale, applied luminescent hour markers and hands in white gold, displays hours, minutes, dive-time measurement and date. The model is available on a black rubber strap with oversized stainless steel pin buckle.

BELL & ROSS

MARINE BR 02-94 CHRONOGRAPH 500 M

As the helium escape valve and screw-down crown make an immediate statement of professional diving functionality, the smooth curvatures of the 44mm satin-brushed steel case begin a tale of aesthetic excellence. Operated by a screw-down piece at 10:00, the unidirectional internal bezel is both easily maneuvered and safely contained beneath the antireflective sapphire crystal. Ensuring optimal visibility, a luminescent coating is applied to the numerals, indexes, hands and bezel pointer. The chronograph, with its 30-minute totalizer at 9:00, allows for a precise and legible measurement of dive and decompression times. Powered by an automatic mechanical movement, this authoritative underwater chronograph features a perfectly integrated discreet date at 4:30 and is worn on a black rubber strap with a satin-brushed steel pin buckle.

GRAHAM

CHRONOFIGHTER OVERSIZE DIVER – REF. 2OVEB.B40A

Integrated into the watch's steel and sapphire bezel in black and silver, the GMT function is read with excellent clarity via a central hand with white luminous tip and red contour. On the left-hand side of the case, coated in black PVD, the famous fast-action Chronofighter start/stop trigger allows for optimal precision in operating the G1733's automatic bi-compax chronograph. The 47mm Chronofighter Oversize GMT Black Steel boasts a power reserve of 48 hours and features a smoked sapphire caseback.

HUBLOT

OCEANOGRAPHIC 4000 TITANIUM – REF. 731.NX.1190.RX

Capable of withstanding the extreme pressure of a 4000m dive, the Oceanographic 4000 Titanium is a downright remarkable push of the diver's concept. While a 6.5mm-thick sapphire crystal provides protection at extreme depths, a helium valve at 10:00 ensures safe escapement of gases during decompression. A coating of SuperLumiNova on the hands, dial, and dive time flange at 2:00 offers clear legibility in the dark, further confirming Hublot's commitment to the creation of a true diver's watch heavyweight.

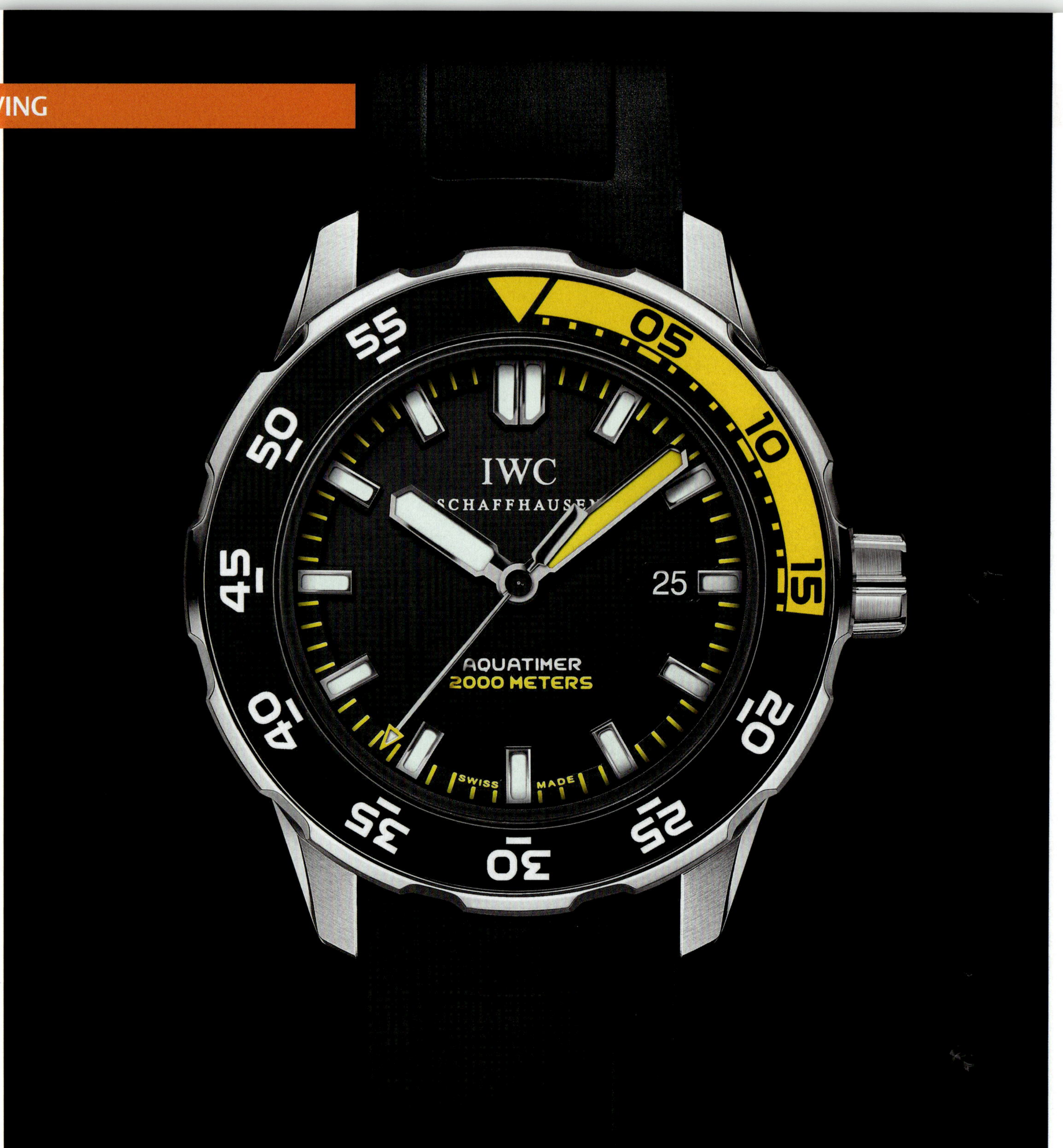

IWC

AQUATIMER AUTOMATIC 2000 – REF. IW356810

The Aquatimer Automatic 2000, with its tested pressure resistance to 200 bar, still holds the horological record for water resistance. Its automatic 30110 caliber contains 40 jewels, beats at 28,800 vph and offers 21 hours of power reserve. The stainless steel watch features a rhodium-plated black dial and a black external mechanical rotating bezel with the familiar luminous yellow 15-minute segment of the previous Aquatimer. Yellow is also used for the minute hand, which indicates the dive time, to ensure a clear distinction. A second variant has a white dial with orange or white numerals on a white or dark blue background on the rotating bezel and an orange hour hand. Shown here on a black rubber strap, the Aquatimer Automatic 2000 is also available on a stainless steel bracelet.

IWC

AQUATIMER DEEP TWO – REF. IW354703

The Aquatimer Deep Two boasts a 46mm case that is pressure resistant to 12 bar. The watch shows not only the actual dive depth, but also the maximum depth reached during a particular dive, doubling as a complete second safety system alongside the dive computer. The Aquatimer Deep Two features a semi-circular indicator on the dial, which records depths down to 50m. Its pressure-measurement system is contained in a second large crown on the left side of the case. The water pressure acts directly on a membrane inside this crown and forces a pin into the interior of the case, triggering a system that results in the depth indicator (blue) moving over the white measuring field as the depth of water increases or decreases. The maximum depth indicator (red) always remains at the greatest depth reached. It can be released by a button underneath the depth-gauge sensor crown on the left side of the case.

PANERAI

LUMINOR SUBMERSIBLE 1950 3 DAYS AUTOMATIC TITANIO – REF. PAM00305

This version of the Luminor Submersible is powered by an exclusively in-house movement, the Panerai P.9000 caliber. The automatic-winding caliber's 197 components and two-barrel system guarantee 72 hours of power reserve. With a 47mm diameter titanium case, it's a professional underwater model, watertight in pressures of up to 30 bar (300m). Distinctive features, in addition to its size, include a substantial counterclockwise, unidirectional bezel with stud and relief markers, as well as a dial with wide baton hands—a design inspiration from historic models. The Luminor Submersible 1950 3 Days Automatic Titanio comes complete with a natural rubber strap.

PANERAI

LUMINOR 1950 SUBMERSIBLE DEPTH GAUGE FOR THE PANGAEA EXPEDITION

REF. PAM00307

Recognized for creating the first professional diver's watches in history and supplying them—along with wrist depth gauges—to the Royal Italian Navy in the first half of the 20th century, Officine Panerai reaffirmed its tradition in the field of professional precision instruments with the combination of these two indispensable measuring devices in a single instrument: the Luminor 1950 Submersible Depth Gauge. Unlike historic wrist depth gauges, which were functional to 30m, this innovative device can measure depths to 120m and record the greatest depth encountered in the course of a dive. This is achieved by an independent, sophisticated electronic device fitted within the 47mm titanium case. In a numbered limited edition, the back is engraved in celebration of famous explorer Mike Horn's Pangaea Expedition.

PANERAI

LUMINOR SUBMERSIBLE – REF. PAM00024

Inspired by the model designed for the Egyptian Navy in 1956, the Luminor Submersible inherits the historic version's striking personality through its characteristic rotating bezel (which enables the duration of a dive to be read quickly) and its reliability under extreme conditions. The addition of an automatic mechanical movement enhances the great functionality of its predecessor, a testimony to Panerai's constant dedication to technical development and quality standards. This 44mm model is water resistant to 30 bar (300m).

ZENITH

DEFY XTREME SEA OPEN

Cased in 46.5mm of black titanium with graduated unidirectional rotating bezel in black titanium, fitted with carbon-fiber inserts, the Defy Xtreme Sea Open is powered by the El Primero 4021 SX automatic chronograph movement with harmonic plate. The caliber consists of 248 parts and 39 jewels. The balance, chronograph and pallet bridges are built of shock-absorbing Zenithium Z+. It has a 30-minute counter at 3:00, small seconds at 9:00, power reserve indicator from the hour axis, and central seconds blue varnished hand. Water resistant to 1,000 meters, the high-tech case features a helium valve at 10:00 and black titanium screw-in pushbuttons with carbon-fiber guilloché patterns and protective crown device. The carbon-fiber dial is a multi-layered construction with shock-resistant Hesalite glass. Composite lateral inserts reinforce the black titanium bracelet with blue-tinted central links.

Brand Directory

A. LANGE & SÖHNE
Altenberger Strasse 15
01768 Glashütte
Germany
Tel: 49 35053 440
USA: 800 408 8147

AUDEMARS PIGUET
1348 Le Brassus
Switzerland
Tel: 41 21 845 14 00
USA: 212 758 8400

BELL & ROSS
8 Rue Copernic
75016 Paris
France
Tel: 33 1 73 73 93 00
USA: 888 307 7887

BLANCPAIN
Le Rocher 12
1348 Le Brassus
Switzerland
Tel: 41 21 796 36 36
USA: 877 520 1735

BREGUET
1344 L'Abbaye
Switzerland
Tel: 41 21 841 90 90
USA: 866 458 7488

BVLGARI
Rue de Monruz 34
2000 Neuchâtel
Switzerland
Tel: 41 32 722 78 78
USA: 212 315 9700

CHANEL
25 Place du Marché St. Honoré
75001 Paris
France
Tel: 33 1 55 35 50 00
USA: 212 688 5055

CHRISTOPHE CLARET
Route du Soleil d'Or 2
2400 Le Locle
Switzerland
Tel: 41 32 933 80 80
USA: 954 610 2234

de GRISOGONO
176 bis Route de St. Julien
1228 Plan-les-Ouates
Switzerland
Tel: 41 22 817 81 00
USA: 212 439 4220

DEWITT
Rue du Pré de la Fontaine 2
Satigny 1217 Meyrin 2
Switzerland
Tel: 41 22 750 97 97
USA: 305 572 9812

DIOR HORLOGERIE
44 Rue François 1er
75008 Paris
France
Tel: 33 1 40 73 59 84
USA: 212 931 2700

FRANCK MULLER
22 Route de Malagny
1294 Genthod
Switzerland
Tel: 41 22 959 88 88
France: 33 1 53 67 44 39

FRÉDÉRIQUE CONSTANT SA
Chemin du Champ des Filles 32
1228 Plan-les-Ouates
Switzerland
Tel: 41 22 860 04 40
USA: 877 619 2824

GLASHÜTTE ORIGINAL
Altenberger Strasse 1
01768 Glashütte/Sachsen
Germany
Tel: 49 3 50 53 460
France: 33 1 53 81 22 68

GRAHAM-LONDON
Boulevard des Eplatures 38
2300 La Chaux-de-Fonds
Switzerland
Tel: 41 32 910 98 88
USA: 213 622 1716

GUY ELLIA
21 Rue de la Paix
75002 Paris
France
Tel: 33 1 53 30 25 25
CA: 310 470 1388
NY: 212 888 0505

HUBLOT
Chemin de la Vuarpillière 33
1260 Nyon 2
Switzerland
Tel: 41 22 990 90 00
USA: 800 536 0636

IWC
Baumgartenstrasse 15
8201 Schaffhausen
Switzerland
Tel: 41 52 635 65 65
USA: 800 492 6755

JACOB & CO.
Rue Pierre-Fatio 12
1204 Geneva
Switzerland
Tel: 41 79 369 77 69
USA: 212 719 5887

JAEGER-LeCOULTRE
Rue de la Golisse 8
1347 Le Sentier
Switzerland
Tel: 41 21 845 02 02
USA: 212 308 2525

LONGINES
Saint-Imier 2610
Switzerland
Tel: 41 32 942 54 25
USA: 201 271 1400

PANERAI
Viale Monza 259
20126 Milan
Italy
Tel: 39 02 36 31 38
USA: 212 888 8788

PATEK PHILIPPE
Chemin du Pont du Centenaire 141
1228 Plan-les-Ouates
Switzerland
Tel: 41 22 884 20 20
USA: 212 218 1240

PIAGET
37 Chemin du Champ-des-Filles
1228 Plan-les-Ouates
Switzerland
Tel: 41 22 884 48 44
USA: 800 628 4344

REBELLION TIMEPIECES
Chemin du Bief
1027 Lonay
Switzerland
Tel: 41 21 802 33 04

RICHARD MILLE
11 rue du Jura
2345 Les Breuleux Jura
Switzerland
Tel: 41 32 959 43 53
USA: 310 205 5555

ROGER DUBUIS
1217 Meyrin 2 Geneva
Switzerland
Tel: 41 22 783 28 28
USA: 888 738 2847

STÜHRLING ORIGINAL
449 20th Street
Brooklyn, NY 11215
USA: 718 840 5760

URWERK
34 rue des Noirettes
1227 Carouge-Geneva
Switzerland
Tel: 41 21 900 20 25
USA: 310 205 5555

VACHERON CONSTANTIN
Chemin du Tourbillon 10
1228 Plan-les-Ouates
Switzerland
Tel: 41 22 930 20 05
USA: 212 713 0707

ZENITH
2400 Le Locle
Switzerland
Tel: 41 32 930 62 62
USA: 973 467 1890